Co-Creating Humane and Innovative Organizations

Co-Creating Humane and Innovative Organizations

Evolutions in the Practice Of Socio-technical System Design

Editors:
Bernard J. Mohr and Pierre van Amelsvoort

Bernard J. Mohr and Pierre van Amelsvoort

Co-Creating Humane and Innovative Organizations
Evolutions in the Practice of Socio-technical System Design

ISBN-13: 9780692510032 (Global STS-D Network)
ISBN-10: 0692510036

Cover design: Ingeborg Mohr
Design: CreateSpace
Design tables and figures: Elly Lemmers (ST-Groep)
Production: CreateSpace

Library of Congress Control Number: 2016905426
Global STS-D Network, Portland ME

Authors

Mohammed Alfayyoumi is director of the System Operations Center for Dominion Virginia Power in Glen Allen, Virginia. He holds a master's degree in electrical and electronics engineering.

Pierre van Amelsvoort studied management science and industrial engineering at the Technical University of Eindhoven (1976–1981). He is an expert in socio-technical systems design and change of organizations. In 1990 he established the Socio-technical Organisation Consultancy Group (ST-Groep). In 1992, he obtained his PhD, and from 1994 to 2007, he was professor by special appointment at the Nijmegen School of Management. Since 2010, he has been a professor at the Catholic University Leuven.

Douglas Austrom is an adjunct professor with Indiana University's Kelley Business School, where he teaches courses on leadership and leading change for Kelley Direct. Doug is also cofounder of Adjutant Solutions Group and Turning Point Associates, consulting firms that specialize in organizational and individual change and increasing organizational and leadership effectiveness. Prior to founding Turning Point Associates, Doug was a full-time faculty member at Indiana University's School of Business, where he won several teaching excellence awards in both the undergraduate and MBA programs.

Betty Barrett focuses on the study of sociotechnical systems despite retirement from MIT in 2015. At the University of Illinois, she was the director of the Center for Sociotechnical Systems in the School of Labor and Employment Relations. She has in-depth background in the auto and aerospace industries as well as innovative work systems.

Peter Bednar is a senior academic and the chair of the Systems and Information Systems research group at the University of Portsmouth. He is also a researcher at the Department of Informatics at Lund University. Educated in engineering, Peter worked in industry before becoming an academic. His main research interests are in the fields of information systems, systems thinking, contextual inquiry into complex and ambiguous problem spaces, socio-technical inquiry and organizational change, knowledge management, information systems security, and sociocybernetics. Peter has written more than one hundred publications in these areas, including journal articles, conference papers, and book chapters.

Kevin Boyle is president and principle of Boyle and Associates, Inc., an organization and professional development firm with key accomplishments in labor-management efforts, participative management, leadership development, strategic planning, and workplace design and redesign in both public- and private-sector business and union organizations. He is a thirty-plus-year member of the Communications Workers of America, and he worked as a lineman and technician, serving as the local union vice president and president in Corvallis, Oregon. Kevin proudly holds a master's degree with millions of others from SFU (Shop Floor University).

Jac Christis studied sociology in Nijmegen. He worked for fifteen years as a senior researcher at the Dutch Institute on Working Conditions. Currently he is an associate professor at Radboud University Nijmegen and a full professor at the Hanze University of Applied Science in Groningen.

He works on organization and job design from a socio-technical perspective (as developed by Ulbo de Sitter). His research concerns the application of socio-technical principles in SMEs, the health care sector, and higher education. He is interested in integrating operations management, Lean production, and socio-technical systems theory from a system theoretical perspective.

Steven Dhondt, a sociologist, is a visiting professor (chair of Social Innovation) at the KULeuven (Belgium). He also is a senior research scientist at TNO in the Netherlands. He is the network coordinator for the European Commission of the European Workplace Innovation

Network (EUWIN).

Pamela Ey is a training consultant with SOS International and founder of The Center for Innovative Decision-making. She holds a PhD in business administration and has a passion for improving the work environment in complex socio-technical systems through behavioral competencies.

Mark J. G. Govers obtained a PhD in management sciences at Radboud University Nijmegen in 2003. He works at the intersection among developing, applying, and teaching knowledge focused on socio-technical issues. Since 2006, he has been an academic scholar at Maastricht University. As visiting professor, he lectures on information, management, and organizational science in the Netherlands and South America (Colombia and Peru). Besides his academic work, he is a senior advisor at his own consultancy firm called Archypel Consulting.

Donald W. de Guerre was appointed to a professorship in the Department of Applied Human Sciences, Concordia University, in 1999, where he teaches human systems intervention in the graduate and undergraduate programs. He was appointed manager of organization effectiveness, Syncrude Canada Ltd., in 1989, where he led a total organization-in-environments redesign process. Prior to Syncrude, Don worked internationally on the development of a democratic organization in various industries and economic sectors. He holds a PhD in human and organization systems and a master of arts degree in organization development from The Fielding Graduate Institute, a master of education degree from the University of Toronto, and an honors bachelor of arts degree in physical and health education from the University of Western Ontario.

Bjorn Gustavsen is a professor emeritus. His main area of interest is work reform and associated strategies for change. He has held academic positions at several institutions and has, alone and with others, published about twenty-five books and several hundred articles on themes like democracy at work, work and health, development processes, and action research. He has been research director for several workplace development programs in Scandinavia and worked closely in particular with the labor-market parties.

Geert van Hootegem is a professor at the Centre for Sociological Research at the KULeuven (Belgium) since 2000, teaching organizational design and change management. Geert obtained his doctoral degree in social sciences at the KULeuven. Throughout his entire career, Geert's academic work has been focused on understanding the impact of organizational structures, division of work, and teams working on various aspects of organizational performance and employee well-being.

His research on teamwork, new socio-technical systems design, and quality of working life is widely published in academic and management journals. Geert is highly regarded as an organizational consultant, supporting companies and social-profit organizations in complex redesign and change programs. He is the founder of Flanders Synergy, a Belgian network of organizations that promote workplace innovation. In 2013 he cofounded Prepared Mind, a consulting firm focusing on total workplace Innovation.

Eric-Hans Kramer is associate professor of human factors and systems safety at the Faculty of Military Sciences of the Netherlands Defence Academy. He has studied various operational processes in the armed forces and operated as an internal consultant of various departments. His work has been published in various journal articles, book chapters, and in the book *Organizing Doubt* (2007). He is a coauthor of a student's handbook on STS in the Dutch language.

Hans Lekkerkerk has been a senior lecturer in organization design and innovation management at Radboud University (Nijmegen, the Netherlands) since 1997. He graduated from the Delft University as a mechanical engineer (MSc) with a specialization in systems thinking and organizational design in 1985. In 2012, he obtained his PhD. He studied the innovation structure from a Lowlands Socio-technical Systems Design perspective. Before joining the university, he worked at the Composite Structures Division of the former Fokker Aircraft Company as an industrial engineer, quality engineer, and project leader, followed by a brief period as an organization consultant and trainer.

Betsy Merck is the founder of Merck Consulting, Inc., a San Francisco Bay Area consulting firm that over the past fifteen years has carried out organization transformation work with all levels of business enterprises in a variety of industries and sectors.

Bernard J. Mohr is a design and innovation practitioner specializing in the development of flexible workplaces that work great and are great to work in. During forty years of professional practice, he has served as a change strategist, thinking partner, and thought leader for clients engaged in reimagining and transforming the way they deliver services and/or create products. His clients are global corporations, not-for-profits, and value networks in health care, education, retail, manufacturing, government, and professional service in the United States, Canada, Central America, the Caribbean, Western Europe, and the Middle East. Bernard's work draws on design thinking, socio-technical systems theory, large-group methods, social constructionism, complexity science, positive psychology, and his experiences as a senior manager. He is the author of three books and numerous articles on designing highly effective and humane workplaces, quality that's built in, and cultures of innovation and engagement at all levels. He is a cofounder of Innovation Partners International.

Matthijs Moorkamp is an organizational psychologist. He is currently working on a PhD thesis in which he aims to develop a safety-management theory for so-called "expeditionary organizations" such as military expeditionary organizations and crisis-response organizations. For his research, Matthijs conducted case-study research within Task Force Uruzgan. He is employed at Saxion University of Applied Science as a lecturer and researcher in security management.

Carolyn Ordowich is the founder of STS Associates, Inc., in Princeton, New Jersey, with more than thirty-eight years as a design practitioner with a wide range of organizations. Using a multidimensional capability set based in STS theory and organization design, design thinking, and participation-based change technologies, Carolyn facilitates large-system transformation work with all levels of enterprise, from the shop floor to the boardroom. Her focus is on *humane, high-performance, ethical organizing* in emerging forms of organization such as reconfigurable teams, networks and ecosystems, and participative governance systems, with specific attention on how digitization of the workplace impacts organization design.

Ike Overdiep has operated since 2010 in a small research and consulting bureau called "Opus 8," focusing on qualification, labor-market policy, and industrial relations. Previously, she worked in a larger consultancy bureau, in the national education department, and in the trade union as a policy advisor on vocational training, employability, and collective agreements. Recently she facilitated the development of new exams for prevocational training as an independent chair, supported several technical branches on the relationship between education and the changing needs of enterprises, and assisted in professionalizing the work organizations in primary schools by stimulating the development and use of intervision and review instruments.

Bert Painter is an independent consulting social scientist, documentary filmmaker, and long-time member of the STS Roundtable.

Pam Posey is the founder and principal of Eyes on Performance in Everett, Washington. She has been consulting in strategic planning, alignment, and organization design for more than twenty-five years. She is widely published in a variety of journals, including *Harvard Business Review*.

Frank Pot, a sociologist, is an emeritus professor of social innovation of work and employment at Radboud University Nijmegen and chair of the advisory board of the European Workplace Innovation Network (EUWIN). Formerly, he was director of TNO Work and Employment and a part-time professor of work and technology at Leiden University.

Rocky Sease is a cofounder and the CEO of SOS Int'l, a leading provider of training and compliance solutions for the power industry. Rocky graduated from Clemson University with an engineering degree.

William E. Smith is an innovator in creating and applying systems theory and practice to the fields of leadership, organization, and social development. While consulting with the World Bank, he created and implemented a natural systems philosophy, process, and model called AIC, named for the three powers of *appreciation, influence,* and *control*.

His book *The Creative Power: Transforming Ourselves, Our Organizations, and Our World* (Routledge, 2009), tells the story of the global development and application of AIC. Bill's work owes much to his mentor, James D. Thomson, author of *Organizations in Action* (1967) and his PhD advisors, Eric Trist, Russell Ackoff, and Hasan Ozbekhan.

Erik Soepenberg studied business administration at the University of Groningen, after which he carried out PhD research on the Workload Control concept, a planning concept suitable for companies producing high-variety/low-volume products. Erik published multiple articles in the *International Journal of Production Economics* and the *International Journal of Production Research* based on this research. At the same time, Erik was project leader of multiple logistical improvement projects in SME companies in the northern part of the Netherlands. Since 2010, he has been a lecturer and researcher at the Kenniscentrum Arbeid of the Hanze University of Applied Sciences. His research focuses on Lean and sustainability.

Wim Sprenger spent many years in the trade-union movement as a trainer/consultant, policy officer, and researcher. His main fields of interest and activity are union policies on changing organizations, quality of work, qualification and employability, flexibility, and security. Since 2001 he has been an independent researcher focusing on labor-market developments, corporate restructuring, continuous qualification, innovation of workplaces, and ecosystems. His favorite themes include unions, boxing, dancing, the movement from management to anticipation of restructuring, how to involve small companies, and the value chain in analysis and design.

Pim Sudmeier is an expert in the field of continuous improvement and teamwork from a socio-technical perspective. As owner of Triaspect, a leading institute for safety and risk management in Dutch health care, he supports cure and care organizations in patient-safety improvement. He develops digital learning and improvement tools for health care teams that enable reporting, analysis, and improvement of processes and knowledge management. Designing ICT with a balance between information needs and information support is the main drive in his work.

Ramkrishnan Tenkasi is a professor of organization change at Benedictine University in Baltimore, Maryland. He is a Fulbright Research Scholar, widely published, with twenty-nine years of consulting experience in organizational change, knowledge management, and innovation.

Christine Welch is a visiting research fellow at Portsmouth Business School, following thirty years' service in further and higher education. She holds a doctorate in systems analysis and has research interests in the fields of information systems, knowledge management, and systems thinking. She has published many articles, conference papers, and book chapters on these topics She is a coauthor of *The Manager's Guide to Systems Practice* (Wiley 2012) and is a former director and president of the UK Systems Society.

Contents

Authors ·v
Preface· ·xv

Chapter 1   Waves of Evolution In Socio-technical Systems Design
            (STS-D)—Bernard J. Mohr and Pierre van Amelsvoort· · · ·1
Chapter 2   Creating High-Performing Organizations: The North
            American Open Socio-technical Systems Design
            Approach—Bernard J. Mohr· ·16
Chapter 3   Open Systems Theory and the Two-Stage Model of
            Active Adaptation—Donald W. de Guerre · · · · · · · · · · ·34
Chapter 4   North American Design of Nonroutine Work
            Systems (1980s–1990s)—Douglas Austrom and
            Carolyn Ordowich ·50
Chapter 5   Human Talent Mobilization: Improving Both Quality
            of Working Life and Productivity by Organizational
            Design in the Lowlands—Pierre van Amelsvoort · · · · · · ·73
Chapter 6   Organizing Innovation and (Strategic) Decision
            Making—L. J. Lekkerkerk ·99
Chapter 7   Socio-technical Systems Design for Coordination of
            Virtual Teamwork—Bert Painter, Pamela A. Posey,
            Douglas R. Austrom, Ramkrishnan V. Tenkasi, Betty
            Barrett, and Betsy Merck· ·123
Chapter 8   STS Designing for a Networked World—Carolyn
            Ordowich and Doug Austrom · · · · · · · · · · · · · · · · · ·145

Chapter 9   The Employee's Voice in the Design of Humane and
             Innovative Work(places)—Kevin Boyle, Wim Sprenger,
             and Ike Overdiep ·167
Chapter 10   Democratic Dialogue—Bjorn Gustavsen · · · · · · · · · · ·186
Chapter 11   Workplace Innovation—Frank Pot and Steven
             Dhondt· ·201
Chapter 12   Purpose and Power in the Evolution of Socio-technical
             Systems Design—William E. Smith · · · · · · · · · · · · · · · ·223
Chapter 13   Evolving Socio-technical Perspectives on Human
             Factors and Safety—Eric-Hans Kramer and Matthijs
             Moorkamp ·241
Chapter 14   Resilience-Centered Approaches for Training Design
             in an Electric Utility—Mohammed Alfayyoumi, Rocky
             Sease, and Pamela Ey ·258
Chapter 15   Enid Mumford: The ETHICS Methodology and Its
             Legacy—Peter Bednar and Christine Welch · · · · · · · · · ·274
Chapter 16   Applying Enterprise Information Technology from a
             Socio-technical Perspective —Mark J. G. Govers and
             Pim Sudmeier· ·289
Chapter 17   Lowlands Socio-technical Design Theory and Lean
             Production—Jac Christis and Erik Soepenberg · · · · · · ·303
Chapter 18   Changing the Nature of Work: Toward Total Workplace
             Innovation—Geert van Hootegem · · · · · · · · · · · · · · · ·326
Chapter 19   The Future of STS-D—Bernard J. Mohr and Pierre
             van Amelsvoort ·344

Preface

The combination of massive economic upheavals, breathtaking advances in technology, widespread political turmoil, unprecedented climate change, radically shifting demographics, and breakthroughs in social relations has left organizations with a full plate of adaptation challenges. The combined demands on productivity, quality, flexibility, innovation, sustainability, and healthy work is driving a revitalized search for innovations in the business and operating models of the workplace—innovations that include but go beyond faster and smaller technology.

The approach of socio-technical systems design has a rich history in creating alternatives to the classical Tayloristic organization in which employees are disengaged, decisions are painfully slow, and silos are powerful dividers. In the past seventy years, the original socio-technical systems design (STS-D) theory and practice have erupted in a rainbow of variations, giving us a kaleidoscope of lenses.

These ideas have influenced many of the most popular change approaches. For example, in both "Lean Thinking" and the "workplace-innovation" movement in Europe, we found STS principles alive and well. While often not well referenced, the philosophy of STS design is very much alive, albeit under different labels and sometimes not as "true" to the original intent as we would like. Regarding these developments around the world, both within the core community of STS practitioners and in the neighboring fields of practice (such as Lean Thinking and Workplace Innovation), most connections were only by chance, yet their underlying purpose and principles seem powerful in their influence.

Bernard J. Mohr and Pierre van Amelsvoort

In the development of the STS-D theory and practices, we can notice three waves. The first wave is about the design of more or less routine work in manufacturing processes, the second is about non-routine work with knowledge workers, and the third is about designing issue-based ecosystems and both internal external value-realization networks. These waves of evolution are not discontinuous but rather like Russian dolls, each working with and encapsulating what has gone before.

Nevertheless, not many organizational designers understand STS design theory and practice well or use it widely. We believe the emerging body of knowledge and practice of STS Design can have a profound impact in understanding and creating innovative and humane communities of work in the twenty-first century.

As a global community of practice, different cultures and colors are represented in our approaches, but we also have a lot in common. At the annual meeting of the North American STS Roundtable in Canterbury, England in 2012, about sixty practitioners and academic scholars joined in conversations about the current state of the art in socio-technical systems design (STS-D) and its evolution all over the world. Since the initial development of STS concepts in the mid-twentieth century, different parts of the world have been home to evolutionary development in concepts, practices, and fundamental theories.

Then, at the STS Roundtable meeting in Boston in 2013, the STS/RT (STS Roundtable) and USI (Ulbo De SitterInstitute in the Netherlands and Belgium) gave birth to a process for creating a network of networks, on a global scale, of STS design practitioners. It includes business leaders, researchers, trade unionists, academics, managers, consultants, and students who share the values, principles, and practices of socio-technical systems theory and a common interest in developing more humane and effective organizations.

This book is one of the initiatives supporting this emerging Global STS-D Network. In inviting possible authors for this book, we cast as wide a net as possible, seeking to find diverse authors representing both past and cutting-edge approaches. Among the authors who accepted our invitations, we created small groups who reflected on each other's contributions and collaborated to improve their respective chapters. We are thankful to the enthusiastic authors who leapt into this process of co-creaion! You will find the result in this book.

In this multifaceted book, thirty authors (academics, union leaders, and practitioners) describe their different lenses on STS-D to shed light on the panoply of past, present, and future thinking and practices that give life to the challenge of "co-creating humane and innovative organizations."

The book is sponsored by the Global STS-D Network, which was cofounded by the STS Roundtable (North America) and the Ulbo De SitterInstitute (in the Netherlands and Belgium).

Hopefully this book is an inspiration for all in the world who share the dream of creating innovative and humane communities of work. We co-creaed this book with passion and a growing mutual understanding. We would like to thank all of the authors for their contributions.

We invite you join our journey and to consider the possibilities. And we hope we can offer a further inspiration to the community that believes in the possibilities for and power of humane and innovative communities of work, be they traditional organizations, value-creation networks, or issue-based ecosystems.

Bernard J. Mohr, Portland, Maine, USA
Pierre van Amelsvoort, Boxtel, Netherlands
July 2016

One

Waves of Evolution in Socio-technical Systems Design (STS-D)

Bernard J. Mohr and Pierre van Amelsvoort

INTRODUCTION

During the second half of the last century, interest in the design and process for designing of organizations increased enormously. The origin of STS design theory dates back to shortly after the Second World War. A number of researchers (Trist and Bamforth 1951, Trist et al. 1963) discovered that technical-economic aspects (i.e., the production processes) could not be entirely understood without understanding the impact of the social structuring of organizations (i.e., the division of labor and grouping of tasks, where labor is understood to include both the production work and management functions of the enterprise). Equally, these social aspects (which include the experience of the human being at work as well as human actions in support of both the production processes and the management functions) can never be viewed without the technical-economic factors. However, at the time, the idea of involving multiple disciplines simultaneously along with those who do the work in intentionally and participatively designing this socio-technical work system was revolutionary. After all, designing production systems was the task of technical engineers, while solving social problems (i.e., problems of assignment and division of labor, motivation, coordination, control, adaptation, and long-term development). And in the organization was the work of management, human resource specialists, psychologists, sociologists, and others.

1

The results of these studies were then disseminated and confirmed all over the world (see Rice 1958, Emery and Thorsrud 1976, and others). Two phenomena are observed:

1) Elements of STS-D (socio-technical system design) theory, (for example, the elimination of non-value-adding levels of management, the streamlining of processes into whole group tasks, the self-managing team concept) recur today in numerous modern approaches such as Lean/Six Sigma, employee engagement/empowerment, and systems thinking/learning organization across the world.

2) STS-D theory has evolved in different ways on different continents (for an intercontinental comparison, see Van Eijnatten 1993).

During the past thirty to forty years, as early ideas of STS-D became absorbed by other approaches to organizational and human performance, STS-D practice has evolved from an approach for job design (micro level) and a "one-size, self-managing teams fits all solution" (meso level) into a broader school of thought in management science, with sound theoretical and research foundations (see chapter 17) and broad global application. We now have more powerful frameworks for analyzing (explaining), designing, and changing whole organizations (macro level), networks, and even ecosystems in an integrated manner.

Contemporary STS-D theory can be defined as follows:

The participative, multidisciplinary study and improvement of how jobs, single organizations, networks, and ecosystems function, internally and in relation to their environmental context, with a special focus on the mutual interactions of the entity's (be it a single organization, network, or ecosystem) value-creation processes (i.e., the technical system composed of all production-related tasks and technologies) and its control/adjustment mechanisms (i.e., the social system composed of its work structure, systems, policies, culture, attributes of people, and their mutual relationships). The goal of all STS-D-based analysis and (re)design is the creation of either jobs, single organizations, networks, or ecosystems that are adaptive, innovative, good to work in, and work well as measured by human, economic, and societal metrics.

EARLY-DAY ROOTS—THE DURHAM CASE

The term "socio-technical system" was first used in the now-famous studies of British coal mines (Trist and Bamforth 1951). These studies were commissioned when it was found that many of the mines introducing new technical-system processes did not improve performance and in some cases reduced performance. With this new technology, management tried to create a production line such as the one found in the automotive industry. In these studies, for the first time, the relationship between the system's technical system and social system was identified.

The coal mine research showed how mechanization of the production process (the technical system) led (unintentionally) in some places to a more fragmented, "siloed" division of labor (the social organization). Before the mechanization took place, teams existed as "natural forms" (flexible whole-task groups) of work organization. Working in a mine underground is a dangerous job with a lot of safety issues, uncertainty, and interference and requires strong collaboration based on trust, internal leadership, and self-organization. The mechanization and the consequence of task division destroyed the teams and had a negative effect on productivity and human side of work in almost all of the sites studied. However, in the course of their studies, the Tavistock researchers discovered the anomaly of Haighmoor seam in the South Yorkshire Coalfield. Eric Trist describes this anomaly as follows: "The work organization of the new seam was, to us, a novel phenomenon, consisting of a set of relatively autonomous interchanging roes and shifts with a minimum of supervision. Cooperation between task groups was everywhere in evidence; accidents infrequent, productivity high. The men told us that in order to adapt with the best advantage [to the newly introduced technology] they

3

had evolved a form of work organization based on practices common in unmechanized days when small groups, who took responsibility for the entire cycle, had worked autonomously."

The twofold eye-opener in these field studies lies first in the realization that "improvements" in one part of the system (in this case, mechanization of the technical system) did not automatically lead to better results and that, even with new technical system design, there is still choice available in how we organize (i.e., how we design the social system). The researchers discovered that many problems in the social system (increased absenteeism and a higher number of conflicts and accidents) were driven by shifts in the mine's new technical system. "Advances" in the technical system had failed to bring about the expected performance increase, due to unintentional design changes in the social system driven by shifts in the mines technical system. The link between this classical form of organization (i.e., increased division of labor) and the negative social consequences (increased absenteeism and a higher number of conflicts and accidents) and the negative economic consequences in terms of low productivity was thereby established. The researchers named this new understanding "socio-technical systems" and proposed that a basis for optimum results is created only by the *joint optimalization* (i.e., the active consideration) of both the technical and social systems (Emery, 1959). These STS discoveries were subsequently confirmed in a range of field studies carried out throughout the world (see Rice, 1958; Emery and Thorsrud, 1976; and others).

QUALITY OF WORKING LIFE

From the onset of socio-technical systems theory, improving everyone's *quality of working life* has been a central goal in organizations and more recently in network and ecosystem design. Quality of working life is seen as an outcome of choices made in the design of a socio-technical system. Through applying the concept of "joint optimization," STS-D seeks to increase both traditional metrics such as cost, safety, quality, and agility and quality of working life. Job satisfaction has long been regarded as a questionable indicator for quality of working life. Alternatively, Fred and Merrelyn Emery offered the six criteria of good work as a way of thinking about, measuring, and designing for improved quality of working life (Emery and Emery 1978). Here are three of the criteria:

- Decision making in one's work
- Variety in one's work
- Opportunities for ongoing learning and growth in one's work

Different people saw these three criteria as desirable to different degrees. A typical approach was to ask, "What do you have, and what do you want?" and then to design for the desired state if it was different from what existed. Their other three criteria were as follows:

- Respect from and of one's peers
- Perceived meaningfulness of one's work to the community and even larger society
- The likelihood that one's work would lead to a desirable future

These last three criteria were considered to be things everyone would want an unlimited amount of. Years later, Marvin Weisbord (1987) suggested a simpler definition of Quality of Working Life: "The experience of dignity, meaning, and community in the workplace."

The question is how the quality of working life should be conceptualized from this perspective. Job satisfaction has long been regarded as a questionable indicator for quality of working life. Instead, De Sitter(1981) argued, based on the theory of Karasek 1979, 1990), for control capacity as a central indicator (see also chapters 5 and 18). STS-D involves the motivation theories that match the concept of control capacity. The importance of the quality of working life is found in many successful practical cases, with a demonstrable increase in involvement, flexibility, and process control.

The importance of quality of working life is attracting more international attention today, and we are convinced that current issues in this field can draw lessons from relatively less well-known developments in the original socio-technical philosophy. Design-related problems are now an issue not only in industry, but also particularly in large organizations in the services sector, in the government, in health care, and in education. This often involves "knowledge-intensive" work or mental work—work in which professional control capacity is needed and limited external-control possibilities exist.

DESIGNING AS A PRINCIPLE-BASED PROCESS

The term "design" can be considered as both a noun and a verb. As a noun, as in the "organization's design," it represents the set of choices made, often over time and often unintentionally, about a range of what we might call (if we were to not use the term "design") the organizational architecture, or perhaps the organization's infrastructure. In any case, the organization's "design" can be thought to include the choices described below in table 1.1 (adapted from W. O Lytle 1998).

Design as a verb—that is, to design—or the designing of a work system or organization, is the activity or process of making decisions/choices about the above elements. Within the STS-D framework, designing is guided by a set of principles, rather than a set of prescriptions, on the assumption that every organization is unique, exists within unique circumstances, pursues a unique set of goals and objectives, and has a unique set of members. Although not initially published until 1976 (and then revisited in 1987), Albert Cherns's *The Principles of Socio-technical Design* was among the most influential set of guidelines used by practitioners, particularly in North America. These principles are summarized in table 1.2 below (adapted from Cherns 1987).

Strategic Management and Organization Renewal	a) How will the organization stay in touch with changing conditions in the business environment? b) How does strategic planning occur? c) What systems will ensure long-term availability of the requisite skills and technology for the organization? d) What mechanisms will we use for the review of organizational culture, structure, and processes?
Role of Management	a) What will the changes be in management roles, levels, and style? b) Which boundaries must be managed and by whom? c) What is the process for identifying breakthrough targets? d) What coordination and goal-deployment tasks are needed, and who will perform them?
Support Systems	a) What information systems (electronic or otherwise) will be needed to support the various teams (e.g., operating teams and specialty teams)? b) What changes are required in our financial-management systems? c) What changes in our human resource systems (selection, development, performance management, reward, compensation, etc.) will be required? d) What new or different administrative systems will we need? e) What separate, new, or different maintenance systems will we need?
Customer Service and Continuous-Improvement Systems	a) How will we bring "the voice of the customer" into every work group? b) What will be our continuous-improvement structures and processes? (What types of continuous-improvement teams will be used? How will improvement projects be identified?) c) What education in continuous improvement will be needed (what tools)? How will it be delivered? d) What will the teams' in-process measures be? e) What will the roles, procedures, and tools for improvement and problem solving be? f) How will we increase the reliability of our processes?
Basic Work System	a) Are there any changes in our core business processes (e.g., the elimination or combination of any existing activities/functions)? b) What should the major organization boundaries/groupings be? c) What will the key measures for the business be? d) What should the department/team boundaries and staffing levels be? e) What will the key measures for each team (operating and resource) be? f) What skills will be needed? How will they be attained? g) What will the key activities be within the work groups/teams? h) What should the layout and technology be like? i) What will the key communication, coordination, and linkage mechanisms be?

Table 1.1 What Gets Designed in an STS-D Process?

Principle	Definition
Joint Optimization	Design for system optimization, not maximization of one aspect at the expense of the other. Design technical, social, and financial systems jointly.
Variance Control	Variance (errors and anomalies) is best controlled by those closest to the origin of the variance.
Minimum Critical Specification	Specify only what is critical, and keep specification to a minimum. Specify what, not how.
Multifunctionality	When possible, accomplish multiple goals or tasks with one design choice.
Boundary Location	Place boundaries only where absolutely required. Do not define boundaries in ways that interrupt critical internal and external information flow.
Information Flow	Information required to control variances should flow first to those best positioned to control those variances. Key information should be shared as widely as possible.
Alignment/Congruency	All aspects of the system must be aligned; support systems must be congruent with overall design.
Equifinality	There is more than one right solution; there are many paths to the goal.
Incompletion	All designs can be improved on and are, in this sense, incomplete.
Self-Direction	People are capable of self-direction when given the information, authority, accountability, and freedom to act.

Table 1.2 Design Principles

INTERNATIONAL DEVELOPMENTS AND WAVES OF EVOLUTION

Trist et al (1963) described (from their research in the coal mines) discovery of a "new paradigm" of work organization, in which "the technological imperative could be disobeyed" (Trist and Murray, 1993), allowing work-group cohesion and self-regulation even in highly mechanized environments (Trist et al. 1963). The ideas of designing work systems for both people and the needs of the organization were applied in the Indian textile industry (Rice, 1953). More exploration of ideas in practice occurred in Norway during the mid-1960s in manufacturing and chemical-process industries (Emery and Thorsrud 1969).

From the early 1970s to the mid-1990s, STS-D was applied (with significant economic and human successes—Davis and Cherns 1975, Kolodny and van Beinum 1983) within North America, Europe, Scandinavia, and Australia. Virtually all of this early work in STS-D was done within organizations where the work could be characterized as "routine" or "linear" in nature—that is, typical of manufacturing, mining, or repetitive service processes such as warehousing. The unique North American variant is described in chapter 2.

The first wave of evolution in the practice of STS-D occurred in Australia and Scandinavia, with the development of a shift from representative participation in the design process to direct participation in the design process. This became known as "participative design" (Emery 1982, 1989), an approach front-ended with a form of strategic planning knows as "Search Conferencing" followed by the direct involvement of the whole workforce in a move to self-managing teams. In Scandinavia, the shift was also toward more collaboration in (re)design through "democratic dialogue" (Gustavsen 1985, 1989). (For more on democratic dialogue, see chapter 10.) In chapter 9, the concept of the employee's voice is discussed in terms of the design of humane and innovative work(places). The employee's voice deals with critical questions of the meaning, structure, fundamental value, and complexity of participation in the design of one's workplace within a complex and turbulent global economic environment. Chapter 6 continues on this issue in discussing organizing for innovation and (strategic) decision-making. It describes the approach more widely known as sociocracy (or "dynamic governance" in North America). Of course the employee's voice always has to do with power. In chapter 12, the relation between STS-D and power is discussed.

The second wave of practice change came about as a result of the shift in the nature of work in North America (not only in the United States). Partially as a result of greater accessibility to computers and the offshoring of much manufacturing, there was a large growth in IT-assisted white-collar service industries such as insurance, banking, R and D, and health care. This shift, sometimes referred to as "the information society," created a large sector in which information rather than material goods was "transformed" by organizations in their value-adding work. New analytic tools (e.g., deliberation and coalition analysis) and concepts were developed to allow STS-D to be more effectively applied to nonroutine/nonlinear and more professionalized work systems (Pava 1983, Taylor et al. 1986) (see chapter 4).

The third wave of practice evolution is the designing of networks of all kinds (including value or supply chains) and even the designing of issue-based ecosystems (the collection of stakeholders, both individual and institutional) who have a shared interest in the management of or solution to complex issues such as global pandemics (e.g., the recent Ebola crisis). This most recent evolution has occurred in response to the reality that individual organizations, while they still exist, almost always, either wholly or largely, operate in various forms of value-realization networks, where there may be one or two dominant players in the network but where no one organization is able to fully provide everything needed by its customers, clients, or patients. More detail about this design practice is included in chapter 8. Of significance also is the Dutch approach, originally named "integral organizational renewal" and now referred to as "Lowlands STS-D." Developed by Ulbo De Sitterin the closing decade of the last century, in the "Lowlands STS-D" practice, a much greater focus is placed on reducing the need for costly coordination mechanisms within complex organizations by creating not only self-regulating work teams but creating them within self-regulating, customer-owning "miniorganizations" that are sometimes referred to as "factories within factories." More on this topic is included in chapters 5, 6, 17, and 18. An important issue is the design of coordination mechanisms, especially in a more virtual world (see chapter 7).

It is important to note that as STS-D has evolved, each wave has augmented but not replaced earlier practices. This means we still see, on occasion, STS-D applied as described in chapter 2. We see occasional use of participative design (as described in chapter 3), as well as the occasional use of Pava's ideas for nonroutine work design (as described in chapter 4). And of course the "Lowlands STS-D" practice continues in use as well.

Retrospectively, one can see these shifts in the context of the following, with each focus being nested in the next, like Russian dolls:

- Moving from task design as the focus to the design of the work system
- Moving from design of the work system to the design of the organization
- Moving from the design of the organization to the design of networks and ecosystems

STS-D, LEAN, AND OTHER MODERN DESIGN APPROACHES:

Socio-technical systems design is perhaps the least known of the most popular approaches to organization improvement, among which Lean is the runaway leader. Some would argue that Lean is nothing more than industrial engineering on steroids and downsizing, while others argue that STS-D is simply about putting everyone on self-managing teams. Both of these characterizations are, of course, caricatures and have little, if any, value as true descriptors.

The reality is that STS-D has been largely eclipsed in the popular discourse as approaches that were marketed more effectively (such as business process reengineering, total quality management, etc.) have come and gone. Lean (along with its Six Sigma cousin), however, has evolved to become, by far, the most-used approach to organizational optimization, while STS-D continues to serve mostly as a body of theory and practice supporting Lean and other such approaches. A useful exploration of the relationship between Lean and STS-D is described in chapter 17. Chapter 18 also elaborates on the integration of Lean and STS-D. In this chapter, a concept for Total Workplace Innovation is presented. In Total Workplace Innovation, Gittel's theory of horizontal relational coordination and the practices of new ways of work (time and place (independent of work) are combined with different approaches. In the past few years in Europe, with the title "workplace innovation," the European Commission policy has focused on the creation of new work systems that are more effective in innovation. Implicit in the STS-D theory and practices are an important base. Chapter 11 describes both a policy concept and its practical manifestation through the European Workplace Innovation Network.

In our society nowadays, information technology takes an important place in life and work. In an early stage, STS-D paid attention to the design of information systems—for example, the ETHICs methodology so nicely described in Chapter 15. However, it is still a huge challenge to merge the design of information systems with STS-D theories and practices. Chapter 16 is about applying information technology from a sociotechnical perspective with arguably the most potent force for workplace change—information technologies. Production systems tend to become more automated and more complex. An important question in this is how can we design jobs so that it is still possible to control these complex technical systems? In chapter 13, several topics are discussed in relation to STS-D, including the evolving socio-technical perspectives on "human factors and safety," in which the perspectives of Normal Accidents Theory (NAT), High Reliability Theory (HRT), the Swiss Cheese Model, Resilience Engineering (RE), and macroergonomics are considered. Chapter 14 discusses a socio-technical systems perspective of resilience-centered approaches for training design in an electric utility. Using a case study, the authors elaborate on some of the ideas presented.

CONCLUSION

In this chapter, we have highlighted some of the important shifts in STS-D theory and practice as they have evolved from their original conceptions at the Tavistock Institute to the many variants now being applied (however sporadically) around the world. This evolution gives a wide variety of different lenses of the STS-D theory and practice developments. We have seen a merger of STS-D with other theories and practices. We hope we have presented an overview of this colorful landscape so that the different lenses and approaches are easier to understand. A more widespread understanding will help us create innovative and humane organizations and networks. We also have new challenges to face (see chapter 19).

REFERENCES

Cherns, A. 1976. "The Principles of Socio-technical Design." *Human Relations* 29.

Cherns, A. 1987. "The Principles of Socio-technical Design Revisited." *Human Relations* 40.

Davis, L. E., and A. Cherns. 1975. *The Quality of Working Life*, vol. 1. Free Press.

Emery, F. E. 1959. *Characteristics of Socio-technical Systems*. London: Tavistock Institute.

Emery, F. E., and E. Thorsrud. 1976. *Democracy at Work*. Leiden: Martinus Nijoff.

Emery, M., and F. Emery. 1978. "Searching: For New Directions, In New Ways...For New Times." In *Management Handbook for Public Administrators*, J. W. Sutherland (ed.). New York and London: Van Nostrand.

Emery, F. E. 1989. *Toward Real Democracy: Further Problems*. Toronto, Ontario: Ministry of Labour.

Karasek, R. 1979. "Job Demand, Job Decision Latitude, and Mental Strain: Implications for Job Design." *Administrative Science Quarterly* 24.

Karasek, R., and T. Theorell. 1990. *Healthy Work: Stress, Productivity, and the Reconstruction of Working Life*. New York, NY : Basic Books.

Kolodny, H., and van Beinum, H. 1983. *The Quality of Working Life and the 1980s*. Santa Barbara, CA: Praeger.

Lytle, W. O. 1998. *Designing High-Performance Organizations*. Plainfield, NJ: Block Petrella Weisboard.

Pava, C. 1983. *Managing New Office Technology: An Organizational Strategy*. Boston: Harvard Business School.

Rice. A.K., 1958. *Systems of Organization*. London: Tavistock Publications.

Sitter, L. U. 1981. *Op Weg Naar Nieuwe Fabrieken en Kantoren*. Deventer: Kluwer.

Taylor, J. 1986. "Long-Term Socio-technical Systems Change in a Computer Operations Department." *Journal of Applied Behavioral Science*.

Trist, E. I., H. Murray, and B. Trist (eds.). 1993. *The Social Engagement of Social Science: A Tavistock Anthology, Vol. II: The Socio-technical Perspective.*Philadelphia, PA; University of Pennsylvania Press

Trist, E., G. W. Higgin, H. Murray, and A. B. Polock. 1963. *Organizational Choice.* London: Tavistock Publications.

Trist, E. L., and K. W. Bamforth. 1951. "Some Social and Psychological Consequences of the Longwall Method of Coal Getting." *Human Relations* (4): 3–38.

van Eijnatten, F. 1993. "The Paradigm That Changed the Workplace." *Social Science for Social Action: Toward Organizational Renewal.* Assen/Stockholm: Van Gorcum/Arbetslivscentrum.

Weisboard, M. 1987. *Productive Workplaces.* San Francisco: Jossey-Bass.

Two

Creating High-Performing Organizations: The North American Open Socio-technical Systems Design Approach

Bernard J. Mohr

INTRODUCTION

Any organizational system is an intricate web of roles, management practices, structures, processes, tasks, technology, and people. How these elements interact with one another determines how successfully an organization can produce a service or product within the constraints of cost, quality, timeliness, safety, and customer requirements. Organizations that continually succeed within these constraints can be considered *high-performing organizations*.[1]

Any measurement of a *high-performing organization (HPO)* must consider the connection between people and organizational-level outcomes. Organizations seeking to become HPOs must design their work systems to ensure that the following three "people conditions" are met:

1. **People must be able to do what is expected of them**. This means guaranteeing the availability of appropriate skills, resources, technology, and opportunities within the work system.
2. **People must want to do these tasks**. This implies a level of individual commitment that can result only from appropriate

---

1 I am indebted to Peter Vaill, whose work on high-performing organizations provides the origins for the notions I present on this concept.

management practices, reward systems, company norms and culture, and work designed to be intrinsically fulfilling.

3. **People must be allowed to do these tasks.** This requires innovations in the management of responsibility and discretion, the elimination of unnecessary boundaries and/or the reformulation of boundaries to support clear ownership of customer groups, and increased access to information needed for operations.

Every work system devises its own way of modifying roles, tasks, processes, and technology to create these conditions. What matters is that this infrastructure exists and that it makes a difference to both the quality of working life experienced by those working in the system and the outcomes the system is able to create. The conscious creation of these conditions—a process called "organization designing"—is how the infrastructure for an HPO is developed.

In addition to knowing about these "people conditions," one should also learn the organizational-level description of an HPO. According to this description, high-performing organizations have the following characteristics:

1. **An HPO largely achieves both its human and business/service goals**. Contrary to some widespread ideas, an HPO is not a "perfect" system that achieves 100 percent of what it strives for. Rather, an HPO performs in the "top range" most of the time. It may not meet every deadline, constraint, or individual need, but observers of high-performing organizations describe them as consistently ranking in the "top ten" of their fields.

2. **An HPO can adapt to changing requirements with minimal disruption to goal achievement and minimal cost (economic or otherwise) to the organization's members and its external stakeholders**. The pace and quantity of changes confronting organizations today are greater than ever before. They must address new demands from employees, customers, competitors, and regulatory agencies. The hallmark of an HPO is its flexibility to modify operations in response to these demands—through ways

other than going out of business. An HPO can adapt to change without incurring the economic, psychological, and emotional trauma often associated with major organizational transitions.

3. **An HPO is characterized by an alignment of the organization's culture, vision, and structure.** We often find organizations that have worked hard to create their own visions. This refers to a widely shared image of an organization's preferred future. A vision becomes the driving force for deciding what kinds of norms, values, and beliefs are to be inculcated. In modifying these cultural elements, organizations frequently find that the structure of work and authority are major factors influencing their cultures. Only when an organization's vision, culture, and structure are "in sync" can it exhibit some of the characteristics of an HPO. For example, an organization in the forest-products industry developed a vision of operating as a series of small entrepreneurial businesses (within the structure of the larger corporation). To attain this vision, management engaged "those who do the work" in designing major structural changes affecting supervision, team composition and roles, and group boundaries, as well as changes in the incentive system and information systems, so that business results would be valued more than individual performance and so that the teams had the resources to accomplish their work. These changes enabled the organization to align its vision, culture, and structure.

4. **An HPO achieves its energy for operation from a high level of individual commitment, which is generated within individuals rather than imposed on them externally through a mechanism of control and punishment.** The underlying premise is that although all organizations require various amounts of human energy, an HPO both requires and generates more of it. Human energy is needed for productivity, and high-performing organizations consume unusually high levels in seeking to be constantly responsive and effective in attaining their goals despite

changing environments and pressures to reduce costs (something faced by all organizations, from governments to health care to the automobile industry). An HPO can consume so much energy only by ensuring that equivalent or larger amounts are constantly generated.

To evaluate the performance of an HPO, the following measurement criteria can be used:

1. **The ratio of resources consumed to the value of what is produced**. This is a basic criterion for evaluating all organizations. Unless the perceived value of an organization's "output"—whether this is a social service, a physical product, information, or, as in the case of a symphony orchestra, a pleasurable experience—exceeds the perceived value of the "input," not only can the organization not be called a high-performing organization, but it will soon cease to exist at all. When examining this criterion, we must not limit our definitions of input and output to traditional monetary ones. Rather, we should refer to a "give/get" ratio. This is the ratio of *expected return on "gives"* (EROG) to *actual returns on "gives"* (AROG), based on the perceptions of stakeholders who provide the resources that enable the organization to operate. When the "gives" include such resources as labor, energy, commitment, electoral mandates, political support, information, physical materials, and money, the "gets" (i.e., return for one's investment) include enhanced power and status in addition to valued products and services, job satisfaction, and money.

2. **The timeliness and quality of the system's output.** No matter how excellent a symphony orchestra is, unless it produces its "product" at the times its customers want to "consume" it, it cannot be considered an HPO. Similarly, a company may offer a highly popular toy, but if it cannot make the toy available in stores until

the week after Christmas, the company cannot be considered an HPO. With respect to quality, the American automobile industry offers classic examples of organizations that are able to meet deadlines but have difficulty ensuring sufficient product quality to maintain their historical shares of the market. Although these companies have put forth major efforts to improve this, they continue to suffer from a perceived "quality gap" in the minds of a significant number of potential customers.

3. **The appropriateness of the output for the primary receiving system**. The primary receiving system consists of those individuals or groups an organization is primarily in the business of serving. A hospital's primary receiving system is its patients; an accounting firm's primary receiving system is its clients. The output of an HPO is typically considered desirable and relevant by its primary receiving system. Examples of organizations meeting this criterion include accounting firms that deliver advice on taxes when asked and provide bookkeeping services on request. An accounting firm that fails to provide its clients with necessary financial planning advice, however—or provides advice its clients consider useless—would not be considered a high-performing organization.

4. **The degree to which the internal individual commitment— rather than control—of organization members is the primary source of energy for operations**. As discussed above in the section on system-level characteristics, the issue is the balance between external control and internal commitment (Walton 1985) as strategies for generating human energy in an organization. All organizations require some degree of internal control as a mechanism of coordination and general management. HPOs tend to rely more on members' commitment to the workplace as a way of achieving necessary behaviors rather than on such controlling tactics as use of time cards, close supervision, piece-rate compensation, and the like.

These four major criteria, along with the description of system-level and "people" characteristics, form the framework for understanding HPOs and for evaluating the extent to which an organization can be considered high performing. The following section discusses how to create (i.e., design) such an organization, whether one is modifying an existing organization or starting a new one.

ORGANIZATION DESIGN, OPEN SOCIO-TECHNICAL SYSTEMS, AND HIGH-PERFORMING ORGANIZATIONS

The opening section of this chapter referred to an organization as an intricate web of roles, management practices, structures, processes, tasks, technology, and people. Organization design is an umbrella term for the conscious creation of an HPO through the systematic and systemic modification of some or all of the above elements making up the "intricate web."

A *systematic approach* is one based on a thoughtful consideration of change and the politics involved with it and on a comprehensive diagnosis of what exists. (This differs from an approach that simply adopts the latest management fad, such as *management by walking around*, TQM, BPR, or the like.)

A *systemic approach* is one based on the recognition of the interconnections of these elements and the tendency of organizations to resist change unless a "critical mass" of the elements is modified to support the change. For example, attempts to modify people's work responsibilities to make them more entrepreneurial are unrealistic unless simultaneous changes are made in the incentives, decision-making processes, and information systems, and unless opportunities are provided to develop required skills.

The rest of this section examines in more detail some of the major organizational elements typically analyzed and modified during an organizational design or redesign process conducted from an "open socio-technical systems" perspective.

Individual skills invariably need development because new work roles require behaviors different from those learned over the years in the organization. The types of skills needing development are skills related to team and interpersonal relations and technical skills. In the case of the redesign of major railway organizations, the number of work-role classifications was reduced from sixteen to eight. Because of this, employees needed extensive retraining in technical skills. For example, individuals who had worked as porters needed to learn how to be waiters, make coffee, and the like. Moreover, the redesigned organization called for work teams to meet at the start of a trip so that members could assign tasks, determine food requirements, and so forth, creating a need to develop skills in problem solving and team decision making.

Organizational redesign affects the availability and allocation of physical and financial resources within the work system. Because the processes for distributing scarce resources can be designed in many ways—each having a dramatically different impact on system performance—the organizational design process requires careful assessment of alternatives. One frequently used option is to assign responsibility for supplies procurement to the work group actually responsible for using those supplies. This movement toward semiautonomous work teams has systemic implications for the traditional staff functions of purchasing and finance. The organizational design process must also note how the roles associated with these functions will need to be modified.

Technology design is another part of the overall design process that can aid in achieving the desired level of total system performance. Technology can be designed to either minimize or maximize the control experienced by the human being or to provide little or much data. For example, when Ford Motor Company sought to improve product quality, it gave each assembly-line operator access to a button that, if pressed, would shut down the line. This modification gave the operators more control over the technology, an important variable of the overall quality-improvement program. Of course, such modifications make sense only if operators have timely access to data enabling them to take action appropriately. Technology can often be designed so that additional "readouts" of information become available to operators.

Modifying management practices is an essential component of organization design. Such practices as determining how decisions are made and the level of involvement of various parties in this process, employing formal goal setting versus an activity orientation, devising incentives to encourage various behaviors, and deciding whether to connect rewards with achievement of results rather than seniority have strong influences on the total system's performance.

As noted previously, the alignment among an organization's culture, vision, and structure is important. All three elements can be changed through the organization design process. In corporate culture, the design process explores and determines the existing norms and values that shape and guide daily activities. The design process identifies organization rites and rituals, the ways culture becomes communicated through management practices, the changes necessary, and how such changes may be implemented. Design mechanisms such as philosophy and mission statements—and statements about what constitutes good management practices—can communicate and guide the design process as it addresses job design and help the remainder of the organization become aware of the new culture.

Perhaps the most visible aspect of an organization's culture is the way it chooses to design individual jobs or work roles. The design process involves making choices about what jobs include or exclude, the extent to which jobs are interconnected, the levels of autonomy associated with various jobs, and the challenges and development opportunities they offer. Choices made involving these elements have some of the strongest impacts on the organization's culture and the concomitant energy levels within it. That is because the daily work required by people's jobs is the setting in which the design process's best intentions either fly or falter.

Along with designing individual jobs, the design process must also consider and choose from among alternatives for connecting and aggregating jobs. This involves answering such questions as the following:

- Should people work individually or as teams?
- How many teams should a unit have? What is the best basis for determining unit boundaries and thus avoiding overfragmentation of the work system?
- How will communication occur within the teams and among teams and units? Who will have the authority to make what kinds of decisions?
- What types of information do individuals require? By teams? By units? By divisions? How can this information be made available so that the necessary data for self- correction are timely and accessible?

All of these decisions must be made as part of the organization design process—but only after extensively assessing how the work system currently performs. Indeed, such an assessment, consisting of the technical-system analysis and social-system analysis, is part of the design process. It must occur, however, before one chooses options in the areas discussed previously.

Both the analysis and subsequent design process seek to consciously and systematically create an HPO having the organizational characteristics described previously and leading to a situation in which:

- People *are able* to do what is expected of them.
- People *want* to do these tasks.
- People *are allowed* to do these tasks.

OPEN SOCIO-TECHNICAL SYSTEMS DESIGN (OSTD)

The North American Open Socio-technical Systems Design approach to designing organizations is composed of a theory and procedure (Pava, 1983) different from those associated with traditional design approaches. According to the perspective of open socio-technical systems, an organization has the following characteristics:

- It is influenced by, and needs to respond continually to, its external environments as it converts input (i.e., raw materials or information) into output (i.e., products or services).
- It is established through a work system composed of a social system interacting with a technical system to convert or transform input into output.
- The technical system consists of any combination of techniques, machines, instructions, or tools used to produce desired output.
- The social system consists of the work-related interactions among persons managing the technical systems (i.e., the transformation of input into output).

North American socio-technical design theory holds that a high-performing organization results from finding, through comprehensive analysis (i.e., designing), the "best match" or most mutually enhancing "fit" between the technical and social systems of an organization.

This theory of designing to achieve "joint optimization"—the best fit—substantially differs from traditional designs such as scientific management, which seeks maximum automation and job simplification. Socio-technical theory assumes that social systems can adapt to the needs of technical systems rather easily. The drawback of the traditional approach is evident in Calvin Pava's description of the General Motors plant in Lordstown:

In 1972...labor strife dramatically underscored the need for a fundamental transformation in how work is organized. At the time, Lordstown housed America's most technologically advanced automotive assembly line. In accord with the Taylorist principles of efficiency, automation was maximized and worker roles greatly simplified. Workers went on strike to protest the low quality of their jobs in this supposedly optimal system. Overoptimization of technology by itself and subpar development of the plant's social system led to deterioration in the overall performance of the facility. The Lordstown episode marked a watershed in American management of human resources. It signified the need to obtain superior performance in ways that depart from traditional reliance upon simple work and purely technological optimization (1983, 128).

The open socio-technical systems approach to organization design not only provides a theoretical perspective but also a specific set of participation procedures for analysis and design activities (see also chapter 3). These activities are carried out in five phases (Cotter 1983):

- Initial planning
- Technical-systems analysis
- Social-systems analysis
- Development of alternatives
- Implementation planning

Technical-systems analysis involves identifying the sequence of the self-contained steps or operations for converting input into desired output. It emphasizes identifying any variances or problems occurring within each operation, how they are currently dealt with, and the consequences for operations "downstream" if variances are not adequately dealt with at the source.

Social-systems analysis involves describing the existing interactions of employees, not only with respect to who controls what variances and how this is done, but also with respect to coordination among groups and individuals, particularly in solving unexpected problems arising from unpredicted events in the organization's external environment. Social system analysis also examines existing organizational processes for recruitment, incentives, performance evaluation, training, career management, and the like and how these influence employees' commitment and the organization's capacity for self-renewal and development over time.

The technical and social-system analyses provide information necessary for considering alternative organization designs. Developing and evaluating design alternatives involves assessing the extent to which possible new jobs and arrangements for connecting them do the following:

- Allow for variances to be controlled as much as possible at their source, thereby minimizing or reducing costly work-flow problems
- Provide meaningful work as defined by the employees themselves
- Create situations in which persons are able to, want to, and are allowed to do the tasks necessary for both the short- and long-term success of the organization

PROCESSES AND STRUCTURES FOR OPEN SOCIO-TECHNICAL SYSTEMS DESIGN

Both the theory and procedures of the open socio-technical systems approach to organization design are of little use when implemented through a traditional process of unilaterally developing—by staff or external consultants—the analyses and recommendations. Alternatively, the open socio-technical systems design approach prescribes a heavily participative process in which the structures for participation are created and agreed to during the first step of the design activity sequence (the initial planning phase). This phase "includes the formation of an approval body and a design team. The approval body is composed of senior managers who have a stake in the final outcome and whose responsibility it is to guide and approve proposals from the team formed to design the new organization. The design team is charged with the task of envisioning the ideal future state, analyzing the current work system, and recommending a new organization design to the approval body" (Ranney and Carder 1974, 171).

PROBLEMS WITH TRADITIONAL APPROACHES TO ORGANIZATION DESIGN

By more closely exploring the dynamics of traditional approaches to organization design, we can also move closer to understanding the role of the methodology, procedures, and theoretical perspective of the open socio-technical systems design approach to the successful design of high-performing organizations.

Managers and employers who have personally been involved in traditional design approaches frequently describe their experiences with them by using statements such as the following:

- "It's what we do every five years—move from centralization to decentralization, or vice versa, often without any lasting impact on the way we really do things around here."
- "That's what those people in the head office do to us when they have nothing else to keep them busy."
- "My job is to get the work done in this business, not to spend my time worrying about academic theories."

Traditional organizational design processes frequently evoke such unflattering images in part because managers and workers (i.e., individual contributors) alike consider them as the following:

- Something done by one group (usually senior management or staff) to another group (usually middle managers and their subordinates)
- Relatively unconnected to the operational problems of the production/service process, partly because they do not include any analysis of the technical or social systems
- Political maneuvers by incoming managers that will have little impact on work done on a daily basis
- Something line managers are not responsible for ("Let the personnel office do it.")
- Belonging to a small set of previously used—and discarded—design "solutions" ("It's either functional, product, or matrix, so why get excited?")

- Focusing only on authority and reporting relationships (i.e., changing the boxes on an organization chart) rather than representing the more comprehensive approach of open socio-technical systems design

Indeed, much of the popular management literature is consistent with these characterizations. For example, much of the past organization-design literature suggest only three or four basic organizational configurations (product, functional, matrix, or geographical) and describe the task of the staff expert (or senior management) to be determining which of these configuration is best for the particular organization.

Experience suggests that the likelihood of successfully designing an HPO by using such traditional approaches is low because such approaches:

- Are not based on a detailed operational analysis of actual, current work practices.
- Have not meaningfully involved those persons closest to the operational process (i.e., workers/individual contributors and line managers).
- Focus on solving only today's—or even yesterday's—problems rather than creating an organization capable of flexibly responding to tomorrow's challenges.
- Do not have the necessary commitment and support of those at lower levels, which are required for successful implementation.
- Are based on the false assumption that modifying only authority/reporting relationships will be sufficient for obtaining intended results.
- Use analytic perspectives that make the "designers" prisoners of their own histories, cultures, and traditions.
- Stem from a constraint orientation emphasizing all that cannot be changed, rather than from an inventive/creative orientation central to effective organizational change.

SUCCESSFULLY IMPLEMENTING THE OPEN SOCIO-TECHNICAL SYSTEM APPROACH TO DESIGNING HIGH-PERFORMING ORGANIZATIONS

The following factors must be present to achieve a successful outcome using an open socio-technical systems design approach:

- The proper analytic perspective, methodology, and procedures for focusing on the right questions (i.e., an open socio-technical systems perspective)
- A design approach characterized by innovation, invention, and experimentation
- Analysis and design activities that involve not only technical/staff personnel and senior management, but also those who will do the actual work
- Recognition by both the participants and those providing resources that the organization design process is a social activity with some human, nonlinear aspects and that it needs widespread, ongoing organizational support

The fourth factor cited above emphasizes the need to consider organization design an activity that, as much as any other key activity, must be managed so that it receives appropriate resources and widespread support and achieves congruence between the process used and the end results.[2]

Table 2.1 presents other implications for action associated with nine key dimensions, moving from a traditional approach to an open socio-technical systems design approach when designing high-performing organizations (Mohr 1984).

---

2 These concepts, often referred to as the set of knowledge and skills related to the "management of organizational change" are discussed in more detail by Beckhard and Harris (1977).

Dimension Movement Required	
1. Participation	Movement from restricting analysis and design to technical specialists and senior managers toward also including operational employees, middle managers, and key organization stakeholders (e.g., union officials, personnel specialists, other staff organization members).
2. Database	Movement from overdependence on individual perceptions and theories as to strengths and weaknesses toward a collection of detailed data on the behavioral and factual aspects of the current operational processes, which consider actual responses to operational problems (i.e., technical system factors) and specific activities of the social system intended to support goal achievement, adaptation to the environment, integration of efforts, and long-term system development.
3. Area of inquiry	Movement from singular, exclusive foci (e.g., those limiting analysis to either structure or equipment or to either procedures or human relations) toward a multiple, inclusive scope of inquiry that includes technology, individual differences, the organization, the environment, and management practices and styles.
4. Causality	Movement from viewing organizational elements as having simple cause-and-effect relationships (e.g., higher pay leads to increased motivation) toward a systemic understanding of multiple causes and effects, not all of which are fully predicted (although one may anticipate their existence)
5. Time orientation	Movement from emphasizing solutions for today's—or yesterday's—problems toward emphasizing the creation of an organizational setting capable of continual, effective progress toward clearly defined goals.
6. Design goals	Movement form an either/or orientation (e.g., calling for choosing between economic and human goals or between short-term responses and long-term development) toward an orientation with multiple goals (e.g., productivity and QWL or short-term results and long-term flexibility)
7. Customization	Movement from a tendency to limit one's choice of design solutions to the three or four structures dominating the literature toward creating a setting uniquely tailored to the organization's own current and future needs
8. Maximization	Movement from designing either the best possible technical system or the best possible social system towards designing the sociotechnical system with the best fit
9. Finality	Movement from expecting the organization design to be completed "once and for all" toward setting a goal of developing the appreciate skills, experience, and flexibility within the organization so that future design activity can be a part of its regular operations, not separate activity

Table 2.1 Implications for Action

CONCLUSIONS

Traditional design approaches for creating high-performing organizations are severely limited by inadequate theoretical frameworks, methodology, and procedures for analysis and design and by their failure to focus on the political processes and organizational structures used for implementing open socio-technical systems theory, methods, and procedures.

Experience suggests that the North American approach, as characterized by the nine dimensions discussed in table 2.1, can help eliminate many of the problems associated with traditional approaches.

Moreover, organizations using open socio-technical systems approach to design will begin to use organization designing, one of management's most powerful interventions for improvement, effectively. To reap the benefits available, however, management must fully understand the essential creative, human, and political nature of the actual design activities, the need for detailed operational analysis, and the need for participative structures for conducting analysis and design.

REFERENCES

Beckhard, R., and R. Harris. 1979. *Organizational Transition: Managing Complex Change.* Reading, Mass.: Addison-Wesley.

Cotter, J. 1983. *Designing Organizations That Work: An Open Socio-technical Systems Perspective.* Unpublished working paper.

Mohr, B. 1984. *Art, Analysis, and Participation: Key Dynamics in Designing Organisations from the Open Socio-technical Systems Perspective.* Unpublished working paper.

Pava, C. 1983. "Designing Managerial and Professional Work for High Performance: A Socio-technical Approach." *National Productivity Review* 2: 126–35.

Ranney, J., and C. Carder. 1984. "Socio-technical Design Methods in Office Settings: Two Cases." *Office Technology and People* 2: 169–84.

Donald W. de Guerre

Three

Open Systems Theory and the Two-Stage Model of Active Adaptation

INTRODUCTION

The main purpose of the version of *open systems theory* developed primarily by Fred Emery, referred to as OST(E), where (E) stands for Emery, is "to promote and create change toward a world that is consciously designed by people, and for people, living harmoniously within their ecological systems, both physical and social" and "to develop an internally consistent conceptual framework or social science, within which each component is operationally defined and hypotheses are testable so that the knowledge required to support the first purpose is created" (Emery 2000).

OST(E) understands that most of our societal problems are expressions of the mechanistic paradigm of organizing called "bureaucracy" and develops an alternative solution that offers a way to move forward toward achieving more desirable futures. Figure 3.1 summarizes the current situation. Treating people as parts in the "big machine" results in negative feelings about the workplace, which starts an irreversible process leading to distress, which over time creates a dissociated, superficial society in which fewer and fewer people vote and we are vulnerable to a new kind of feudalism. Emery calls that society "tele and tinny," meaning coming home from work and picking up a bag of potato chips and a beer to "zone out" on television for the night.

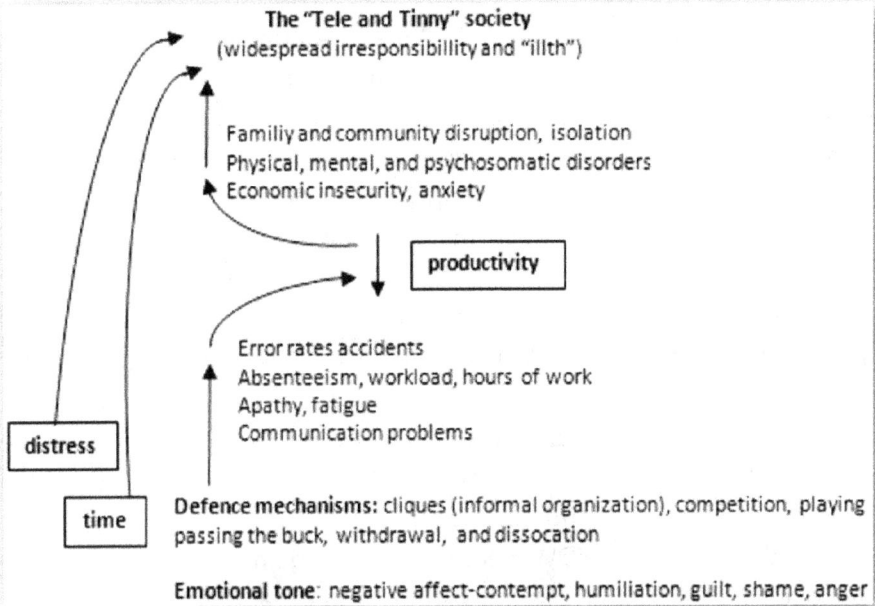

Figure 3.1 Bureaucracy as the Organizational
Expression of Mechanism Produces

Socioecology simply means "people in environment," and if the social environment is structured as a hierarchy of personal dominance, then changing that social environment to a more participative, democratic, appreciative one would create a healthier and more effective society.

When we say that OST(E) is a socioecological systems theory that includes socio-technical systems, we mean that the unit of analysis and design is always the "system in environment," and it is always about more positive and less negative effects and better human relations at work. Research shows that this is what leads to productivity, quality, innovation, and human health (de Guerre and Emery. et al. 2007, de Guerre and Emery 2008, Emery 2008). Figure 3 describes the practical reality of how to create a new, more stable environment populated by true active, adaptive learning organizations that are good for people, the economy, and the planet.

Stage 1 of the two-stage model of active adaptation is the "search conference" (SC). It examines the system in environment over time and elicits ideal seeking behavior, creating an alignment between organizations and their environments. SC is a participative, active, and adaptive planning process. The active, adaptive enterprise actually proactively plans and prepares to improve the environment socially, economically, and ecologically (person, planet, profit), not just the organization. In today's world, actively adapting person, planet, and profit by planning to improve the environment is the new reality for organizations as members of larger innovative ecosystems. At the same time that active, adaptive, innovative organizations begin Stage 2, the participative design workshop (PDW), to align people and the work they do, thus making the organization agile, resilient, and healthy for people.

Combined, SC and PDW create the two-stage model of active, adaptive planning to democratize our paradigm of organizing that permeates how we design workplaces, schools, health care systems, families, etc. This two-stage model is very flexible and can be used in organization

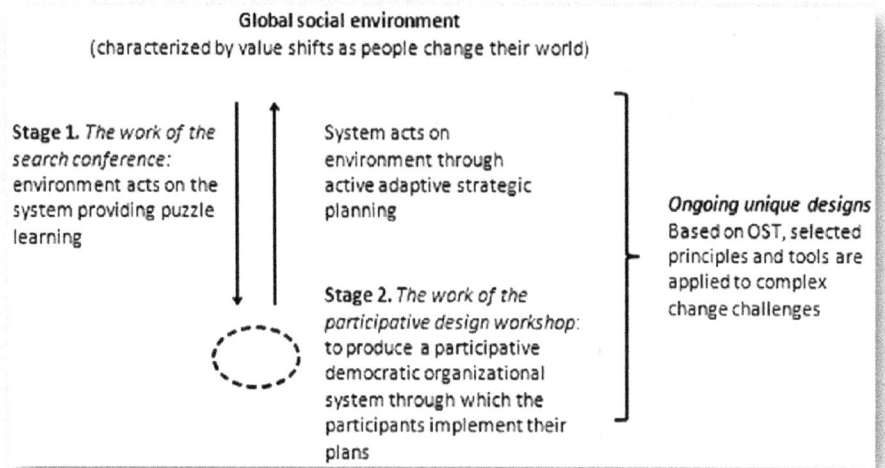

Figure 3.2 The Two-Stage Model of Active Adaption

design, community development, and larger social systems. To do this both requires and develops a new paradigm of organizing that is contextual rather than mechanistic. In this complex structural change process, many unique participative events are required. Keeping a common set of principles, notions, and values helps members of the organization or larger social system develop a common language and common understanding—a new paradigm.

THE SEARCH CONFERENCE

The first step of the two-stage model of active adaptation is a *search conference* (SC). In organization design and redesign, the people who are going to redesign their organizational structure in the second step need to be involved in the SC because it is here that the organizational strategy and business model are developed. The purpose of Stage 2 is to design an organization to deliver on that strategic model, and the designers need to understand it. The SC is also often the first experience of working in a democratic organization structure and thus provides the opportunity for learning about how to participate collaboratively to make decisions and choices.

Because the SC is based on open-systems theory, the key elements of the planning and design process are understanding the system, learning about the environment, and integrating what is learned about these into action plans to produce an active, adaptive system and environment (fig. 2). The process is one of integrated learning and planning. The implicit structure underlying this process is designed to develop high trust levels and ideal seeking. When done well, this results in collaborative creativity and innovation. Figure 3.3 shows the explicit structure of an SC from environmental scanning to diffusion after the search.

Diffusion is an essential distinguishing characteristic of a search because without effective diffusion, any time spent developing strategic plans is virtually worthless. In a search, the participants develop action plans in such a way that their implementation includes effective diffusion of the goals and their underlying ideals. This strategy of diffusion is an important element of performance for world-class systems.

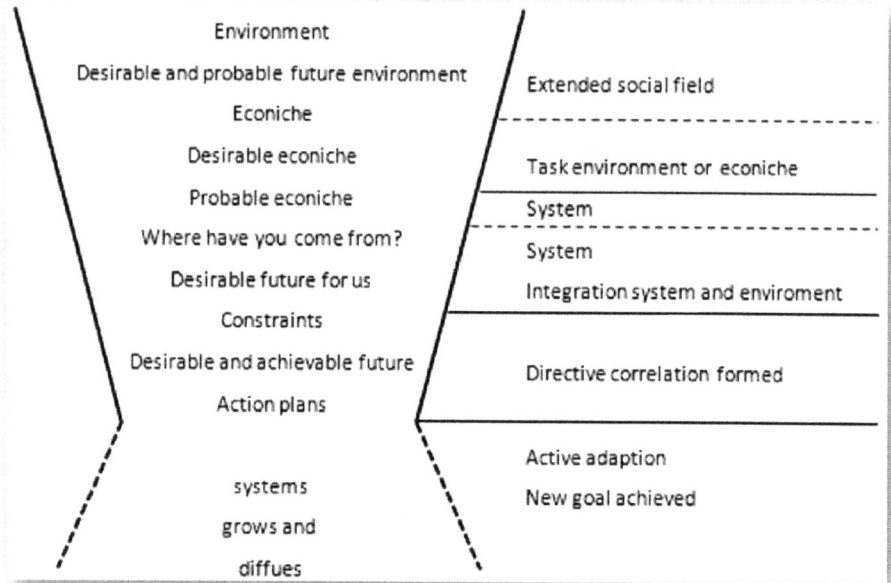

Figure 3.3 Seatch Conference Schematic Framework

The picture of a funnel is a good analogy because at the start of a search, participants consider all possibilities and gradually focus on their choices, most effective strategies, and actions. They start broadly from possible implications of changes in the social field, and as the search progresses, they gradually narrow their focus to a set of specific ends and the means to achieve their future as an adaptive system that influences its surrounding environments.

The SC is a community-building event, not a small-group event. Any small-group work must be integrated in large-group plenary sessions to become community property. Integration includes the process of rationalizing conflict so that the common ground is crystal clear (Emery, 1999).

Conducting an SC does not necessarily result in a transformational path of significant change for the entire organization. It does, however, represent a fundamental change in the way most organizations do strategic planning. The one overriding guiding principle is that the SC is an opportunity for people to start taking more control over their affairs and their destinies. Every aspect of theory and practice is geared to this end.

Strategic-planning searches for organizations usually consist of senior management—those who get paid to take responsibility for the health and direction of the organization. Other participative events or unique designs may be required before and after the organizational search. However, organizations also use search conferences for kicking off major projects, as the first stage of important organizational redesigns and to establish organizational networks and ecosystems to tackle big issues in interorganizational domains. Since the development of the two-stage model of organizational and community change in the early 1990s, most searches have added a participative design workshop (Emery and de Guerre 2006).

THE PARTICIPATIVE DESIGN WORKSHOP

While the SC establishes an active, adaptive enterprise strategy, that is not enough to create a new, more stable environment for people in environment to be healthy and wise. A learning organization that is agile, resilient, innovative, and productive is required to deliver on today's active, adaptive strategies. The PDW is the tool for that purpose. It is participative because the people doing the work are their own best designers, and usually every employee is involved in the participative design exercise. It usually consists of at least one SC, several PDWs, and other participative unique events to adapt support systems, develop new technologies, and establish new policies aligned with the new paradigm. For organization design and redesign, the most important elements of OST(E) are the organizational design principles and the intrinsic motivators (six factors for productive human activity).

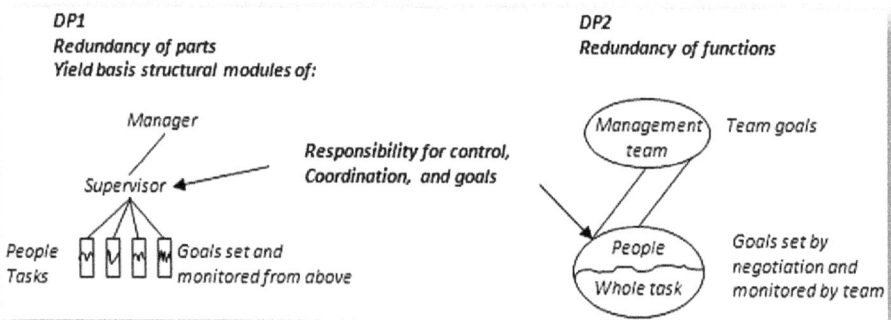

Figure 3.4 Organization Design Principles

There are only two genotypical organization design principles or paradigms. The first one (DP1) is bureaucratic and has the key characteristic that work is always controlled and coordinated at least one level above where the work is done. This principle is the organizational expression of mechanism and creates a hierarchy of personal dominance and at scale and, over time, the tele and tinny society (fig. 3.1). It is called "redundancy of parts" because spare parts (people and machines) are always available. The organization always has more parts available to it than are required and thus can add and subtract parts quickly.

The second organization design principle (DP2) is called "redundancy of functions" (or skills) because people always have more skills than are used in any one task and can carry out different functions when the organization needs to be flexible and adaptive. This is a jointly optimized socio-technical system rather than the fragmented and segmented one seen in DP1. The work team sets its own goals in negotiation with management and then not only does the work but also records, analyzes, and plans to improve the way work gets done. Thus, when applied, this principle yields a flat hierarchy of functions in which people are learning and growing all the time, and no one is in charge of anyone else. Rather, people work together, feel good about themselves and their organization, and develop good human relations. As mentioned, the design process used to create this organization is called a "participative design workshop" (PDW) and is the second stage of the two-stage model of active adaptation.

The PDW is an organization design process with the single purpose of producing an organizational structure based on the second participative democratic design principle. When it is applied, it yields a hierarchy of functions or skills in which people design back into their organizations the human dimension of work that is summarized by the psychological requirements of productive activity. These six criteria, described below, are the *intrinsic motivators* (Emery 2000). When these are present, there is much positive, appreciative affect and better human relations in the workplace. In these structures, people are motivated to produce quantity and high quality, regardless of whether they are producing widgets, services, or ideas. Because the PDW entails a transfer of all the conceptual knowledge and tools required for organizational design and redesign, the participants also learn how and why to maintain DP2 and its consequences.

The intrinsic motivators for employee engagement and productive human activity are as follows:

1. **Adequate elbow room**. This is the sense that people are their own bosses and that, except in exceptional circumstances, they do not have some boss breathing down their necks. The tension between too many and too few degrees of freedom has to be managed.
2. **Opportunity to learn on the job and keep on learning**. Such learning is possible only when people are able to do the following:
   a. Set goals that are reasonable challenges for them.
   b. Get feedback of results in time for them to correct their behavior.
3. **An optimal level of variety**. People can vary the work to avoid boredom and fatigue and to gain the best advantages from settling into a satisfying rhythm of work.
4. **Mutual support and respect**. Conditions should exist in an organization such that people can and do get help and respect from their coworkers. This means that it is important to avoid the creation of conditions in which people do not assist one another, where people are entangled in destructively competitive relationships, and where the group interest denies the individual's capabilities.
5. **Meaningfulness**. This characteristic refers to a sense of one's own work meaningfully contributing to the "greater good." People see the whole product and their contribution to it, and they have pride in knowing how they have added value.
6. **A desirable future.** People want work that allows personal growth and increases skill levels.

The PDW comes in two basic forms, one for redesigning existing DP1 structures and the other for designing a new structure from scratch. For employing organizations with an existing structure, the PDW follows an agreement that the design principle will be formally changed and that this will result in a participative democratic organizational structure to which all policies and support systems such as pay will be adapted. For large organizations, a series of PDWs is designed for a total systemic structural redesign (de Guerre 2000; Purser and Cabana 1998). The form for design rather than redesign is used to create a new organization where none existed before.

If people are to accept responsibility for self-management, it is important that they have been involved in designing the organization of their section or area of the company. In a one- or two-day PDW, participants analyze their existing work organization, develop a new proposal, and outline detailed changes that need to occur before the new design can be implemented. Through the process, all participants learn a great deal about the work that others do and learn about organizational choice— that there is not one best way and that the choice of how to organize ourselves to get work done is critical to business success, people's health, and planetary survival. With this kind of learning, skill development, and appropriate support systems, self-managing groups are more effective on all measures than one-person/one-task DP1 structures (de Guerre, Emery, et al. 2007).

In a PDW, the first phase is an analysis of what currently exists, phase two develops a new organization design proposal, and phase three covers all of the practical matters that need to be in place to ensure the new organization's effectiveness.

In phase 1, the PDW manager does a briefing on the six criteria, DP1, and its consequences. In design teams, the participants then analyze the effects of the existing structure in terms of human motivation and current distribution of skills. In phase 2, the manager does a briefing on DP2 and its consequences and the DP2 structures appropriate for specialist, as well as potentially multiskilled self-managing organizations. Participants briefly draw up the work flow through their section of the organization to ensure that everyone knows what happens in the section as a whole and where critical decisions about control and coordination are made. They then draw up the formal legal structure of their section and redesign that structure. When they have the best possible DP2 structure, they move on to phase 3. In phase 3, they prepare a first draft of the goals that will control the work of that section or the groups within it and then work out their detailed training requirements and anything else required to make the new structure work in practice. They also prepare a first draft of a new career path based on skills, as it would apply to them in their work. These drafts are later negotiated and agreed on with whatever designated organizational authorities. A professional career-path designer will design a final career path based on payment for skills. The final system design will be individual to the organization's people and to the organizational strategic goals (from the SC in stage 1). It will be the unique and local variation of the implementation of the second design principle aligned to the business environment and the planet. The design principles are genotypic and descriptive, not prescriptive. There are many variations or phenotypes that get built up through the participative design process (de Guerre 2000).

Implementation is usually seamless because everyone has been involved in creating it, and almost everyone understands and is committed to the structure that has been agreed to be implemented. Sometimes it is implemented as a prototype to be tested, validated, and refined over a year, with the final decision a year from the implementation date. Sometimes teams need to meet to complete a kind of detailed design for their team—ho does what, when, and with whom—the kind of operational and tactical planning any self-managing group would have to do. Sometimes in the final part of the PDW, new technologies are suggested, or perhaps new products or services are identified in the SC and worked through in the PDW so that there is some work to do before the new organization structure (socially and technically) can be fully implemented. Because people have learned through the process how to work together and make decisions using the rationalization of conflict, it is pretty easy for them to design a staged implementation process that integrates ongoing learning and planning into the process. Each situation is unique, and each organization has to write its own story.

CASE EXAMPLE

An open-pit mine with three hundred employees redesigned itself using the two-stage model. After some time exploring OST and its methods, management communicated to all employees a set of principles and minimal critical specifications for the new design and the design process. After some time discussing these, the employees agreed to engage the design process to create a new DP2 organization. Not every employee thought this was a good idea because being able to blame management would no longer be an option, but enough were prepared to engage that management decided to go forward.

Four participative strategic planning search conferences were held with about thirty-five employees in each. A set of eight desirable future themes were agreed to, and these were posted for everyone to see. However, the implicit learning that occurred through the process about the need to change to meet future business demands was invaluable and deeply appreciated by all who participated.

PDWs were explained to all employees in small groups as working sessions in which the people who work there redesign the social and technical structures, the work and the decision-making processes of the organization. The number of workshops held was not predetermined. Rather, it was agreed that they would continue until all employees had a chance to participate. After each PDW, the designs were published as proposals and consequently formed an ongoing conversation about the relative merits of each design.

After three PDWs, a diagonal-slice management group made up of managers, area supervisors, and frontline supervisors held their own PDW, from which two quite different redesign proposals were put forward into the mix. However, like the shop-floor redesign proposals, both of these had significantly fewer supervisors than the existing organization. Following a few more frontline PDWs in which the management redesign was discussed, a second management PDW was held. In this PDW, only supervisors were involved, and they designed themselves into teams to support the shop-floor teams, with a monitoring and mentoring role, aimed at assisting the workers in taking control of their own work.

Following the PDWs, an implementation team used a simple affinity process to sort the designs into three basic design themes. These were discussed with all employees in small groups to validate that their input had been included and nothing was left out. However, all three basic designs were incomplete, none had placed people into the work teams, and there were areas of work that were not agreed on. Modified PDWs were held to modify the incomplete designs.

When all three basic designs were complete, management withdrew a design that did not meet the minimal critical specifications; it was not based on the second design principle. Management was surprised that no one complained about them taking that unilateral decision, but when everyone has been involved in the process, everyone knows what is right. The participants saw management as simply doing what had been previously agreed to in the SC process of stage 1. A town-hall meeting for all employees was planned to choose between the two remaining designs.

At the town-hall meeting with about three hundred people present, the key criteria for choosing a design was that all people had to be able to support the new design in a fashion that would enable them to work hard to make it work well. To accomplish this, table groups developed rationale for their preferred design choice, and three reasons for their choice. All of the table groups were polled for their choice, and their rationales were tallied. Of the thirty-one groups, twenty-seven favored design "A." The meeting participants were then asked if anyone present could not live with design "A." No one indicated that they could not live with it. Following a bit more dialogue to make minor adjustments, the new organization was chosen and was implemented soon after the town-hall meeting.

As a consequence of an ongoing organization dialogue through preparation to search, four search conferences, and an integration conference, eleven PDWs produced forty-four proposed designs. An implementation task force found the designs to have three main themes in common: the rejection of one design because it did not meet the minimal critical specifications, a couple of additional PDWs to complete design details, and a town-hall meeting involving all employees. Organization choice had been made with consensus to proceed. What is important to stress about the design process is that it was not an intellectual engineering exercise; it was very much a political and emotional process for all involved. Some called it "painful learning." However, the euphoria and commitment to the new organization design, not to mention the pride of accomplishment and sense that this new organization was theirs gave management the confidence that they had a high-performing organization. In other words, the participative redesign process used was a generative learning process involving individual, team, and organizational learning at the operational, business, and political levels.

CONCLUSION

Search conferencing and participative design have been used around the world in every industry since the 1970s, and the two-stage model have been used since the 1990s. Marv Weisbord popularized SC in North America with his version called "Future Search." There are many other copies and adaptations of the original SC that were developed primarily by Fred and Merrelyn Emery. Today the two-stage model is very popular in community development for innovation and sustainability because it is one of the most reliable methods to design and develop innovation ecosystems that are sustainable. It can reliably help communities adapt to global climate change. Merrelyn Emery and her colleagues in Australia have developed a new version specifically for ecological strategy development. SC or unique variations are used often in organizations to integrate learning and planning in strategic direction, project design, and management for example. The theory and method are very flexible and can be adapted in many ways.

For organizations, the main legacy of OST(E) and its methods is the notion of organizational choice and the insight that organizations are perfectly designed to deliver what they do. Consequently organization design and redesign are now established fields of study and practice, and there are lots of different approaches, both conceptual and methodological. However, with a good understanding of OST(E) and its methods, one can see whether the organization theories and models being touted are truly participative democratic models (DP2) or not. OST(E) has established over the years that participative democracy is more effective than autocracy or representative democracy (DP1). Consequently, a multitude of participative practices are shaping the future of governance. OST(E) gave us the principles, notions, and methods to pursue truly inclusive and diverse democracies. The challenge to implement remains, and OST(E) and its methods continue to be of value as we create a positive, appreciative future for everyone.

To learn more about OST(E) and its methods, contact the author. The classic textbook is *Searching: The Theory and Practice of Making Cultural Change* by Merrelyn Emery. A good introduction for practitioners is *Participative Design for Participative Democracy*, edited by Merrelyn Emery. For an application to a big issue in today's world, see *The Future of Schools: How Communities and Staff Can Transition Their School Districts* by Merrelyn Emery.

REFERENCES

de Guerre, D. W. 2000. "The Codetermination of Cultural Change over Time." *Systemic Practice and Action Research* 13 (5): 645–63.

de Guerre, D. W., and M. Emery. 2008. "Modern Forms of *Laissez Faire* Organisations." International Academy of Open Systems Theory. Accessed January 24, 2015. http://www.academia.edu/3111094/ Modern Forms_of_Laissez-Faire_Organization.

de Guerre, D. W., M. Emery, et al. 2008. "Structure Underlies Other Organizational Determinants of Mental Health: Recent Results Confirm Early Socio-technical Systems Research. *Systemic Practice and Action Research* 21 (8): 359–79.

Emery, M. 1999. *Searching: The Theory and Practice of Making Cultural Change.* Philadelphia: John Benjamins.

Emery, M. 2000. "The Current Version of Emery's Open Systems Theory." *Systemic Practice and Action Research* 13 (5): 685–703.

Emery, M. 2008. "The Determinants of Creativity and Innovation at Work." International Institute for Open Systems Theory, Montreal. Accessed June 10, 2011. www.thelightonthehill.com.

Emery, M., and D. W. de Guerre. 2006. "Evolutions of Open Systems Theory: The Two-Stage Model and Unique Designs for Active Adaptation," in P. Holman, T. Devane, and S. H. Cady (eds.), *The Change Handbook: The Definitive Resource on Today's Best Methods for Engaging Whole Systems.* San Francisco: Berrett-Koehler.

Four

North American Design of Nonroutine Work Systems (1980s–1990s)

DOUGLAS AUSTROM AND CAROLYN ORDOWICH

INTRODUCTION

The North American approach to nonroutine work design is set in the context of the 1980s, during which time the developed world was undergoing a major structural transformation from industrial to postindustrial society. Daniel Bell (1973) argued that postindustrial society would be information-led and service-oriented and that it would replace the industrial society as the dominant system. He further argued that postindustrialism would entail a shift from manufacturing to services and the centrality of new-science or information-based industries.

The salient characteristics of the preindustrial, industrial, and postindustrial eras such as key economic activities, strategic resources, core technologies, critical skills, and the primary modes of work, are summarized in table 4.1. As table 4.1 shows, the nature of work in postindustrial society shifts from a reliance on fabrication activities, financial capital, machine technology, and the division of labor to information activities, human capital, knowledge processes, intellectual technologies, human interaction, and networked labor.

Major eras, key economic activities	Strategic resources	Core technology, critical skills	Primary modes of work	Methods and methodology
Preindustrial era Extraction activities such as agriculture, mining, fishing, timber, oil and gas	**Raw materials** converted to outputs by the natural power of wind, water, draft and human muscle	**Craft** technology; artisans, manual, laborers, farmers.	**Physical labor**	Common sense, trail-and-error, experience
Industrial era Fabrication activities such as goods production manufactured durables and nondurables, heavy construction	**Financial capital** converted to output using manufactured energies (steam, electricity, coal, oil, gas, nuclear power)	**Machine** technology; industrial engineers, semi-skilled and skilled workers	**Division of labor**	Empiricism and experimentation
Postindustrial era Processing and information activities • transportation and utilities • trade, finance, insurance, real estate • health, education, government, recreation, entertainment	**Human capital** Converted into outputs via information, knowledge processes, programming algorithms, computers, exchange, data transmission, human interaction	**Intellectual** technologies; scientist, technologist, professionals, other highly skilled workers	**Networked labor**	Models, simulation, decision theory, systems thinking

Table 4.1 Emergence of Post Industrial Society (adapted from D. Bell, 1973)

Virtually all of what Bell (1973) predicted has been realized, and probably more profoundly than anyone could have imagined forty years ago. We have witnessed the rapid deindustrialization and offshoring of manufacturing in North America and much of the developed world and a dramatic, although bifurcated shift to well-compensated "gold-collar" work in information and knowledge-intensive workplaces and to poverty-level "iron-collar" work and wages in the bourgeoning service industry.

The new tools of this era were word processors, integrated voice/data switches, portable computers, and fax machines. By the 1980s and 1990s, work increasingly involved processing data and information and translating it into knowledge rather than transforming raw materials into tangible products. The primary task of knowledge work is nonroutine problem solving that requires a combination of convergent, divergent, and creative thinking (Reinhardt, Schmidt, Sloep, and Drachsler 2011). Knowledge work is typically nonrepeated, unpredictable, and emergent and primarily involves the management of unstructured or semistructured problems (Keen and Morton 1978) characterized by imprecise information inputs, varying degrees of detail, extended or unfixed time horizons, dispersed information formats, and diffuse or general scope.

The practice of socio-technical systems design from the 1950s through the 1970s reflected the predominant workplaces of that era, process and manufacturing industries, and work processes that tended to be fairly routine and consistent. But by the end of the 1970s, the structural transformation from an industrial society to a postindustrial society was accelerating, along with the fundamental nature of work and the workplace. Given the success of Socio-technical System design initiatives in process-industry and manufacturing settings, attention moved to office and administrative settings to provide a more comprehensive approach to organization design.

Tom Cummings (1978) suggested that STS's shop-floor heritage and its language, concepts, and orientation limited its application in office settings.[3] He also claimed that the relatively lower reliance on technology in

---

3 It should be noted that Pava commented that Cummings's critique of STS in office settings was not fully correct for routine or even semiroutine office or clerical work. According to Painter (2015), STS analysis and design had been used very effectively,

the office—at least, at that point in history—created an imbalance between the social and technical systems and rendered the analytic tools less useful.

Eric Trist (1984) and Cal Pava (1986) echoed these concerns when they argued that conceptually, STS design had fallen into a rut and that over-reliance on customary practices such as the nine-step method had stifled innovation and restricted STS's applicability to the emergent workplace.

The North American approach to nonroutine work-system design was formally introduced in 1983 with the publication of Pava's seminal book, *Managing New Office Technology: An Organizational Strategy*.

In this chapter, we explore the broader context and the changing nature of work and work systems that prompted Pava's approach to designing nonroutine work. We discuss the STS principles that served as the foundation of his approach and provide an overview of nonrou-tine work-system analysis—in particular, deliberation analysis. We high-light two practical applications and several research studies that have incorporated deliberation analyses. We also discuss the contribution of Pasmore and colleagues to the field with their introduction of the con-cept of knowledge-management barriers as an elaboration and neces-sary evolution of the traditional STS notion of variances.

In subsequent articles, Pava (1985, 1986) recognized that the distinctions between blue-collar and white-collar work was decreasing due to increased reliance on knowledge work in both the office and the factory, especially given the emergence of "smart" equipment, advanced manufacturing, arti-ficial intelligence, and the emerging integration of computer and commu-nications technology. He argued forcefully that to be relevant and valuable in the 1990s and beyond, STS design concepts and methods themselves needed to be redesigned. We conclude this chapter with a discussion of the impact of Pava's thinking on the current theory and practice of STS.

In assessing this emerging organizational landscape, Pava recognized two key shifts in the nature of work that would require "an overhaul in STS design: the shift from long-link mechanical technologies to integrated

though not often, in settings such as an office automation project with airline-ticket processing and public-service redesign in Ontario.

information and a shift in the function of labor because of this techno-logical transition" (1986, p. 202). He and others further articulated the key differences in the nature of work between the industrial and postin-dustrial periods that undermined traditional STS design approaches (see table 2 for a summary of his discussion and visual representations com-paring routine, linear work and nonroutine, nonlinear knowledge work).

As opposed to routine work such as manufacturing, in which the con-version processes were linear and the steps were reasonably predeter-mined, nonroutine work systems such as research and development (R and D) or market research involve a high level of equivocality in terms of their nonlinear conversion processes. Given this emerging reality, Pava cogently made this observation: "Altogether, these conditions invalidate key assumptions supporting conventional STS design: definable inputs and outputs, sequential flow of conversion, cascading one-way variances, and pooled group identity with transferable skills. Attempts to accommo-date these conditions by rigidly adhering to the nine-step model and the autonomous work-group template ignore the major differences between linear and nonlinear work" (1986, p. 206).

CORE CONCEPTS OF PAVA'S APPROACH

Pava responded to these challenges, and in so doing, he played a pivotal role in defining the second generation of STS thinking by extending it to the nonroutine work processes characteristic of knowledge work and the service economy. In Pava's view, the digital revolution presented such a challenge that neither the purely "soft" approaches of behavioral science nor the "hard" approach of industrial engineering could engender and sustain organiza-tional learning and change as did the new unique approach of STS, which had already proven to "more effectively organize in the most uncertain steps of the conversion process and at the most problematic interfaces with a system's environment," which is the new context of work. The heart of the socio-tech-nical systems approach is the critical match between the technical and social subsystems in the performance of the work system as a whole. As the work shifted to knowledge work, it became more difficult to discern the elements of the technical and social subsystems because both related to people.

	Routine work	Nonroutine work
Nature of work		
Context	Stable environment	Unstable environment
Nature of the technical system	• Long-link, mechanical processes • Unitary, convergent, linear, sequential conversion process with a programme series of steps • Largely unvarying tasks wit limited variety • Defined • One specified way • Sequential interdependence of subtasks • Repetitive, short cycle task	• Unstable environment • Integrated information processes • Multiple concurrent, nonlinear non-sequential conversion processes with poorly structure problems and un-programmed activities • Highly variable tasks with unclear inputs and outputs anc too much variety • Undefined • Many potential ways • Saturated, pooled or team interdependence • Nonrepetive, long cycle tasks
Nature of the social system	• Work groups with shared identity	• Highly trained professionals with specialized expertise • Individualistic orientation
Nature of the governance system	• Hierarchical authority-based • Position-based authority • Clear shared goals	• Lateral, consensus-based • Expertise-based authority • Multiple, competitive goals
Variance analysis	• Obvious • Downstream with clear cause-effect relationships • Recognizable patterns	• Hidden • Multidetermined and multidirectional causal linkages • Largely un-patterned
Typical design options	• Autonomous work groups • Job enrichment • Multiskilling	• Discretionary coalitions/role networks with explicitly defined responsibilities • Job simplification to reduce the equivocality of problems • Reticular organization with fluid distribution of information and authority

Table 4.2 Changing Nature of Work (Pava 1986; Pasmore and Gurley 1991)

SOCIO-TECHNICAL DESIGN PRINCIPLES FOR NONROUTINE WORK SYSTEMS

To develop a socio-technical design process for nonroutine office work, Pava revisited and reconfirmed the general theory of socio-technical systems and its core tenets. Specifically, he stated that a work organization is an open system that meets these criteria:

- Interacts with a complex environment (transactional and contextual) and transforms inputs into outputs via a sequence of conversions.
- Benefits from an optimal match of the social and technical subsystems.
- Emphasizes redundant function over redundant parts.
- Can self-regulate many of its own activities through feedback (without excessive supervision because of shared goals).
- Must generate a level of variety that matches the level of flexibility required to achieve its purpose in its environment.

Furthermore, Pava reinforced the STS precept that the design process is as important as the design product and that it must be self-designing because only the participants in the "system" can determine its nature, purpose, and boundaries before designing its details. The participative design approach itself is a prototype of the managerial style required to realize the benefits of a socio-technical systems design. The design process is based on *minimal critical specifications*, where only those things that must be defined are and is open ended because it must adapt the design as changing circumstances make the existing design obsolete.

Pava's approach focuses on *deliberations* as the unit of analysis for examining the nature of nonroutine work processes (Pava 1983; Taylor, Gustavson, and Carter 1986). The focus on deliberations implicitly expresses a core value of STS—that is, *to advance the connections between the principles of democracy and the social and economic objectives of organizations.* The idea of deliberation is built on the notion of *participative governance,* where *reasons* and *inclusion* are the two central aspects that realize "just" or "legitimate" outcomes. The more people exchange reasons and foster an ethic of inclusion, the more likely the participants are to change their position, and thus the more likely a solution is to be derived based on collective intelligence and implemented with community consensus. Deliberation is a social, not a rational, process (Habermas 1990). The best articulation of deliberation is that by Fung and Wright (2003): "In deliberative decision making, participants listen to each other's positions and generate group choices after due consideration. Participants ought to persuade one another by offering reasons that others can accept. Real-world deliberations are often characterized by heated conflict, winners, and losers. The important feature of genuine deliberation is that participants find reasons that they can accept in collective actions, not necessarily ones they completely endorse or find maximally advantageous."

To analyze and redesign nonroutine office work and the interactions among people in the work system, Pava recommended mapping the sequence of *deliberations* that he defined as "reflective and communicative behaviors regarding a particular topic" (1983, p. 58). He further described deliberations as "equivocality reducing events" that are critical to nonroutine work systems, especially those involving knowledge generation and knowledge utilization. However, deliberations are not simply the equivalent of decisions or meetings; they are sense-making exchanges (Weick 1994), communications, and reflections that are integral to the nature of nonroutine work.

Rather than ignoring or minimizing the complexity of nonlinear conversion processes, deliberation analysis provided STS researchers and practitioners with a way to trace the sequence and type of deliberations in terms of the key *topics* or problematic issues to be addressed; the *forums* in which they occur; which ones may be structured, semi-structured, or unstructured and ad hoc; the *participants with specific points of view,* both those who are currently involved and those who ideally should be involved in the deliberation; and *discretionary coalitions* whose purpose is to obtain the best outcomes from the inputs of multiple perspectives.

The deliberations or sense-making conversations often cut across formal departmental boundaries and involved informal patterns of exchange, which were specific to a topic. Thus, Pava coined the term for the social system, "discretionary coalitions," which were flexible alliances of interdependent parties formed to make intelligent tradeoffs that enable attainment of overall objectives; different coalitions are associated with different deliberations. It was and is a novel organizing principle because it overlays or pushes the static positions of the organization chart into the background.

Unlike routine STS, the nonroutine approach emphasizes *reciprocal understanding* rather than a shared goal and *coalition formation* rather than group identity as one finds in self-managing teams that are permanent entities in the social system. Identifying major deliberations and the discretionary coalitions needed to manage them helps gain better alignment between the major lines of contention and the overall viability of an enterprise in a turbulent environment.

Deliberations are the key design element in the socio-technical analysis of nonroutine knowledge work systems. *Deliberations* are patterns of exchange and communication in which people engage with themselves or others to reduce the equivocality of a problematic issue. Deliberations form a collectively built framework that creates clarity without denying complexity.

Also, when developed collaboratively, the *deliberation dialogical process* builds community and fosters more extended application and testing. Deliberations are not simply talking or giving opinions; reasons offer a justification for a stated position related to the topic under debate, an answer to the question, "Why do you say that?" Inclusion also means more than simple participation. Although talking is one part of including oneself in a group interaction, it is important that one's contribution be on topic and purposeful and that one makes the effort to ask opinions of others or to reference previous points of view made by others in the group. Coalitions are network structures that are a different form of organizing than the traditional hierarchical forms.

STS ANALYSIS OF NONLINEAR KNOWLEDGE WORK SYSTEMS

The diagnostic steps of open socio-technical systems design, according to Pava (1983, 1986) include analysis of the business, analysis of the technical subsystem, and analysis of the social subsystem.

CONDUCTING AN INITIAL SCAN AND MAPPING THE SYSTEM

The purpose of an initial scan is to discern the mission or goals of the system and the governance processes and coordination mechanisms that enable or inhibit collaboration in pursuit of the mission. The mission and governance system provide the impetus for a self-regulating system of players who define and iteratively evolve the technical subsystem in terms of the key deliberations or issues they need to address to achieve the mission.

TECHNICAL ANALYSIS

Pava (1983) described deliberations as choice points that are critical to work systems involving knowledge generation and knowledge utilization. From this general description, Purser (1990) defined deliberations in product development as "social interactions in which knowledge is exchanged to define or solve a problem, make a decision, or implement a solution." A deliberation is identified by the existence of an equivocal topic that is explored in different types of forums, involving a particular group of participants who either contribute important information or take-away important information. Deliberation analysis assesses the values and perspectives of participants within forums, as well as "the interpretative dynamics among interdependent parties who must forge a discretionary coalition" (Pava 1983) to make intelligent tradeoffs from their respective values, priorities, and cognitive orientations (Tenkasi 1994, 2000).

Deliberations in knowledge work such as R and D can be viewed in terms of intellectual bandwidth (Nunamaker et al. 2001, 2002, Qureshi et al. 2002) and the ability to mobilize intellectual assets in deliberations to create value. The STS model of nonroutine work-system design provides a framework for measuring the extent to which an organization can create value from its intellectual assets by looking at two key elements in deliberations. The first is the process of understanding the data and available information and translating it into knowledge. The second addresses the interdependence of efforts and whether it is primarily an individual work mode, a collected work mode and the sum of individual work, a coordinated work mode in which there is sequential interdependence, or a concerted work mode in which everyone works in concert to produce joint deliverables.

SOCIAL ANALYSIS

The social system is defined in terms of discretionary coalitions that are needed to conduct the deliberations effectively. These coalitions make the important tradeoffs in creative work that is made necessary by the presence of useful but inherently divergent values and perspectives. For example, in traditional research environments, scientists typically compete against one another for limited grant money and to publish articles in top journals, neither of which enable the effective functioning of coalitions in a virtual project. The social-system design does not try to eliminate differences, but rather tries to create a mutual understanding and a common orientation so that tradeoffs can be settled on an intelligent and ongoing basis. Coalitions are to nonroutine work what work groups or teams are to more routine work. Roles and responsibilities can be defined for the parties involved in the coalitions, as well as other changes in the coordinating mechanisms in a way that supports and rewards the sort of integrative perspective necessary to successful coalition functioning.

FROM VARIANCES TO KNOWLEDGE BARRIERS AND DYNAMIC SYNCHRONIZATION

In traditional Tavistock-North American socio-technical systems analysis, the focus is on addressing and eliminating variances in work processes and performance. However, in nonroutine knowledge-work systems, Ron Purser and colleagues discovered that variances manifest as knowledge barriers—that is, any factor that inhibits or undermines building the pool of shared knowledge and new insights in timely fashion. Purser (1990) conducted an in-depth STS analysis of a nonroutine work system—the research and development function of a major corporation. He used quantitative methods such as surveys and qualitative methods such as observations to analyze key deliberations and discover critical variances that contributed to delays on research projects. Purser discovered that delays occurred when there was a lack of critical knowledge or information to make decisions, when there was inadequate time to make thoughtful decisions, and when information was missing due to poor documentation of previous projects. All of these variances were, in fact, knowledge barriers. Purser, Pasmore, and Tenkasi (1992) subsequently used factor analysis to identify four main categories of "barriers" obstructing and delaying collaborative knowledge development: lack of a common frame of reference, failure to share knowledge, lack of knowledge, and failure to use knowledge. Let's look at each category of barriers more closely.

The *lack of a common frame of reference* includes cognitive frame-of-reference barriers typically associated with differences in functional expertise, values, cultural norms at both the corporate and national or ethnic levels, and language. This knowledge barrier is most likely to occur when the discretionary coalitions span company, sector, and national and cultural boundaries. One of the most often overlooked yet critical design activities is to establish a common lexicon or shared language.

1. The lack of a common frame of reference contributes to the second knowledge barrier: *failure to share knowledge*. Failure to share knowledge occurs when key participants are not included

in the deliberation or when the participants in the deliberation are unwilling to cooperate. In highly competitive organizational cultures with "knowledge is power" norms, participants may be reluctant to share what they know. Similarly, when there are conflicts or distrust between groups or among individuals, relevant information is often withheld. This knowledge barrier is often exacerbated when there are unrealistic time frames and other time pressures that serve to narrow a person's focus to his or her immediate task at the expense of sharing knowledge that might benefit other participants in the deliberation.

2. The third knowledge barrier is *lack of knowledge* about the work, the procedures and processes, or the capabilities that can slow or derail progress regarding the deliberation topic(s).

3. In the case of the fourth knowledge barrier, the failure to use knowledge, the knowledge for completing the task, deliberating, and making decisions exists but is either ignored or used improperly.

Purser and colleagues (1992) determined that these knowledge-management barriers were due to poorly designed and mismanaged deliberations. To improve deliberation efficacy and ensure that relevant parties are involved in key deliberations and that they have a common lexicon and adequate time, Purser and colleagues offered the following recommendations:

1. Align the most useful skills of participants with the various deliberations.

2. Ensure that reward systems foster knowledge sharing.

3. Implement a participative learning system.

4. Allocate sufficient time for learning in the early stages of product development.

5. Design deliberations that promote knowledge development and learning.

Pasmore (1994) confirmed Pava's earlier work that the differences between variances in routine and nonroutine work are so significant that they require new STS thinking—more specifically, that adequate preparation and problem definition are critical so that people can organize themselves to deliberate effectively on the questions they have identified. He also further elaborated the characteristics of effective and ineffective deliberations. See table 4.3 below.

Effective deliberations	Ineffective deliberations
<ul><li>Knowledge highly developed and readily available</li><li>Knowledge utilized fully and without bias</li><li>Apolitical discussion of facts and alternatives</li><li>People with most knowledge present</li><li>Disruptive or inappropriate people absent</li><li>Discussion held alt key choice points</li><li>Goals clear and shared</li><li>Challenging but realistic time frames</li><li>Decision-making procedures clear</li><li>Appropriate attention to external environment</li><li>Minimum bureaucracy</li></ul>	<ul><li>Lack of knowledge</li><li>Failure to use knowledge</li><li>Lack of cooperation</li><li>Missing parties in key discussion</li><li>Wrong parties in key discussion</li><li>No key discussion at all</li><li>Lack of goal clarity</li><li>Time frame too short or too long</li><li>Procedures unclear or non-existent</li><li>Inadequate attention to external environment</li><li>Too much bureaucratic structure</li></ul>

Table 4.3 Characteristics of Effective and
Ineffective Deliberations (Pamore 1994)

Adler and Docherty (1998) extend this shift in thinking regarding variances in knowledge work from minimizing them to seeking "dynamic synchronization." This is a concept Purser and Pasmore (1992) introduced that is based on maintaining a balance between order and disorder. Order affords the systemic coherence needed for the technical and social subsystems to achieve task requirements, while disorder can actually be beneficial to the extent that ambiguity and uncertainty trigger opportunities for creative learning. For example, serendipitous findings that are typically outliers or unexpected results—and would be considered variances in routine work systems—are often critical in creating scientific breakthroughs.

ILLUSTRATIVE EXAMPLES OF NONLINEAR STS IN PRACTICE

Pava provided the most illustrative cases of the application of deliberation analysis: the software engineering group in a moderate-sized computer systems firm (1983) and the customer service and support unit in a rapidly growing microcomputer device company (1986). In the case of the microcomputer device company, management had decided to install a new computer system. However, they were not convinced that the recommended system requirements would achieve the desired levels of customer support. An STS design effort was initiated, and business, technical, and social analyses were conducted. The design team proposed that the customer support unit be reorganized into market team structure. Six regional support teams were established to provide full line service and to acquire customer and market data for their region. There was a modest amount of cross-training and a moderate degree of job enrichment, along with a pay-for-skill ladder. All would be shared with the team first. At the end of the first year, customer satisfaction had improved significantly, and the teams had achieved unexpectedly high scores on the performance measures they had jointly established during the redesign.

While other STS practitioners have employed elements of Pava's nonroutine STS design in their work, there have been relatively few documented cases of the formal application of deliberation analysis and redesign. There have, however, been several qualitative research studies that have focused on the conditions that contribute to deliberation efficacy. Most recently, the Socio-technical Systems Roundtable, in collaboration with the University of Illinois, received a grant from the National Science Foundation to study deliberation efficacy in three virtual research projects: the Orchid Project, which is a collaborative project among physicists from research universities around the world and basic research on the

R-and-D continuum; the Uniform Data Set Project (UDS), which is a joint project among twenty-nine Alzheimer's Disease Centers across the United States and began at the advanced development stage; and a Large Video Game Project, which involved some startup, but mostly scale-up development activities such as art-asset production, engineering, and testing activities shared among the game developers and vendors around the world (Barrett, Austrom, Merck, Painter, Posey, and Tenkasi 2013).

Barrett and colleagues focused on understanding the influence of virtuality on deliberations and knowledge-development barriers at various stages of the R-and-D continuum. This comparative study of virtual, geographically dispersed RD projects reinforced the importance of understanding and managing the challenge of coordinating work and knowledge across time and space. Building on the theory of organizations as information-processing and knowledge-utilization systems, the research identified different types of coordinating mechanisms and their effect on managing knowledge-development barriers across the R and D spectrum.

THE LEGACY OF PAVA'S APPROACH TO DESIGNING NONROUTINE WORK SYSTEMS

Pava had the foresight in 1983 to see extensive network organizing in the future that was a natural fit with socio-technical systems thinking, built on a foundation of self-regulation to deal with the complexities and uncertainties emanating from an increasingly turbulent environment (Emery and Trist, 1965). He called to our attention a new kind of knowledge work that went beyond a focus simply on decision-making to a wide range of cognitive methods and techniques that managers and professionals use to resolve complex issues that are the essence of their work. Finally, he also warned us that increasing computerization could result in a technocratic imperative and thereby erode our ability to generate what Bright and Fry (2013) called "humane, high-performing, and ethical organizing."

Pava provided us with a template for a truly *holistic organizational architecture* based on the precepts of self-regulation. Trist (1983) stated in the afterword in Pava's book that the concept of self-regulation was meant to be extended to every control level so that the organization as a whole was seen as a series of mutually articulated self-regulating systems, which would make it both flatter and leaner. He articulated three types of work and organizing forms for this *holistic organizational architecture*, as follows:

- **Routine work**—Primary task work becoming digitized and regulated by *self-managing teams*
- **Hybrid (routine and nonroutine) work**—*Project teams* (for innovation, change, and research work, as has been more traditionally used, as well as for realizing customer orders in project-based companies and in those companies in which the primary task is done at exceptional speed requiring very agile coordination)
- **Nonroutine work**—Deliberations and *discretionary coalitions* that describe the interactive character of a great deal of day-to-day work of managerial, professional, and even primary task groups in which work is based on high uncertainty and complexity.

In so doing, Pava combined and integrated self-managing work teams (routine), project teams (hybrid), and discretionary coalitions (nonroutine) into a reticular organization (network/ecosystem) with participants jointly creating value and their future. And in our iVUCA (interconnected, volatile, uncertain, complex and ambiguous) postindustrial era, this is critical to the survival of the enterprise because as Peter Drucker argued in 1966, everyone must be a contributor: "Every knowledge worker in a modern organization is an 'executive' if, by virtue of his position or knowledge, he is responsible for a contribution that materially affects the capacity of the organization to perform and to obtain results."

While most people instinctively knew there was a difference between routine and nonroutine work, few were able to describe its core content as cogently, and those who tried put too much focus on decision making to the exclusion of a whole range of cognitive activities that occur in the unprogrammed work of professionals and managers. But as robust as this approach to designing contemporary work systems has been, Pava's warnings about complacency in STS design appear to have gone largely unheeded. There are several factors that may account for this outcome, not the least of which was the failure of STS design to keep pace with changes in the fundamental nature of work and work systems. As Pava argued, it may have been due to an overreliance on traditional methods. Also, the paucity of documented cases using STS design for nonroutine work systems attests to the fact that we have not generated pragmatic methods with tangible steps that others can follow. As Pava observed, "Without grounded concepts and usable methods, the aspirations of STS design become an unfeasible litany" (1986, 209).

The variegation of the field with numerous derivative or related methodologies has also been a factor, to the point where STS design in North America has effectively been supplanted by other methodologies that share STS values and principles to a greater or lesser degree. Examples include appreciative inquiry (Cooperrider 1990), democratic dialogue (Gustavsen 1992), Lean thinking, Ackoff's democratic hierarchy (1999), and more recently, sociocracy (Endenburg 1998) and holacracy.

CONCLUSIONS

Pava's STS shows us how to design a *dynamic emergent organization*, which is a much better fit with today's iVUCA environment. Further, he claimed it is the only way to design "healthy organizations" in today's technologically driven workplaces because it goes to the heart of the structural and cultural issues that must be designed to achieve both humane and high-performance workplaces.

Pava warned us about what he foresaw as a relentless technology drive that, if left unchecked, would result in *artificial rationality* that is characterized by the belief that human shortcomings can be "engineered out" with technology and rational methods. He also warned us about *micromyopia*, which "seeks analytically to rationalize nonlinear work into discrete components to increase the efficiency of parts based on the belief that this will increase the efficiency of the whole set of work activities" (Pava 1983, 53). What Pava could not fully envision was the scope, scale, and pace of the digital revolution, especially the advent of smart devices and how pervasive "bring your own device" would become in the early twenty-first century. These and numerous other technological innovations comprise the burgeoning field of information and communication technology (ICT). But except for a few notable exceptions (cf. Mumford, 1995), relatively little work has been done on deepening our understanding of the relationship between ICT and socio-technical systems in the analysis and design of contemporary work systems. This is clearly an area of inquiry that warrants considerable attention.

Finally, nonroutine work and work systems today are more complex than ever. To respond to these dramatic changes, organizations have had to "learn and change" in ways that have been far more profound than the traditional methods such as training and procedural enhancements. A new paradigm for managing and leading was, and is, needed. But Pava did not directly address this. In a later chapter, we discuss how STS first principles provide us with a new paradigm for designing, organizing, and leading and how this paradigm becomes the foundation for network design and organization.

REFERENCES

Ackoff, R. L. 1999. *Recreating the Corporation—A Design of Organisations for the Twenty-First Century.* New York: Oxford University Press.

Adler, N., and P. Docherty. 1998. "Bringing Business into Socio-technical Theory and Practice." *Human Relations* 51: 319–45.

Barrett, B., D. Austrom, B. Merck, B. Painter, P. Posey, R. Purser, and R. Tenkasi. 2013. National Science Foundation Program, "Virtual Organizations as Socio-technical Systems (VOSS)," grant number NSF OCI 09-43237.

Bell, D. 1973. *The Coming of Post-Industrial Society: A Venture in Social Forecasting.* New York: Basic Books.

Cooperrider, D. L. 1990. *Appreciative Management and Leadership: The Power of Positive Thought and Action in Organizations.* San Francisco: Jossey-Bass.

Cummings, T. G. 1978. "Socio-technical Experimentation: A Review of Sixteen Studies." In W. Pasmore and J. J. Sherwood (eds.). *Socio-technical Systems.* La Jolla, Calif.: University Associates.

Drucker, P. 1966. *The Effective Executive.* New York: Harper and Row.

Endenburg, G. 1998. *Sociocracy: The Organization of Decision Making.* The Netherlands: Eburon Academic Publishers.

Fung, A., and E. O. Wright. 2003. *Deepening Democracy: Innovations in Empowered Participatory Governance* New York: Verso.

Gustavsen, 1992. Dialogue and Development. *Social Science for Social Action: Toward Organizational Renewal, Vol. 1.* Stockholm: Arbetslivs Centrum and Assen: Van Gorcum.

Habermas, J. 1990. *Moral Consciousness and Communicative Action: Studies in Contemporary German Social Thought*. Boston: MIT Press.

Keen, P. G., and M. S. Scott-Morton. 1978. *Decision Support Systems: An Organizational Perspective*. Reading, Mass.: Addison-Wesley.

Mumford, E. 1995. *Effective Systems Design and Requirements Analysis: The ETHICS Approach*. London: Macmillan.

Nunamaker, J. F., Jr., N. C. Romano, and R. O. Briggs. 2001. *A Framework for Collaboration and Knowledge Management in the Proceedings of the Thirty-Fourth Hawaiian International Conference on System Sciences (HICSS)*.

Nunamaker, J. F., N. C. Romano, and R. O. Briggs. 2002. "Increasing Intellectual Bandwidth: Generating Value from Intellectual Capital with Information Technology." *Group Decision and Negotiation* 11 (2): 69–86.

Painter, B. 2015. Personal communication.

Pasmore, W. A., and K. Gurley. 1991. "Socio-technical Systems in R&D: Theory and Practice," in R. Kilman (ed.) *Making Organizations More Productive*. San Francisco: Jossey-Bass.

Pasmore, W. A. 1994. *Creating Strategic Change: Designing the Flexible, High-Performing Organization*. Hoboken, NJ: John Wiley and Sons.

Pava, C. 1983a. "Designing Managerial and Professional Work for High Performance: A Socio-technical Approach." *National Productivity Review* 2: 126–35.

Pava, C. 1983b. *Managing New Office Technology: An Organizational Strategy*. New York: Free Press.

Pava, C. 1985. "Managing New Information Technology: Design or Default?" In R. E. Walton and P. R. Lawrence (eds.). *HRM: Trends and Challenges*. Cambridge: Harvard Business School Press.

Pava, C. 1986. "Redesigning Socio-technical Systems Design: Concepts and Methods for the 1990s." *The Journal of Applied Behavioral Science* 22 (3): 201–21.

Power, J. 1973. "The Reticulist Function in Government: Manipulating Networks of Communication and Influence." *Public Administration (Australia)* 32 (1): 21–27.

Purser, R. E. 1990. *The Impact of Variances and Delays on Nonroutine Decisions and Knowledge Utilization in a Product Development Organization*. PhD Thesis. Cleveland, Ohio: Case Western Reserve University.

Purser, R. E., and W. A. Pasmore. 1982. "Organizing for Learning." In W. A. Pasmore and R. W. Woodman (eds.). *Research in Organization Change and Development* (Vol. 6). Greenwich, Conn.: JAI Press.

Purser, R. E., W. A. Pasmore, and R. V. Tenkasi. 1992. "The Influence of Deliberations on Learning in New Product Development Teams." *Journal of Engineering and Technology Management* 9: 1–28.

Qureshi, S. V. Hlupic, G. J. de Vreede, R. O. Briggs, and J. Nunamaker. 2002. "Managing Knowledge in a Collaborative Context: Experiences and Future Directions." In V. Hlupic (ed.), *Knowledge and Business Process Management*. Hershey, PA: Idea Group Publishing.

Reinhardt, W., B. Schmidt, P. Sloep, and H. Drachsler. July/September 2011. "Knowledge Worker Roles and Actions—Results of Two Empirical Studies." *Knowledge and Process Management* 18 (3): 150–74.

Taylor, J. C., P. W. Gustavson, and W. S. Carter. 1986. "Integrating the Social and Technical Systems in Organizations," in D. D. Davis (ed.), *Managing Technical Innovation*. San Francisco: Jossey-Bass.

Tenkasi, R. V. 1994. *The Consequences and Antecedents of Cognitive Simplification Processes in New Product Development Teams.* Doctoral dissertation. Cleveland, Ohio: Case Western Reserve University (thesis advisor: William Pasmore).

Tenkasi, R. V. 2000. "The Dynamics of Cognitive Oversimplification Processes in R&D Environments." *International Journal of Technology Management* 20, (5/6/7/8): 782–98.

Trist, E. L. 1983. Afterword. In C. Pava, *Managing New Office Technology: An Organizational Strategy.* New York: Free Press.

Weick, K. E. 1994. *Sensemaking in Organizations.* Thousand Oaks, Calif.: Sage Publications.

Five

Human Talent Mobilization: Improving Both Quality of Working Life and Productivity by Organizational Design in the Lowlands

PIERRE VAN AMELSVOORT

INTRODUCTION

In the Netherlands and Belgium, STS-D developed into an overall organizational design theory. We will call this "STS-D in the Lowlands"
(STSL). This chapter gives an overview of the development of STS theory
in the Netherlands and Belgium. We focus on design, which is, of course,
a limited part of the participative change process as a whole. Other
recent developments in the Lowlands are workplace innovation and Lean
Thinking. The importance of workplace innovation, based on the STS-D
insights, for Europe is emphasized in chapter 11 by Pot and d'Hond. In
some practices, we see a merger of STSL and Lean, which van Hootegem
discusses in chapter 18 and Christis discusses in chapter 17.

Ulbo De Sitterdeveloped the socio-technical systems theory of
the Lowlands (STSL) (De Sitter1994; De Sitteret al. 1997; Kuipers, van
Amelsvoort, and Kramer 2010) in response to the limitations of the job-
design approach. The focus is the design of the division of work in the core
work and control processes to create flexible, innovative organizations
that mobilize human talent. Business demands are the starting point of
the design process. STSL provides a practical and integral framework for
designing organizations that focus simultaneously on improving involvement (quality of working life), as well as the quality of the organization:

increasing productivity, flexibility, and the innovative capacity of the organization, quality of working relations: participation, mutual respect, openness, trust, and fairness and also partnership between the management and the working council and social responsibility (Achterbergh and Vriens 2009).

THE LACK OF SUSTAINABILITY IN EARLY SOCIO-TECHNICAL EXPERIMENTS

In spite of the positive results of these early STSL experiments, success in the revitalization of organizations and dissemination of the philosophy was limited. Eventually, hidden, conservative forces prevailed over those arguing for successful change. Some of the main reasons for this—still important to keep in mind—include the following:

- The experiments usually took place in a confined setting or in an isolated part of the organization, approached at departmental level. They were tolerated by management, but rarely with active support and direction. The experiments came under pressure from opposing forces in the rest of the organization, which were not involved but were affected (Davis 1975).
- The consequences for the organization as a whole of increasing job control in the operational process were not correctly foreseen. Managers in particular felt threatened by a bottom-up change strategy for organizational development. This translated into resistance (Kuipers and van Amelsvoort 1990).
- Although from the start, improvement in both the quality of working life and productivity was key, discussion centered on the humanization of work. An endless, ideologically influenced discussion rapidly emerged in which managers saw the idea of humanization as an "open-sandals-and-woolly-socks" philosophy, in particular because it was not possible to establish precisely in advance what the results of this kind of change would be. Within

this context, the fear that participation would drift into "worker self-management" and lead to unmanageable chaos also played a part. During the 1960s and '70s, the business climate did not favor organizational modernization. The strategic focus was limited to efficiency and mass production. Democratic emancipation within organizations was not well developed, and a great deal of energy was devoted to the development of formal and indirect employee participation, grounded by legislation. The idea that workers could be a valuable resource rather than extensions of machines or computers was not widespread. Management involvement in the experiments was limited. From the workers' point of view, too, job and organizational design were low on the strategic agenda (De Sitter1981).

- Management attention was focused on achieving short-term economic benefits. During the 1960s and '70s, the market position of many organizations could be characterized as emphasizing efficiency requirements in which mass production was key (Bolwijn and Kumpe 1989). In this context, classic forms of organization are adequately effective, and there was little reason to make changes. Looking at both the sales and the labor markets, the strategic need for organizational modernization in this period was therefore minimal.

This analysis of the limited sustainability of early STSL experiments and the lessons learned also gave the impulse to develop a more fundamental theory, STS-D.

STSL'S THEORETICAL FOUNDATIONS

The founder of STSL, Ulbo de Sitter, was not satisfied with the original STS theory and tools, so he rethought and reformulated the theory based on cybernetics, especially Ashby's law of requisite variety: "Only variety can absorb variety" (Ashby 1969).

DESIGN AS A STRATEGIC ISSUE INSTEAD OF OPEN SYSTEMS

According to the open-system principle, the design of organizations is strategic, forming a rich point of view, including all stakeholder perspectives. Achterbergh and Vriends see focus only on the shareholders' value as a poor perspective (2009). Diagnosing, designing, and changing organizations takes place in relation to environmental conditions and strategic business choices. These choices impose requirements on the organization, the "burning platform," as well as dictating the desired direction (see also Adler and Docherty 1998). Bureaucratic principles are neither false nor good; rather, depending on strategic choices, they support and create constructive or destructive organizational conditions for realizing the organization's strategic goals. In repetitive core work processes with a limited focus on job efficiency, these classic principles of mass production are still useful for productivity, but less so for healthy and humane work environments. If the need arises for flexibility, innovation and a healthy work environment, traditional organizational design is destructive in realizing strategic goals. Dramatically demographic developments in Europe forecast a growing number of older people and future shortages in the labor market. Attention also has to be paid to healthy aging and longer working lives in creating effective strategies.

DIVISION OF WORK INSTEAD OF SEPARATED SOCIAL AND TECHNICAL SYSTEMS

Originally, a distinction was made in STS-D between social and technical systems. According to the principle of joint optimization, equal attention must be paid to both systems. De Sitterpoints out that the definition of the social and technical system was not clear (De Sitteret al. 1997). The starting point of STSL is the fact that a separation between technical and social subsystems creates a false distinction. Both a system with people but without technological instrumentation and a technical system without people are empty systems. Human and technological factors can indeed be distinguished from each other, but they cannot be separated! A dynamic systems-theoretical perspective of work and organization is central to STSL. As a result of the division of core work processes into tasks and roles, the organization can be seen as an interacting network with external and internal components. Structure in STSL is defined as the formal and informal division of core work processes and (strategic, tactical, and operational) control activities into tasks and roles allocated to equipment, people, teams, departments, business units, support staff, etc. This creates an interacting network that can be seen as the basis of technological and human factors. These interaction networks, which can be thought of as Siamese twins, is made between (a) the structure of executing activities (production structure of the value-based processes—PS) and (b) the structure of controlling activities (control structure—CS) (De Sitteret al. 1997).

COMPLEXITY OF THE INTERACTING NETWORK

The organization can be seen as an interacting network of jobs with technological instrumentation, with jobs as nodes interacting with other interdependent nodes (see fig 5.1). The nodes are both internal and external interaction partners in both business and quality-of-work-life balance. The organization can be understood as a social network. At the nodes, input is transformed into output or outcome. Interaction between nodes is necessary for the exchange of information or materials to create knowledge, give orders, plan, coordinate, or deliberate. For productivity and to respond to customer demands, the various interactions need to be established at the right moment, between the right jobs, and at the right place. A balance between demand and limited transformation capabilities is necessary. In stable interaction networks, demand and capabilities are in balance, and all losses can be decreased. If the business demand is unchanging or predictable, all losses can be detected and solved to create an efficient system by preestablished rules and standards. In real life, this type of accurately balanced, stable network is a utopia because networks and business demands are dynamic. Nowadays, it is rare for customer demand to be unchanging and predictable. A node has to cope with the following factors:

- External variety: Input variety; lack of information; communication errors; customer demand changing both in quantity and type; incomplete input; conflicting, ambiguous, or competing demands
- Internal variety: Human errors, technical disturbance, invalid and inflexible capabilities, shortage of resources

The unplanned nature of the different interactions interfere with stable and stationary networks. Of course, attempts to minimize interference can be made through continuous improvement, but it will not remove the cause of the interference in the design of the interaction network (PS). Therefore, it is necessary to create a robust organization by reducing the cause of the interference (PS) and increasing local control capabilities that can deal with unpredictable inferences (CS) through a decentralized organization. If a node lacks control, there is higher possibility that an interference will negatively affect the desired output in time, cost, quality, safety, stress, work-life balance, and loss of motivation. Internal and external job control is necessary to reduce the negative effect of the inference. If not, the interruption will be transferred or escalated, with increased risk of amplifying negative effects: the "bullwhip effect." Complexity in PS is important in STSL for various reasons:

- To a large extent, the risk of interference is influenced by the complexity of the interaction network and especially the production structure.
- In complex interaction networks, the contribution of individual parts to the purpose is smaller than the purpose of the whole system. As a result, it is difficult to create purposeful or meaningful work.
- In a complex interaction network, the possibilities for local control at the nodes are limited, and the need for central control increases.

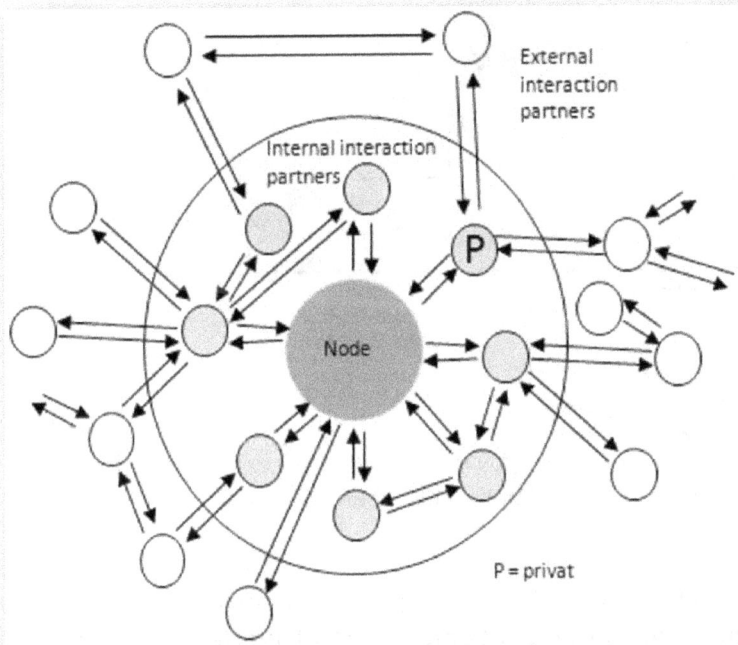

Figure 5.1 The Interaction Network with Nodes

JOB CONTROL CAPABILITIES (AUTONOMY)

According to Ashby's law of requisite variety, control capability at an intersection is necessary to resolve interference there and to prevent or reduce quality problems, delivery-time deviations, productivity losses, and so forth. Decentralized control also influences the interference sensibility. If interference cannot be handled at the source, it can have a negative effect on other nodes. Lack of control is an amplifier for minor interferences and can have major consequences. Operational control capability is the combination of internal job autonomy—formal decision-making authority, technological variation possibilities, flexible access to means—and external control—coordination, team members' support, recognition, feedback, and influence. Strategic control is necessary to reduce frequent interference through organizational design. In dynamic situations, control also includes learning.

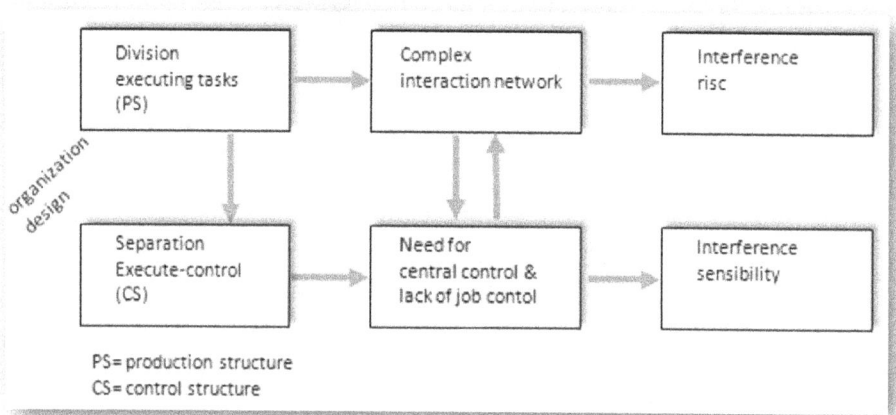

Figure 5.2 The Relation between PS Design and CS Design

The structure of the division of work determines the complexity of the interaction network and not only the risk of interference but also through interference control sensibility (fig. 5.2).

SIMULTANEOUS FOCUS ON QUALITY OF THE ORGANIZATION, QUALITY OF WORKING LIFE, AND QUALITY OF WORKING RELATIONS

Organization design is a determining factor in relation to strategic choices in achieving results in the quality of the organization, working life and working relations.

QUALITY OF ORGANIZATION

The quality of the organization concerns the ability to cope with strict external demands, customers' demands for variety (product mix), and uncertainty about both short- and long-term planning. In addition, the capacity to meet business demands, includes requirements in relation to efficiency, quality, flexibility and innovation. The degree of division of work (structure) and formalization and standardization (systems) in the interaction network will be conserved in the culture (habits and values) and in people's behavior. The organization's culture influences structure and systems design, creating a regime of social and technical aspect systems. The division of work has consequences for information-processing capacity (Galbraith 1977) and organizational behavior. In the functionally divided organization, departments and teams become silos with a focus on fragmented goals and interests. A healthy organizational regime depends on the organization's demands. In a situation of low business demands (low variation and high predictability) with repetitive processes, division of labor can help with efficiency; a bureaucratic regime can be healthy. On the other hand, if business demands are high, a bureaucratic regime is unhealthy.

In practice, unhealthy organizations are facing problems. Here are some examples (Kuipers and van Amelsvoort 1990, De Sitter1994) (see also chapter 18):

- Unreliable and long lead times due to poorly harmonized processes
- Slow response time
- Difficulty in quality assurance due to insufficiently managed processes and poor communication
- Bad cost control because actual costs cannot be monitored and (too) much interference occurs
- Slow and blind decision-making
- Expensive coordination and control mechanisms
- Lack of innovative capacity due to poor communication among the business functions and a lack of initiative

In general, the traditional, bureaucratic response to these problems is to tighten control and implement more stringent rules and procedures. These measures are counterproductive because the source of the dysfunctions is simply aggravated. This, then, is the vicious circle of the division of labor (De Sitter1981). The organization becomes entangled in the stranglehold of bureaucracy. Naturally, STSL is not a panacea for all of these problems. However, tackling unnecessary complexity at least begins to address the source of the failures described above. In a robust organization, continuous improvement or learning is more effective.

QUALITY OF WORKING LIFE: NOT SATISFACTION BUT INVOLVEMENT AND HEALTHY WORK

The structure of the division of labor can be related to simultaneously improving productivity and the quality of working life. Control capability is, after all, also an important predictor for involvement. In STSL, the quality of working life is defined in terms of objective and dynamic structural characteristics. The theory forecasts involvement and the development of intrinsic motives in organizations with sufficient control capacity. Conversely, the theory also forecasts a unilateral orientation toward extrinsic incentives such as money or promotion, where opportunities for the development of involvement and intrinsic motivation in the work itself are lacking. In a bureaucratic structure with little control in the workplace, there is therefore hardly any opportunity for involvement and intrinsic motivation (Hirschhorn, 1988), and a unilateral orientation toward external incentives emerges. The quality of work is determined by the extent to which the structure creates opportunities and conditions for involvement, motivation, and development.

De Sitter's ideas about the quality of work oppose what we refer to here as the "fit theory" of motivation (De Sitter1994). Behind the static ideas, which STSL rejects, lies the assumption that people bring fixed motives and needs to the workplace.

There has to be a "fit" between what employees want and what the organization has to offer. If their work fulfills their motives, they are satisfied; if the work does not, they are dissatisfied. This reasoning concurs with content theories of work motivation originating in industrial psychology (with major founders including Maslow [1954], McGregor [1960], Hertzberg [1966], and McClelland [1961)]. The quality of working life and motivation are approached from an individual psychological or sociopsychological perspective. In this view, quality of work is subjective. (Implicitly) widespread, it is often intuitively determined and more myth than insight.

Obviously, this perspective is important. However we are missing something essential if we are not able to approach these questions also from a structural perspective. According to the "fit approach," satisfaction is the principal quality of a work indicator. However, invariably, according to De Sitter(1994), the result of research into work satisfaction is that most people (70–80 percent) are satisfied, regardless of the organization, the nature of the job, or working conditions. Moreover, virtually no relationship exists between work satisfaction in organizations and indicators such as absence through illness, turnover, stress, or performance. Rather, satisfaction is an indication of the adjustment that people make, and it says little about whether human talents are being used fully or whether people are being challenged to develop them further (Davis, 1975). In contrast to work satisfaction, STSL prefers to use internal and external job-control autonomy as a central indicator of the quality of working life. De Sitter(1994) shows that control capacity leads to involvement and motivation, which translates into positive effects on indicators such as absenteeism, turnover, and stress. The lack of (formal and informal) job control leads to workarounds, hidden cost, increased need for management, late response time, loss of engagement, and so on. This idea is supported by Karasek's Job Demand-Control model (Karasek, 1979; Karasek and Theorell, 1990) (see also chapter 19). In it, a link is demonstrated between high and low job demand and high and low job control, striking a balance between the potential control over the task and the conduct during the working day. Specifically, evidence has been found that high job demand and low job control—exhausting work—are important predictors of psychological stress and illness. Also, we found evidence that the combination of high job demand and high job control in the form of active work is a predictor of an innovative organization.

The Karasek model was the start of a now-flourishing line of research into positive organizational psychology (see, for a state-of-the-art discussion, Bakker and Demerouti 2007). The Job Demand-Control model has developed into the Job Demand-Resources model. Job demand can be seen in terms of stressors such as work overload, unpredictable demands, time pressure, role ambiguity, interference, and emotional and physical demands. Job control has expanded into job resources such as autonomy, craftmanship, support from colleagues, constructive performance feedback, variation possibilities, leaders' appreciation and support, accurate information, and communication. This dynamic model incorporates specific stressors and resources for different occupations. Various international studies have demonstrated the importance of the broad concept of control on employee commitment.

QUALITY OF WORKING RELATIONS AND SOCIAL RESPONSIBILITY

The quality of working relations is defined as the way people work together in terms of mutual respect, openness, trust, and fairness and also the way in which partnership is built among management, works councils, and unions. Organization design also influences the way in which various parties work together. The traditional division between thinking and doing is also expressed in the relationships between groups and departments in the organization.

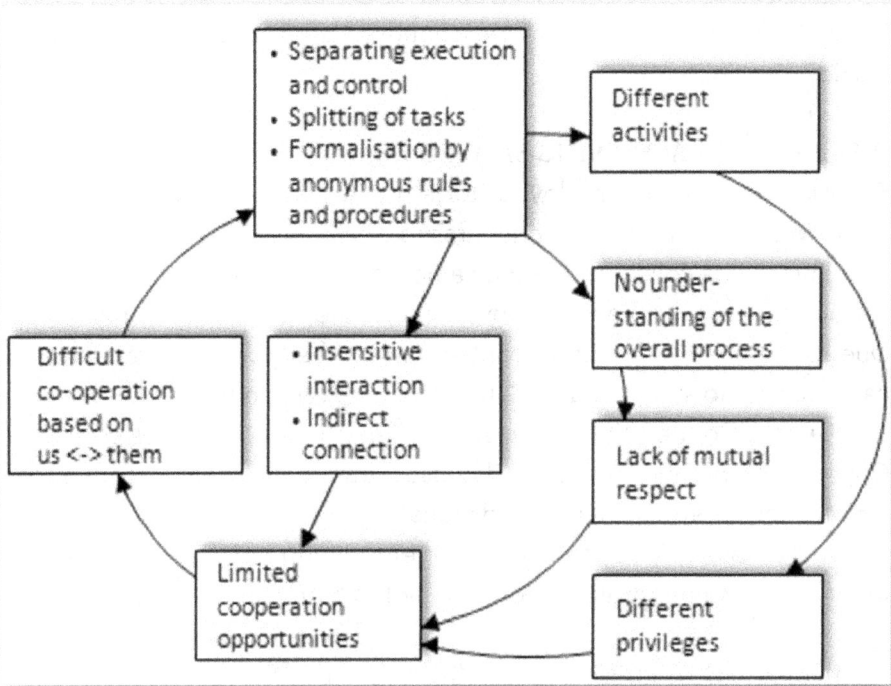

Figure 5.3 The Relation between Design and Working Relations

The traditional relationship between thinkers and doers is typified by the master and servant analogy. There are four important dysfunctions, briefly discussed below, due to inadequate division of labor in the field of working relations (van Amelsvoort 2000).

THE EMERGENCE OF DIFFERENT WORLDS

In the traditional organization, only central management has an overview of and insight into the complete process and into the organization as a whole. Different worlds emerge—for example, that of the executing employees versus that of the management group and support employees. Differences in the nature of the work, which can be typified on the one hand as physical labor (doers) and on the other hand knowledge work (thinkers), result in mutual ties between people doing similar types of work. The privileges allocated exclusively to a particular party promote the division between parties. An "us and them" situation arises, which forms the basis for difficult cooperation and leads to distrust among the parties (see fig. 5.3).

DIFFICULTY IN ACHIEVING SHARED GOALS
Focusing on bringing employees together into a single group or department with a common goal encourages social identification and bonds with immediate colleagues in the same department or group. The closer the bonds with the immediate environment, the weaker the overall bonds. Due to the absence of direct contacts with other parties, internal bonds can become so strong that isolation from the remainder of the organization occurs. Cooperation between the departments becomes confused. Consciously or unconsciously defense strategies emerge focused on maintaining or strengthening individual interests in organizations under external pressure. This can lead to finger pointing, risk-avoidance behavior and passing the problems on to a higher hierarchical level.

AN INEFFECTIVE POWER CULTURE
The degree of division of work between management and employees who execute the tasks also determines power position. This division of power arises because the controllers have greater insight and overview and more authority. Commonly held images of superiors and subordinates are linked to behavioral characteristics, as if in a predeterminded mechanism. Subordinates are expected to be attentive, compliant, and loyal, while superiors are expected to show initiative, management identification, control, and guidance. Managers are expected to solve problems. Under pressure, "two bags" are necessary to bring order to day-to-day problems (exploitation) and strategic projects (exploration). According to the theory of ambidexterity in this situations, exploitation has priority. Exploration and thus innovation is not effective to realize (Smith and Tushman 2005).

TENSION IN INDUSTRIAL RELATIONS
The consequences of bureaucracy are also visible in the field of industrial relations. The need for the employee's voice is fed by the power

concentration at the management level, the social separation between them, and the lack of employee involvement. This is expressed in the representative structure of indirect employee participation (see chapter 9). Historically determined distrust between these parties emphasizes the tensions between management and employees, with management being seen as an extension of the shareholders.

DESIGNING STRATEGY AND SEQUENCE

In STSL, the following design principles have been developed:

1. **Reduce complexity in the division of labor in the core work processes by focusing on customer-order families**. This kills two birds with one stone. On one hand, the complexity of the relationship network declines drastically. The pressure for harmonization (standardization) is greatly reduced, and the risk of interference declines. On the other hand, the professional space for self-control and self-organization in the workplaces can be drastically increased (see point 2.)

2. **Increase the local (job) control capability by decentralization.** Designing organizations is aimed at increasing productivity, flexibility, and innovation on one hand, and on the other, improving conditions for involvement and maximizing opportunities for involvement and intrinsic motivation, as well as opportunities for the development of competencies and social bonding. Maximum control in the workplace can cover the entire work process, including all preparatory and support activities. It can include not only day-to-day operational problems but also achievement of tactical improvements in the work process or in the product itself, and even accomplishing strategic changes. At the team level, far-reaching possibilities exist for building control capacity into the design. This also determines the opportunities for involvement and intrinsic motivation in a meaningful work process.

3. **Congruent infrastructure and HR systems: minimum critical specification (Cherns, 1987).** Technical instrumentation has to follow and support the logic of the structural design. The technological choice should, as far as possible, follow the logic of the socio-technical organization architecture (Kuipers and van Amelsvoort 1990). In other words: structure first and then automation. Technical tools are fitted into the design of the organization, such that the dominance of the customer process is the overall hallmark. Organizational units have access to the installations, which are embedded in the relevant process. The capacities of the technical tools meet the volume and flexibility requirements that are imposed within the unit. The control, programming, resetting, and maintenance of equipment are areas the unit bears responsibility for and has the regulation to allow it to live up to these responsibilities.

These design strategies can be applied at various levels: design of the organization, the teams, or the individual job.

REDUCTION OF COMPLEXITY: CUSTOMER ORDER PROCESS FLOW ORGANIZATION

To reduce complexity, the processes linked to customer orders are central to organization design (de Sitter, 1994) (see fig. 5.4). The reduction of the need for control can be achieved not by confronting the entire system with all possible environmental variations but instead by having part of the system process part of the variety. Processes are unraveled from customer groups, market areas, or technological differences—product-market-technology combinations—and a shift occurs from a functional organization to a process-oriented organization (parallelization). According to the theory of group technology (Burbidge 1985), different communities and teams can focus on specific customer "family groups," while maintaining variety in customer demand. The various processes can no longer interfere with one another and can progress at their own "market rhythm." The number of transfer points is also drastically reduced. Each organizational unit can concentrate on relevant groups of customers, products or services. This establishes opportunities not only for increasing operational control, but also for responding proactively to customer requirements. Instead of individual activities, the central focus in an organizational environment is the total work-process flow for a customer order (lines of business).

The preferred option in this connection is homogeneous order flows. Based on these work flows, organizational units can emerge, within which effective and efficient cooperative routines can be developed. However, as a result of variation and uncertainty, order flows are often heterogeneous in the case of innovative organizations. As a result, temporary groups emerge to develop cooperative routines rapidly, such that major demands are placed on the skills of the changing (external and internal) partners. In such a situation, the learning curve for cooperation will have to be completed at an accelerated rate.

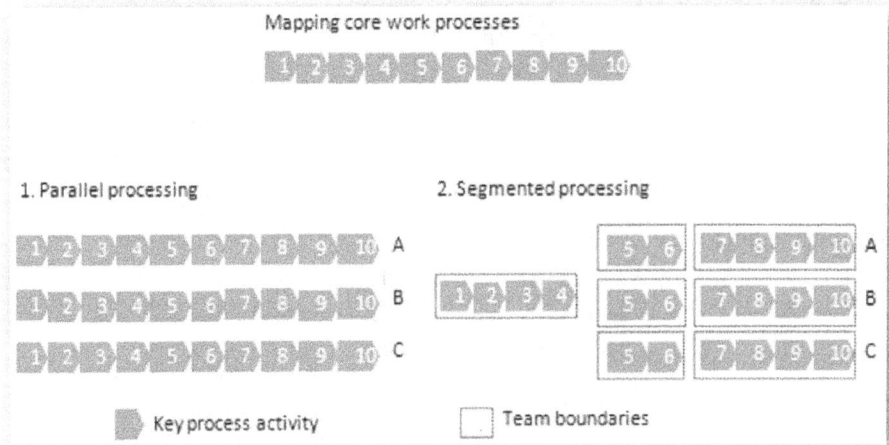

Figure 5.4 Designing the Core Work Process

If process complexity is still too high, the process is divided into highly interdependent segments. The activities within these process components are knit tightly together, and a recognizable, measurable contribution is made to the finished product, service, or customer. The interrelations between the various process segments are relatively minor. Product function is achieved as a whole task, and these segments can be seen as components of the process. Only those activities that, because of economic, technological, or strategic considerations, must be executed on a large scale, are concentrated. For example, opportunities for parallelization are limited within the process industry, in which installations from a technological/economic viewpoint are often difficult to split. Segment boundaries within the process must be sought so that process components can be viewed as the task domain for the organizational building blocks. It is worth splitting the unit into smaller segmented or parallel teams if the staff scale of the parallel work units becomes too large for a close social group (a maximum of twenty people).

INCREASING LOCAL CONTROL CAPABILITIES: DECENTRALIZATION AND SELF-ORGANIZATION

The units of the organization emerge in the PS and become complete building blocks as components of the organization by allocating sufficient control capabilities to regulate the process. Control capacity, however, can be substantially increased only if the complexity of the primary process is reduced. Within a process-oriented organization, small-scale and independent work groups and work communities can be created. Within these self-managing teams, opportunities arise for controlling and improving the process. Opportunities also occur for creating challenging work. The concept of self-managing teams is elaborated in STSL (van Amelsvoort and van Amelsvoort 2000).

Interference and variation in the process can be controlled within the work units through the introduction of feedback and feed-forward control cycles. Local regulation capacity influences the reactive capacity necessary to function successfully in a turbulent environment.

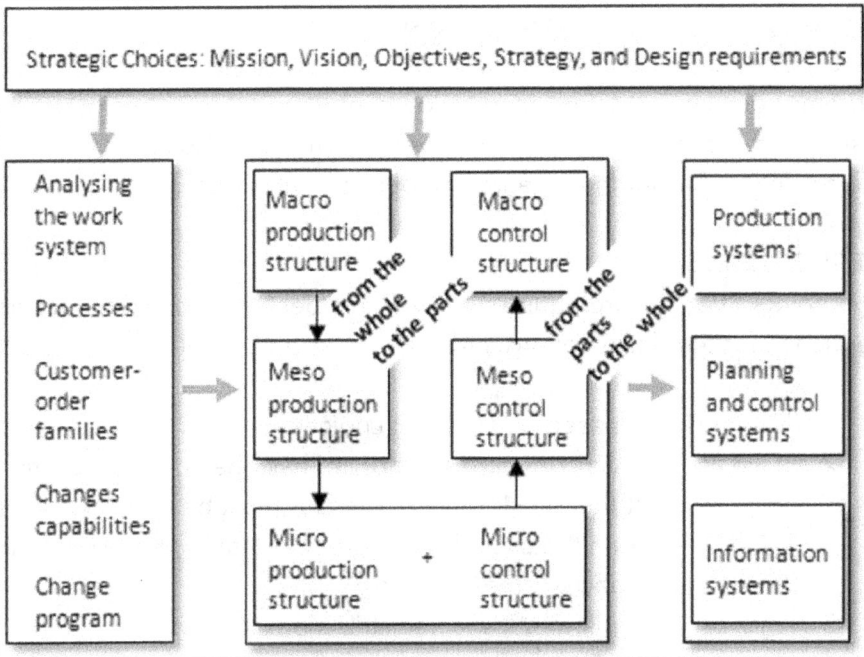

Figure 5.5 The Design Sequence Rules

MINIMAL CRITICAL SPECIFICATION

So far in this paper, emphasis has been placed on control capacity as the condition for productivity, flexibility, innovation, involvement, and motivation. Control capacity is necessary but not sufficient. In addition to the structure, (computerized) systems also have to be organized so that they too offer sufficient scope to enable structurally in-built control capacity to be used in practice. In fact, this applies not only to HR systems but to all (computerized) systems in organizations (see chapter 15), such as those handling protocols, production systems, planning systems, quality systems, and budgeting systems. Many of these systems are based on the principle of maximum specification. This means that they can be a straitjacket when it comes to action. Control capacity can be neutralized once more. From our perspective, the issue is to set up systems as much as possible based on the principle of minimum critical specification (Cherns, 1987). All HR systems (recruitment, selection, development, remuneration, etc.) must do justice to the person as a source of diversity. That can also have far-reaching consequences for the organization of existing HR systems.

DESIGN SEQUENCE
The points of departure outlined above have been supported by design sequence for the design of organizations (fig. 5.5) (De Sitteret al. 1986):

1. The design is based on strategic choices.
2. If we assume that strategic positioning has been carried out, first and foremost the transformation process must be designed. This takes place from the overall picture to the details (from the whole to the parts: macro > meso > micro).
3. This can be followed by a redistribution of control capabilities through the design of the management structure. The control structure is designed in reverse—in other words, from the parts to the whole (i.e., determination is first made of what can be controlled at the local, or micro level, subsequently what can be organized at the level of a larger organizational operating unit, or meso level, and finally what has to be controlled within the organization as a whole at the macro level. Subsequently, the consultation and decision-making structure can be further elaborated on. These rules of design sequence are regularly interpreted incorrectly, with a top-down approach being used for the redesign of the production structure and a bottom-up approach used for the control structure.
4. Finally, the various technical systems are implanted in the new architecture (see chapter 3). In practice, the rules of order are often still "violated." For example, in many automation projects, management is designed from coarse to fine, and the organization is simply adapted to the systems.

CONCLUSION

STS-D theory and practices have, since the 1970s, played an important role in the development in the Lowlands in changing the workplace. The waves in the development of the North America STS-D approach have mirrored those in the Lowlands (see chapter 1). In the Lowlands, we have seen a change in practices of STSL from profit to social-profit industries, such as health care and education organizations.

The original theory of job design has developed into a theory about organization design (see table 5.1). STSL was the basis for legislation relating to healthy working environments and formal, indirect democratic participation by workers, as well as in developing theory and practices in relation to designing organizations. STSL is still involved in academic studies and education in universities such as Eindhoven, Maastricht, Nijmegen, and Leuven. But widespread diffusion, or perhaps marketing, of the STSL theory as a brand is still problematic.

	Original STSL (1970s)	STSL today
Context	Efficiency Repetitive manufacturing Surplus labor market	Efficiency, quality, flexibility and innovation Custom made and knowledge work War on talent and healthy aging
Objective	Humanization of work	Business demands Quality of working life Quality of organization(al) health Quality of working relations
Subject	Job design (micro level)	Organization design and designing
Concepts	Open systems Joint optimalization of social and technical systems Bottom-up change	Design and change as a strategic competing (meaningful- sense making) factor Division of work: twin concepts of production and control structure Education for self design, cocreation, combination of top-down and bottom-up
Instruments	Variance control matrix Analyzing the social and technical processes	Stakeholders' demands Customer order grouping in "families" Understanding events that interfere with work Worker conditions analysis Analysis of the interdependencies of processes activities (tight analysis) Principles for self-organizing teams Concepts for designing the control structure

Table 5.1 Comparison of the Original and the Current STSL Approaches

STSL is not a commonly used term, but it provides common ground for "modern" movements. At the moment, the popular Lean Thinking approach is dominant, but successful applications of Lean Thinking have many similarities to the STSL approach (see chapter 17). Recent developments in the Lowlands and Europe called "workplace innovation" of organizations has a strong foundations in STSL philosophy (see chapter 11). In Flanders, in Belgium, Flanders Synergy has had an important role in promoting and supporting organizations that want to create innovative labor organizations with healthy working environments. STSL projects are ongoing in about one hundred organizations. Around eighty consultants have been educated in the STSL theory.

Although we have focused in this chapter on developments in design and the approach of the change process, it changes from bottom up to combinations of bottom up and top down (van Amelsvoort, 2000). Participation in change process has strong roots in the various roundtable conference methodologies (Axelrod 1992, Weisboard 2011, and many others). The STSL change approach has a special place for educational elements for creating participating workers as "experts" for co-creaion in organizational design in the practice of changing organizations and workplaces (De Sitteret al. 1997).

The central tenet of the STSL approach is to move from complex organizations with simple jobs to simple organizations with complex jobs (De Sitteret al. 1997).

REFERENCES

Achterbergh, J., and D. Vriens (2009). *Organizations: Social Systems Conducting Experiments*. Dordrecht: Springer.

Adler, N., and P. Docherty.1998. "Bringing Business into Socio-technical Theory and Practice." *Human Relations* 51 (3).

Ashby, W. R. 1969. "Self-Regulation and Requisite Variety." In F. E. Emery, *Systems Thinking*. London: Penguin Books.

Axelrod, R. 1992. "Getting Everyone Involved: How One Organization Involved Its Employees, Supervisors, and Managers in Redesigning the Organization." *Journal of Applied Behavioral Science* 28 (4).

Bakker, A., and E. Demerouti. 2007. "The Job Demands—Resources Model: State of the Art." *Journal of Managerial Psychology* 22 (3).

Bolwijn, P., and T. Kumpe. 1991. *Marktgericht Ondernemen: Management van Continuiteit en Vernieuwing.* Assen: Van Gorcum/Stichting Management Studies.

Burbidge, J. L. 1975. *The Introduction of Group Technology.* London: Heinemann.

Cherns, A. 1987. "The Principles of Socio-technical Design Revisited." *Human Relations* 40.

Davis, L. E. 1975. "Developments in Job Design," in P. Warr (ed.), *Personal Goals and Job Design.* London: John Wiley.

de Sitter, L. U. 1981. *Op Weg Naar Nieuwe Fabrieken en Kantoren: Productie-Organisatie en Arbeidsorganisatie Op de Tweesprong.* Deventer: Kluwer.

de Sitter, L. U. 1994. *Synergetisch Produceren, Human Resources Mobilization in de Productie: Een Inleiding in de Structuurbouw.* Assen: Van Gorcum.

de Sitter, L. U., J. F. Hertog, and B. Dankbaar. 1997. "From Complex Organizations with Simple Jobs to Simple Organizations with Complex Jobs." *Human Relations* 50 (5).

Emery, F. E., and E. Thorsrud. 1976. *Democracy at Work: The Report of the Norwegian Industrial Democracy Program*. Leiden: Martinus Nijhoff.

Galbraith, J. R. 1977. *Organization Design*. London: Addison-Wesley.

Hertzberg, F., B. Mausner, and B. B. Snyderman. 1959. *The Motivation to Work*. New York: John Wiley.

Hirschhorn, L. 1988. *The Workplace Within: Psychodynamics of Organizational Life*. Cambridge: MIT Press.

Karasek, R. 1979. "Job Demand, Job Decisions Latitude and Mental Strain: Implications for Job Design." *Administrative Science Quarterly* 24: 285–307.

Karasek, R. A., and T. Theorell. 1990. *Healthy Work: Stress, Productivity, and the Reconstruction of Working Life*. New York: Basic Books.

Kuipers, H., and P. van Amelsvoort. 1990. *Slagvaardig Organiseren, Inleiding in de Socio-techniek als Integrale Ontwerpleer*. Deventer: Kluwer.

Kuipers, H., P. van Amelsvoort, and E.-H. Kramer. 2010. *Het Nieuwe Organiseren, Alternatieven Voor de Bureaucratie*. Leuven: Acco.

Maslow, A. 1954. *Motivation and Personality*. New York: Harper and Row.

McClelland, D. C. 1961. *The Achieving Society*. New York: Van Nostrand Reinhold.

McGregor, D. 1960. *The Human Side of Enterprise*. New York: McGraw-Hill.

Mumford, E. 2006. "The Story of Socio-technical Design: Reflections on Its Successes, Failures, and Potential." *Information Systems* 16.

Smith W. K., and M. L. Tushman. 2005. "Managing Strategic Contradictions: A Top Management Model for Managing Innovation Stream." *Organization Science* 16.

van Amelsvoort, P. 2000. *The Design of Work and Organization.* Vlijmen: ST-Groep.

van Amelsvoort, P., and G. van Amelsvoort. 2000. *Designing and Developing Self-Directed Work Teams.* Vlijmen: ST-Groep.

Weisbord, M. 2011. *Productive Workplaces: Dignity, Meaning, and Community in the Twenty-First Century.* New York: Wiley.

Six

Organizing Innovation and (Strategic) Decision Making

L. J. LEKKERKERK

INTRODUCTION

This chapter explains ideas about the integration of the design of the "innovation structure" in the redesign of the organizational structure. The ideas build on the Lowlands STS-D tradition and are based on my recent work (Lekkerkerk 2012). To be able to design a structure, one needs to know what work has to be done, divided, and hence coordinated. Using the Lowlands STS-D guidelines, the production structure, and the operational layer of the control structure—together labeled the "primary process"—can be designed (see chapter 5).

Then the question is how to design the innovation structure and how to link it to the structure of the core work process, including how to involve workers having the greater part of their job. A possibility is to let the shop-floor employees participate in decision-making, but a practical way to do that is needed. Sociocracy is presented and proposed as a practical way to organize the involvement of making the various types of innovation (and strategic) decisions.

Sociocracy seems to fit quite well to Lowlands STS-D. It has an answer to the question of how to integrate multiple viewpoints from various layers of the organization representing different disciplines as well, in making these nonoperational decisions as good as possible. Incorporating sociocracy in the approach to designing the upper layers of the control structure enhances STS-D. Sociocracy, also known as the "circular organization," was originally developed in the early 1970s by Gerard Endenburg, a Dutch entrepreneur. Because it inspired "holacracy," this recent approach to decision making is briefly described too.

Lowlands STS-D, described in a previous chapter and compared with Lean (see chapter 16), uses the Ashby-view of an open system that should have control, design, and operational regulation of some primary transformation to maintain its separate existence (Ashby 1956). It uses slightly different terms, as shown in figure 6.1 below.

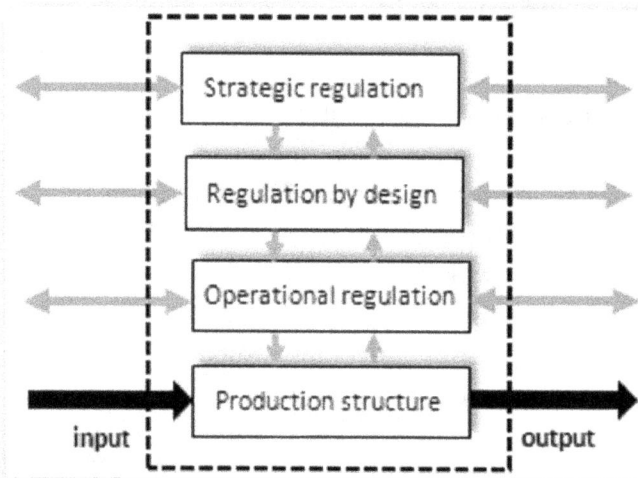

Figure 6.1 STSL Open Systems View of an
Organization (based on Ashby 1956)

Lowlands STS-D aims at an integral (re)design of the organizational structure (division of labor and coordination). As van Amelsvoort explained (chapter 5), first the production structure, responsible for the primary transformation, is designed top down, and then the control structure is built bottom up to coordinate and control. Key to this production-structure design is the formation of autonomous units that ideally function as minicompanies serving a subset of customers. As Christis (chapter 17) explains, the flows that Lean systems designs are similar (Womack and Jones 2003). Ashby and Beer advocate creating simple (production) structures with complex jobs (De Sitter et al. 1997) and label this design-principle "attenuation."

But even all these autonomous teams need the three types of control, so they need to be (self-) managed, and to that end the control structure with the three layers must be designed. Preferably it is one that amplifies the regulatory potential of the system. Controllability can be regarded as a central design target of Lowlands STS-D.

The design of the control structure starts with the operational regulation layer by assigning operational control activities—for example, for quality, logistics, and finance to the lowest possible level (i.e., usually to the team—either to a team supervisor or to different members of the team). Interdependencies between teams require operational coordination too. The primary process consists of the production structure plus the operational layer of the control structure.

Then the upper two control structure layers need to be designed to complement the primary process, enabling the organization to (1) adapt its goals by strategic regulation, either to respond to changes in its environment or to implement strategic choices of its own, and (2) adapt its primary-process infrastructure to enable reaching the (partly new) goals.

The latter is called "regulation by design," and this type of regulation can also be triggered "from below" when recurring operational problems demand an innovative solution. This rest of this chapter focuses on the design of the "regulation by design" control structure—what it is and how it is done.

Let us now take "regulation by design" as the system in focus for which we want to design a substructure. There are two basic questions when designing an organizational structure:

1) What is the work that needs to be done, and how can it be divided over groups or individuals?
2) How can the work best be coordinated?

The term "regulation by design" may seem a bit vague and abstract. "Design" sounds like creative ideas and exciting new possibilities and has a feel of new products that may have a "designer" do the aesthetics.

Also, information and communication technology or process equipment may be designed and implemented. And changes in social systems, like human resource policies, a new set of performance indicators (Balanced Score Card, Global Reporting Initiative), or the organizational structure, can be "designed" too. So "regulation by design" has to do with innovation and planned change. Its results are changes in the primary process, either by replacing an element and adapting surrounding ones to the new element or by adding a new operational unit (e.g., one responsible for a new geographic market or for a new product-service combination, involving a new business model and new equipment (like the PC division for IBM in the early 1980s). This kind of "change work" is typically project-based, knowledge-intensive, and done by professionals while involving other people from various disciplines. It is leading to something new and thus deals with more uncertainty than the primary process. Because of this, Achterbergh et al. (1999) renamed the "regulation by design" substructure responsible for these innovation activities "innovation structure."

Now we have a brief idea of the answer to the first question for regulation by design. These activities are necessary in any organization, whether small to extremely large, publicly held, cooperative or privately owned, as long as the organization wants to remain viable or simply to stay in business.

Of course the subquestion "How can it be divided?" can be answered only for the innovation structure of a specific organization because of all the contingencies involved in organization design. It goes without saying that the innovation structure must be tightly linked to the primary-process structure (its target) and to the strategic regulation layer of the organization (its supervisor).

Strategic regulation, which Ashby named "control," is the top layer of the control structure, and its task is to formulate the higher purpose of the organization and the vision, mission, and goals that follow from the purpose and the desires of the stakeholders involved. For the twenty-first-century organization, we may safely say that its goals express multiple value creation for multiple stakeholders (Mackey and Sisodia 2014).

The rest of the chapter is structured as follows. First we explain the work to be done within the innovation structure, and briefly the strategy work. After that, the "model innovation and organizational structure" is presented as linking these functions. Then we turn our attention to the decision-making part in the work of these two upper layers of the control structure, to proceed by explaining "sociocracy" as a systematic way to involve employees from all levels and disciplines in nonoperational decision-making.

INNOVATION WORK

What activities belong to the innovation structure? Textbooks on innovation management (cf. Tidd and Bessant 2009) describe the innovation process as consisting of three basic steps or phases: *Search, select, and implement.*

Search, according to Tidd and Bessant (2009), includes looking for and finding ideas for innovation, evaluating them (by doing some preliminary investigations), and turning the promising ones into a project proposal or business case. This stage is sometimes referred to as the "fuzzy front end" of innovation (Koch and Leitner 2008; Kurkkio et al. 2011).

The selection process should figure out which of the business cases presented will probably contribute most to the realization of the goals of the organization. This implies that strategic criteria are needed to make a selection. Selection leads to a portfolio of innovation projects, and this portfolio needs to be balanced against several criteria.

Then the implementation process carries out the project plans of the selected business cases, and most are changed to adapt to developing insights. In innovation management, the notion of the ambidextrous organization is relevant, which refers to an organization capable of doing both radical-explorative and incremental-exploitative innovation and change projects (March 1999, O'Reilly and Tushman 2004). Tidd and Bessant state that both types of innovation projects need their own "search-select-implement" funnel, using a different approach to the work and different sets of criteria to choose and control the projects. Because different types of work require different activities and talents, this distinction is useful for the organization designer.

STRATEGIC REGULATION WORK
Strategic regulation involves various activities, and it may be done according to ten different schools (Mintzberg et al. 1998). Defining the primary goal, the reason why the organization is in business, or its higher purpose (Mackey and Sisodia 2014), is an important part. Christensen et al. (2009) prescribe that the function for the customer rather than the (temporary) product or service should be described. So instead of delivering "the ultimate coal heater," the purpose should be supplying "a comfortable home."

The higher purpose relates to the customer as an important stakeholder. Henry Ford (1922) already put the customer first, and Alfred Sloan (1963) mentioned serving various GM stakeholders without neglecting the shareholder. Identifying the stakeholders and the multiple values to be created to serve all as good as possible is a strategic activity. Although very important, these activities count for only a small fraction of the overall headcount in full-time equivalent (but more in terms of employees involved). For the organization designer, the task is quite different from designing the primary-process structure and the innovation structure. For the "strategy structure," designing may involve organizing a lot of individuals contributing a minor part of their working time to strategic decision-making (e.g., from various employees who devote most of their working hours to the primary or the innovation process).

This brief outline should enhance understanding of what strategic regulation work (mainly decision-making) entails and enable readers to appreciate what sociocracy brings to this later in the chapter.

THE MODEL INNOVATION AND ORGANIZATION STRUCTURE (MIOS)

We now proceed to present and explain the Model Innovation and Organization Structure, using the acronym "MIOS" from now on. The MIOS was developed using several insights from cybernetics and socio-technical systems thinking.

A "function model" of an organization is an organizational cybernetic concept. Function here refers to the contribution of an element or sub-system to the system it is part of (In 't Veld 1994, Veeke et al. 2008). So it should not be confused with function referring to "an individual's job" or to a functional (or activity-based) structure. And "model" refers to a simplified representation of the complex reality to highlight certain aspects—in this case, the different functions that are needed to keep an organizational system "viable,"

Beer (1994, 2000) developed a function model known as the Viable System Model (VSM). Like de Sitter, he is building on Ashby (1956). Based on systematic reasoning, not challenged to date (Achterbergh and Riesewijk 1999), Beer claims that his VSM incorporates "necessary and sufficient" functions for viability of a system, making it a powerful diagnostic device. And it incorporates the logic of recursion that fits well with the socio-technical idea of a production structure consisting of (near) autonomous units, which (depending on the size of the organization) may be further and further divided in again (near) autonomous subunits (Bee 2000, In 't Veld 1994).

A drawback of the VSM is the fact that it contains only five functions, and only two are directly involved in innovation, with a third as a strategic innovation control function. For a detailed diagnosis of innovation structures, and to guide redesign, that is not sufficient. Also, its abstract nature and terminology prevent many practitioners to understand it intuitively. So a VSM-based model containing more functions to represent the innovation structure and giving all functions names that appeal to practitioners was deemed necessary.

In 't Veld (1994) supplied ingredients for development of the new model. He developed two models, based on systems thinking and pragmatic engineering logic, that contain more innovation-related functions, using understandable names (Veeke et al. 2008). Secondly, innovation-management literature supplied the steps in any innovation process: search, select, implement, capture (Tidd and Bessant 2009, 44). Also used was the distinction between exploration and exploitation (March 1999), linked to radical and incremental innovation, with the idea that any organization should do both in an "ambidextrous" way (O'Reilly and Tushman 2004).

Closely linked to ambidexterity is the notion of a balanced innovation portfolio of projects (Kester et al. 2009, 328). Combining newly developed and existing knowledge is related to innovation (Hislop, 2005); therefore, organizational memory is important to store its knowledge. Lekkerkerk (2012) presents the full line of reasoning behind the resulting model, which is named, as mentioned earlier, "the Model Innovation and Organizational Structure" (MIOS). Figure 6.2 presents the model. The names of the functions contain a verb, according to system theory custom. The codes added to the names, with I, C, and V for innovation, central, and supply (*voortbrengen* in Dutch) respectively and a number, serve as a practical shorthand when discussing how functions are assigned.

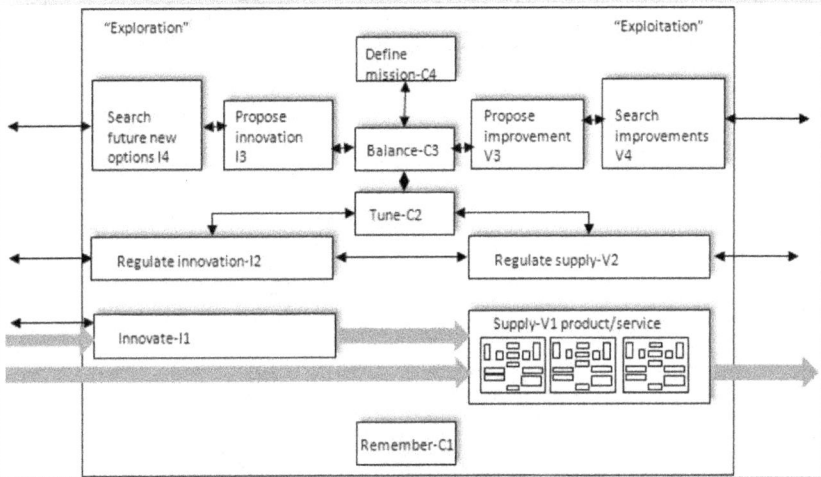

Figure 6.2 The New Function Model: the Model Innovation
and Organizational Structure, or "the MIOS" (Lekkerkerk 2012,
296). (Some relations, such as those of Remember-C1 with all
other functions, are omitted for clarity of the drawing.)

The contributions of the twelve functions of the MIOS to an organizational system are summarized in table 6.1. Being based on the logic of Beer's VSM, this new model also contains "necessary and sufficient" functions. Hence, an organization that implements all these functions and their relations in its structure, and of course assigns them to competent employees who execute them well, is able to remain viable. That is, the organization is "able to maintain its separate existence" (Beer 1994, 113). Like the VSM, the MIOS incorporates the idea of recursion, meaning that the Supply-V1-function may consist of separate, independent parts that are (or should be) viable subsystems. In figure 6.2, the small versions of the MIOS within the function Supply-V1 symbolize this recursion.

Bernard J. Mohr and Pierre van Amelsvoort

Name-code	Contribution of function to organization
Supply product service-V1	Represents the primary process supplying products and/or services by transforming inputs in output Includes order-related activities: logistics, process planning, sales, finance, procurement, etc Includes supporting activities: maintance, HR, facilities management, etc.
Regulate supply-V2	Conduct operational regulation of the various aspects of the primary process, including continuous improvement
Propose improvement-V3	Make project proposals for the best opportunities for improvement received from V4
Search improvement-V4	Search and find ways to improve exploitation of current products, markets, facilities, etc
Innovatie-I1	Carry out all improved innovation projects and improvements projects
Regulate innovation-I2	Conduct operational regulation of individual innovation projects and operationally manage the portfolio of projects in progress
Propose innovation-V3	Make project proposals for the best future options for innovation received from I4
Search future new options-I4	Explore environment and search for future options for innovation aimed at new and existing markets
Remember-C1	Organizational memory storing codified knowledge relevant for the organization
Tune-C2	Tune V1 and I1 enabling smooth implementation of innovation and tune the upper six functions contributing to the strategic planning process
Balance-C3	Balance the project portfolio by strategically choosing which new proposals (from V3&I3) should be funded and at the same time which of the projects in progress should be continued, paused or aborted
Define mission-C4	Define the mission, vision and strategy for the company and deriving lower level strategies for supply and innovation including performance indicators and budgets
Continuous improvement	Set up small scale improvement or 'kaizen' activities. These important activities (Bessant 2003, Womack, Jones 2003) are embedded in each function's operational regulation

Table 6.1 Brief Description of the Functions in the MIOS (Lekkerker 2012)

The twelve MIOS functions are related to innovation management and to socio-technical literature. The generic innovation process (Tidd and Bessant 2009, 44) mentioned above links to the MIOS functions in the following ways:

Search: Both Search-functions (V4/I4) and both Propose functions (V3/I3)

Select: Preliminary selection is part of both Search and Propose, with final selection of proposals by Balance-C3

Implement: Carrying out and operationally managing the selected innovation projects by Innovate-I1 and Regulate innovation-I2

The Lowlands socio-technical theory matches the MIOS functions in the following way. The production structure as defined by De Sitterequals Supply-V1. The three layers of his control structure are incorporated, of course. Regulate Supply-V2 is his operational regulation layer, and Define mission-C4 equals strategic regulation. The remaining functions are detailing the layer regulation by design or the innovation structure. Remember-C1, or the organizational memory, is supporting all other functions.

DECISION MAKING IN THE UPPER LAYERS OF THE CONTROL STRUCTURE

As already described, at each layer of the control structure, decisions have to be made, which is part of the work. And because of our bounded rationality, each decision may be seen as an "organizational experiment" with an inherent risk of failure (Achterbergh and Vriens 2009), which is illustrated by the high failure rate of innovation projects. Due to the topic of this chapter, we left operational regulation out.

When looking back at the discussion of the work involved in the innovation structure, it may already be clear that you don't need to be a full-time innovator for your organization to be able to contribute to the innovation-related functions. Employees may pick up ideas from any-where, may be granted some working hours to further develop their ideas (10 percent at 3M and even 25 percent at Google), present their business case to those responsible for the function Balance-C3, and if they desire and are deemed competent, they may even carry out the approved inno-vation project (probably with others), temporarily acting as a project man-ager (Laloux 2014). These examples are innovation work, so they relate to the "innovation production structure," but there is also an "innovation control structure" (De Sitter1998). For the sake of simplicity, we assume that the innovation control structure has an operational control function.

A basic control activity for innovation is similar to quality control in operations. The question "Does the product conform to specifications?" equals the question "Does the idea, the business case, the result of a project stage (still) match strategic and innovation portfolio criteria?" The business cases that are chosen need operational control per project and over the set(s) or portfolios of active projects. Delays and budget overruns are commonplace when developing new results, and a project that is delayed may influence the start of another project that needs the employees still on the delayed project team.

More strategic innovation decisions, like "Which of the project pro-posals should we choose?" and the go/no-go decisions at the develop-ment gates, need to be looked at from various perspectives. To involve employees representing these perspectives, sociocracy appears to be a systematic way.

SOCIOCRACY OR THE CIRCULAR ORGANIZATION

Sociocracy was invented and developed in the Netherlands in the 1970s and has since spread around the world without being implemented on a large scale. It also has a more recent US adaptation named "holacracy," which we discuss later in the chapter. Sociocracy leaves the production structure, or primary-process structure, largely as it is at the moment an organization starts its implementation. Sociocracy is a consistent approach to involve employees (including managers) from different hierarchical levels in making nonoperational decisions. These decisions may be about strategic choices, including innovation and change. Sociocracy can be regarded as an approach to organize decision-making within the innovation structure and for strategic regulation (Endenburg 1974, Buck and Endenburg 2004).

BACKGROUND OF THE SOCIOCRATIC APPROACH

When an organization employs a lot of people, a large number of processes are carried out. To keep the processes in control and the organization viable, both operational decisions and policy (or strategic) decisions should be taken. Sociocracy presents a solution to deal with these policy decisions, using a layered and linked structure of so-called circles. Decisions are made by the circle at the right level and by consent of its members. Although the term "sociocracy" was borrowed from sociology (and means something completely different there), this approach was originally developed at a Dutch firm founded by the parents of Gerard Endenburg. They were influenced by Kees Boeke, a Dutchman inspired by anthroposophical ideas of Rudolf Steiner.

In 1974, Endenburg wrote his first book on sociocracy, and later he devoted his PhD research to it (Endenburg, 1998) to give his system a scientific foundation. Endenburg, being a professional electrotechnical engineer, was also familiar with organizational cybernetics (Romme and Endenburg 2006, 290), and used system dynamics to inspire his ideas on decision making (Romme 1998, 159).

CORE IDEAS AND CONCEPTS OF SOCIOCRACY

To explain the working of the core idea, we assume an organization existing of at least some departments or groups. Each group has a hierarchical manager who reports to a higher manager. For operational decisions, this group manager has authority and may delegate this (partly) to his/her subordinates. Usually the group manager represents the ideas and interests of the group when strategic decisions are discussed and taken at a higher management level. Consequently, group members are not directly involved.

Sociocracy names groups of people at the shop or office floor "circles," and, depending on the size and the operational division of labor, there is a hierarchy of circles (e.g., operational circle, business unit circle, top circle). Members of a circle elect one of them (the manager excluded) to represent them and their views in a higher-level circle, which is linking various related (floor-level) circles. Depending on organizational size, a number of layers may be formed until the top circle is reached at top management team level. So a "circle organization" not only has a normal chain of command hierarchy for operational matters, but also a parallel structure of "circles" for strategic or policy decision-making that also serves as a bottom-up feedback channel, increasing the information-processing capacity of the organization. An interesting and crucial feature about sociocratic decision making is the principle of "consent." Romme and Endenburg explain it this way: "Informed consent, defined as 'no reasoned and paramount objection,' governs all decision-making on policy issues in circles. This means a policy decision can only be made if nobody raises a reasoned and paramount objection against it" (Romme and Endenburg 2006, 292).Because circles have a size-enabling, fruitful discussion that all take part in, there is room for raising objections and for trying together to adapt the decision to take the objections away. It seems obvious that "informed consent" is different from democratic, majority decision-making. However, decisions need not be consensual or unanimous because having no objections does not imply wholehearted agreement with a decision. On the other hand, maintaining a reasoned and paramount objection comes close to the right of veto. Another feature of the circle organization is the delegation of strategic decisions to the lowest possible level. If a strategic decision (e.g., a redesign of its service, entering a new market, would have no consequences beyond an operational circle so then that circle decides). Of course, if it needs a substantial amount of investments to carry out its decision, other (higher) circles are immediately involved. In bigger organizations, the word "strategic" may be confusing because the operational circles are involved in "local policy" decisions (e.g., about the procedure to make the schedules for the members, or who works when).

THE SOCIOCRATIC APPROACH IN PRACTICE

The description of the core idea already incorporates most of the design rules. Romme and Endenburg (2006) summarize these rules as follows. To build organizational capacity for self-regulation and learning, apply the following rules to create a circular design tailored to your organization:

1. Decisions on policy issues are taken by informed consent (defined as "no reasoned and paramount objection").
2. Every member of the organization belongs to at least one circle, a unit of people with a common work objective. Each circle formulates and updates its objective(s); performs the directing, operating, and measuring/feedback functions; and maintains its skills/knowledge base by means of integral education.
3. The double link (i.e., the vertical connection between two circles), is constituted by the participation of at least two persons in both circles—including the functional leader and at least one elected delegate from the lower circle.
4. The circular structure, defined in the previous rules, is added to the administrative hierarchy. This administrative hierarchy, as a sequence of accountability levels, contains all functional leaders who are responsible and accountable for implementation of policies made in circles.
5. Circles elect persons only on the basis of informed consent, after an open discussion (Romme and Endenburg 2006, 296).

Apart from the "circular design rules," Romme and Endenburg present a number of conditions that must be met to make a sociocratic design work (2006, 296). The goal of the organization must be to stay economically and socially viable, and at least top management, including the board, should embrace this sociocratic idea. Also, any information is available to all members of the organization (with only well-motivated exceptions). The accountability levels in the hierarchy must be clearly laid out, differentiating higher and lower-level issues. Because the CEO's leadership style must conform to the rules of consent, his or her support for a redesign is quite important. Implementation of sociocracy is regarded as a change project, may use outside experts, and requires a number of pilots in which employees, after being trained in the rules of consent decision-making, are experimenting with the circle structure supported by the project team. After the pilots have proved successful, top management can make a decision on organizationwide implementation, and it is advised to create statutory safeguards (2006, 296) preventing the CEO's successor from throwing sociocracy overboard and going back to a command and control hierarchy.

According to Romme and Endenburg, its original theoretical roots in cybernetics are complemented by grounding sociocracy in political science, organizational learning and control, unanimity rule, employee commitments, and organizational property rights (2006, 294).

There are a number of collaborating national sociocratic organizations that hold regular national and international meetings and provide training for novices. This way, tools, instruments, and methods are spread and further developed within the community. (See reference section for links.) The company founded by Endenburg's parents was ailing when he took over in 1968, and upon implementing the circular structure, which in fact enables using all (or at least a greater part of) available talent and insight, the situation improved, leading to further development of the idea (reported in Endenburg, 1974, 1998). Romme and Endenburg present data based on "thirty-two organizations" (2006, 292), the largest to successfully implement it having about fifteen hundred employees. Most are Dutch, but companies from Canada, the United States, and Brazil are also described. And "many other organizations" experimented with it (Romme and Endenburg, 2006, 292). The various websites present a number of different cases, and there is a decent article on *Wikipedia* at http://en.wikipedia.org/wiki/Sociocracy. It is obvious that making well-informed strategic and lower-level policy decisions in organizations, seen as socio-technical systems, is very important for their survival. Sociocracy presents a systematic way to involve more employee talents than is usual in ordinary administrative decision-making processes. Members of higher circles represent their lower-level circle, so they will discuss the higher-level decisions with them too. Because roles and responsibilities are clearly defined and assigned to individual organizational (circle) members and can even be institutionalized in statutory arrangements of the organization, it seems that implementing a circular design is a permanent change. Other options to involve large groups in decision making, like open space or world café, seem to have a more ad hoc nature.

What remains less clear is whether the circular design supposes a particular organizational structure for the primary process of the organization. Decentralizing decision-making to the lowest level in an activity-based (or functional) structure also complicates the circle structure on top of that because many strategic decisions (including innovation and investment) in such a hierarchical structure have implications for many, if not all, operational groups and thus circles. This implies that the top circle may end up being the only real strategic decision-making circle. The most-used references for this chapter—Romme (1997, 1998) and Romme and Endenburg (2006)—do not address this issue. Romme explained that as soon as a circular structure is implemented, the existing administrative hierarchy or structure may be taken up by the circles when the members think the structure is causing problems that may be solved by a redesign (personal e-mail, 2014).

In the jargon of the Lowlands socio-technical systems design by de Sitter, sociocracy presents additional guidelines for designing the organization of decision-making for strategic regulation and "regulation by design" and involving shop-floor employees in it via the circles. These are needed because a systematic way to involve operational employees in activities belonging to the higher control structure layers is not available in de Sitter's work (1998) or in recent handbooks by Kuipers et al. (2010) or van Hootegem et al. (2008).

The Dutch Sociocratic Foundation and the related international groups seem to further develop sociocratic design actively. Romme, who holds a chair in entrepreneurship and innovation at Eindhoven University of Technology, seems to be one of the leading academics on the topic.

An "offspring" of sociocracy in the United States is "holacracy." Between 2001 and 2006. Brian Robertson developed his "holacracy"™, which is apparently influenced by sociocracy, as comparisons between the approaches on the website show. For policy decision-making, holacracy uses a similar set of circles. For operational decision-making, holacracy borrowed from agile software development, which is no surprise given the fact that at that time, Robertson ran a software development company. (Further information is available at http://holacracy.org/.)

CONCLUSION

Diagnosing and designing an innovation structure using the MIOS as a guideline fits in the Lowlands STS-D tradition. Further research of successful innovation structures, and how they are embedded in the overall organizational structure, will lead to a more detailed set of design guidelines for this important substructure, which are still lacking.

Looking at the innovation process using the MIOS as a lens, we described the various types of innovation decisions. These decisions can be made well only by using various perspectives and by involving various disciplines and maybe external stakeholders. A systematic way to involve all kinds of employees is found in sociocracy. The fact that sociocratic thinking can be incorporated into the Lowlands STS-D approach should be clear from this explanation, but it remains to be done.

This chapter presented two ways to further develop the Lowlands socio-technical systems design approach. Some other options for further development are worth mentioning here:

- Find a way to incorporate a multiple-stakeholder approach in setting organizational goals (for multiple value creation) that the structure to be designed should help achieve.
- Link (corporate) governance by external (government) agencies and internal boards of directors to the design of the control structure.
- Adapt the design rules to designing at the network level of collaborating parties (companies, NGOs, individuals, government),

where hierarchical power is lacking, which poses change-management challenges.

Further developments of Lowlands STS-D may be coordinated by the Ulbo De SitterKnowledge Institute, founded in 2012 to honor the late de Sitter, a partner of the global STS-D network. (See http://www.ulbodesitterkennisinstituut.nl/kennisinstituut/).

REFERENCES

Around the sociocratic ideas, an active international society exists, and it started an educational process for becoming a certified sociocratic professional. More information is included in texts, papers, and links to YouTube videos via websites, both in Dutch (http://www.sociocratie.nl/) and English (http://www.sociocratie.nl/global/).

The US organization: http://www.socionet.us/

The *Wikipedia* article: http://en.wikipedia.org/wiki/Sociocracy

About Holacracy™: http://holacracy.org/

The Ulbo De SitterKnowledge Institute (in Dutch only): http://www.ulbodesitterkennisinstituut.nl/kennisinstituut/

Achterbergh, J., B. Dankbaar, H. Lekkerkerk, and W. Martens. Juli/Augustus 1999. "Bestendiging Door Vernieuwing, Over Functies en Structuren Voor Innovatie." *Management and Organisatie*, Themanummer Innovatie, 53e jrg. (nr. 4), 1999: 147–62.

Achterbergh, J. M. I. M., and B. Riesewijk. 1999. *Polished by Use: Four Windows on Organization*. Eburon, Delft, PhD thesis, Radboud University.

Achterbergh, Jan, and Dirk Vriens. 2009. *Organizations: Social Systems Conducting Experiments.* Springer Verlag, Berlin.

Ashby, W. R. 1956. *An Introduction to Cybernetics.* London: Chapman and Hall. http://pcp.vub.ac.be/books/IntroCyb.pdf.

Beer, S. 1994. *The Heart of Enterprise.* The Stafford Beer Classic Library. Chichester: Wiley. (First edition 1979.)

Beer, S. 2000. *Diagnosing the System for Organizations.* The Stafford Beer Classic Library. Chichester: Wiley. (First edition 1985.)

Bessant, J. (2003) *High-Involvement Innovation: Building and Sustaining Competitive Advantage through Continuous Change.* Chichester: Wiley.

Buck, J. A., and G. Endenburg 2004. *Sociocracy: The Creative Forces of Self-Organization.* www.sociocratie.nl.

Christensen, C. M., J. H. Grossman, and J. Hwang. 2009. *The Innovator's Prescription: A Disruptive Solution for Health Care.* New York: McGraw-Hill.

de Sitter, L. U. 1998. *Synergetisch Produceren: Human Resource Mobilisation in de Produktie: Een Inleiding in de Structuurbouw,* second revised edition (first edition 1994). Assen: Van Gorcum, Assen.

de Sitter, L. U., J. F. den Hertog, and B. Dankbaar. May 1997. "From Complex Organizations with Simple Jobs to Simple Organizations with Complex Jobs." *Human Relations* 50 (5): 497–534.

Endenburg, G. 1974. *Sociocratie: Een Redelijk Ideaal.* Zaandijk: Klaas Woudt.

Endenburg, G. 1998. *Sociocracy as Social Design.* Edited PhD thesis, Eburon, Delft.

Ford, H. 1922. *My Life and Work.* BN Publishing Reprint.

Hislop, D. 2005. *Knowledge Management in Organizations: A Critical Introduction.* Oxford: OUP.

Kester, L., E.-J. Hultink, and K. Lauche. 2009. "Portfolio Decision-Making Genres: A Case Study." *Journal of Engineering and Technology Management* 26: 327–41.

Koch, R., and K.-H. Leitner. 2008. "The Dynamics of Self-Organization in the Fuzzy Front End: Empirical Evidence from the Austrian Semiconductor Industry." *Creativity and Innovation Management* 17 (3): 216–26.

Kuipers, H., P. J. van Amelsvoort, and E. H. Kramer. 2010. *Het Nieuwe Organiseren: Alternatieven Voor de Bureaucratie.* Leuven: Acco Uitgeverij.

Kurkkio, M., J. Frishammar, and U. Lichtenthaler. 2011. "Where Process Development Begins: A Multiple Case Study of Front-End Activities in Process Firms." *Technovation* 31: 490–504.

Laloux, F. 2014. *Reinventing Organizations: A Guide to Creating Organizations Inspired by the Next Stage of Human Consciousness.* Brussels: Nelson Parker.

Lekkerkerk, L. J. 2012. *Innovatie en Organisatie Structuur: Ontwikkeling en Test van Een Functiemodel Voor Structuuronderzoek en Diagnose.*

PhD thesis, Radboud Universiteit, Innovatica Nijmegen. Full pdf with summary in English available at http://repository.ubn.ru.nl/handle/2066/93601.

Mackey, J., and R. Sisodia. 2014. *Conscious Capitalism: Liberating the Heroic Spirit of Business.* Boston: Harvard Business Review Press.

March, J. G. 1999. *The Pursuit of Organizational Intelligence.* Oxford: Blackwell Business.

Mintzberg, H. B., and Ahlstrand J. Lampel. 1998. *Strategy Safari: The Complete Guide through the Wilds of Strategic Management.* New York: FT-Prentice Hall.

O'Reilly III, C. A., and M. L. Tushman. April 2004. "The Ambidextrous Organization." *Harvard Business Review.* 1–8.

Romme, A. G. L. 1997. "Werken, Leren en Cmmuniceren." *Tijdschrift Voor BedrijfsAdministratie,* jrg. 101, oktober, nr. 1206: 340–46.

Romme, A., and L. Georges. 1998. "Toward the Learning Organization: The Case of Circular Reengineering." *Knowledge and Process Management* 5 (3): 158–64.

Romme, A. G. L., and G. Endenburg. March–April 2006. "Construction Principles and Design Rules in the Case of Circular Design." *Organization Science* 17 (2): 287–97.

Sloan, A. P. 1963. *My Years with General Motors.* New York, NY: Currency Doubleday.

Tidd, J., and J. Bessant. 2009. *Managing Innovation: Integrating Technological, Market, and Organizational Change,* fourth edition. Chichester: Wiley.

van Hootegem, G., G. van Amelsvoort, G. van Beek, and R. Huys. 2008. *Anders Organiseren and Beter Werken: Handboek Sociale Innovatie en Vrandermanagement.* Leuven: Acco.

Veeke, Hans P., M. Ottjes, A. Jaap, and Gabriël Lodewijks. 2008. *The Delft Systems Approach: Analysis and Design of Industrial Systems.* London: Springer Verlag.

Veld, J. In 't. 1994. *Analyse van Organisatieproblemen: Een Toepassing van Denken in Systemen en Processen*, sixth revised edition (first edition 1975). Stenfert Kroese/EPN: Houten.

Womack, J. P., and D. T. Jones. 2003. *Lean Thinking: Banish Waste and Create Wealth in Your Corporation*, fully revised and updated edition (first edition 1996). London: Free Press.

Seven

Socio-technical Systems Design for Coordination of Virtual Teamwork

BERT PAINTER, PAMELA A. POSEY, DOUGLAS R. AUSTROM,
RAMKRISHNAN V. TENKASI, BETTY BARRETT, AND BETSY MERCK

INTRODUCTION

Cross-industry, cross-discipline, network-based organization has become central to the emerging practice of science and engineering (Nobelius 2004). Hence, the US National Science Foundation and many others believe it is now vitally important to improve design of work systems for innovation and knowledge work that is interdependent yet not colocated.

Coordination has been described as "the major challenge" of global software development (Herbsleb 2007). Others contend that there is a "cost to overcome" with global projects and multiuniversity research and a key cost driver is coordination (Binder 2007, Cummings et al. 2007).

This comparative study of ongoing research-and-development (R-and-D) projects conducted by virtual, geographically dispersed teams reinforces the importance of managing the challenge of coordinating knowledge work across time and space. The organizations and projects studied represent different stages in an innovation process continuum, ranging from basic research to scale-up and commercial development. Using socio-technical systems (STS) analysis as a methodological approach, the research has focused on understanding the influence of virtuality on deliberations and knowledge development at various stages of the innovation continuum. Our research aim has then been to learn more about the effective coordination of this knowledge development by teams working across time, space, and changing environments.

RESEARCH SITES AND METHODOLOGICAL APPROACH

Three ongoing virtual R-and-D projects are included in this study; each project is in a different industry, and each deals with different challenges based on the type of virtual work being done. R and D has been characterized as an intrinsic learning system (Purser et al. 1992) with multiple stages. Each stage is defined by the degree to which participants do or do not know the "what" (objective) or the "how" (method or means) of their knowledge development and synthesizing activities. These stages form an innovation continuum[4] that ranges from high uncertainty tasks in which participants don't know *what* is the objective in concrete terms and don't know *how* to operationalize it—to projects with low uncertainty in which participants know "what" they need to achieve and also know *how* to achieve it operationally (see fig. 7.1).

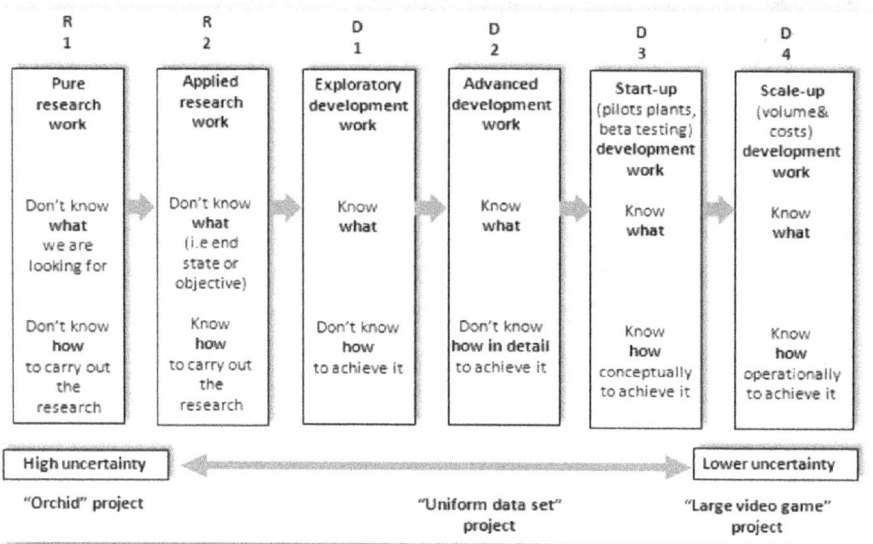

R 1	R 2	D 1	D 2	D 3	D 4
Pure research work	Applied research work	Exploratory development work	Advanced development work	Start-up (pilots plants, beta testing) development work	Scale-up (volume & costs) development work
Don't know what we are looking for	Don't know what (i.e end state or objective)	Know what	Know what	Know what	Know what
Don't know how to carry out the research	Know how to carry out the research	Don't know how to achieve it	Don't know how in detail to achieve it	Know how conceptually to achieve it	Know how operationally to achieve it

High uncertainty ← → Lower uncertainty

"Orchid" project   "Uniform data set" project   "Large video game" project

Figure 7.1 Six-Stage Continuum of the Inovation Process, with Location of Case Study Projects

4 Carolyn Ordowich (personal communication, March 26, 2009) outlined an innovation continuum adapted from a research portfolio model originally developed and deployed at Bell Laboratories (Revkin 2008).

Each project in this study is located at a different stage on the continuum of the innovation process, and each displays a different level of uncertainty in the project work. The "Orchid Project" was a pure research project (R1) on the innovation continuum. The "Uniform Data Set Project" was initially studied in the early development stage (D1) and more substantially at the advanced development stage (D2) on the continuum. The "Large Video Game (LVG) Project" was primarily positioned in the scale-up stage (D4), although the engineering aspects of this project more closely aligned with the start-up stage (D3) of development. In addition to being clearly identified as R-and-D projects, each of the projects has been conducted by teams in a virtual organizational setting. In each case, work is composed of interdependent knowledge-based tasks conducted by teams that are dispersed across space and time and are unable to collaborate face-to-face all or most of the time. Thus, each case exemplifies the primary characteristics as identified in prior studies of "virtuality" in teamwork processes (Dixon and Panteli 2010, Gibson and Gibbs 2006, Chudoba et al. 2005, Lojeski 2008).

THE RESEARCH SITES

The Orchid Project represents the field of fundamental, basic research and appears at position R1 on the innovation continuum; it is a collaborative project among theoretical and experimental physicists from research universities around the world. The project, funded by the US Defense Advanced Research Projects Agency (DARPA), is led by a team of scientists from Caltech and includes other teams of physicists from universities in the United States, Austria, and Germany. It is a pure research study in which the researchers *don't know what* they are going to find and therefore *don't know how* to design a research project that will actually be effective. The degree of virtuality is high in the patterns of interaction between faculty and students or postdoc staff.

The Uniform Data Set(UDS) Project is a joint project among twenty-nine Alzheimer's Disease Centers across the United States and the National Institutes of Health. At the outset, in the development of the "minimal data set," the project was positioned at D1 on the innovation continuum—the parties knew *what* their goal was but *didn't know how* to accomplish it. Based on this experience, this has evolved to a mature development project (D2) that is expanding its investigation based on earlier accomplishments. The chief participants have worked together for a number of years under overall guidance of the National Alzheimer's Coordinating Center. In addition, there are substantial professional ties within and across the centers because the membership consists of a majority of the world's experts in Alzheimer's disease treatment.

The Large Video Game (LVG) Project involved some Start-Up Development (D3) and mostly Scale-Up Development (D4) activities; it incorporates art-asset production, engineering, and testing activities shared among the game developer and teams of vendors around the world. Clarity of purpose and outcome is crucial in the D4 positioning of LVG, and though uncertainty about the what and, to a somewhat lesser extent, the how of the process is low, there is a high degree of virtuality and relatively low face-to-face collaboration in this project.

THEORETICAL BACKGROUND AND METHODOLOGICAL APPROACH

In virtual organizations that involve innovation, work is nonlinear and knowledge-based. This means much of the work is conducted through discussions and choice-making interactions that are often not face-to-face; these are referred to as "deliberations" in socio-technical systems theory. Deliberations are "patterns of exchange and communication...to reduce the equivocality of a problematic issue" (Pava 1983, 1986). They are not discrete decisions—they are a more continuous context for decisions. They have three aspects: topics, forums, and participants. Finally, a deliberation is a unit of analysis (like "unit operations" in linear processes)—the input, conversion, and output at these "choice points" is what moves knowledge work forward. The value of deliberation analysis to identify sources of variances and delays in new-product development has been demonstrated (Shani and Sena 2003, Purser 1992, Pasmore and Gurley, 1991). This NSF research project aimed to extend use of Pava's second-generation STS analysis of key choice points into research settings in which equivocality is even greater to identify how uncertainty shapes virtual projects and outcomes across the full innovation continuum.

An extensive review of the literature on virtual organization helped frame the context and focal questions for this research. Researchers then conducted scoping interviews conducted in each organization to gain an understanding of the projects and teams involved in the virtual work. Through a combination of structured interviews and observation, researchers identified and tracked key deliberations in each worksite to gather core data about the innovation process and outcomes. Finally, the team conducted follow-up interviews to assess the quality and outcomes of the deliberations process.

STS analysis provided a powerful lens through which to view knowledge generation and sharing, highlighting both social and technical systems of coordination in virtual work environments.

COORDINATION MECHANISMS

Coordination mechanisms are developed or emerge because of the need to manage interdependence among work activities (Herbsleb 2007, Gibson and Gibbs 2006, Malone and Crowston 1994) while minimizing barriers that affect the capacity to reduce equivocality in deliberations. Purser et al. (1992) identified four main categories of "barriers" obstructing and delaying collaborative knowledge development:

1. *Knowledge-sharing and planning* barriers, such as lack of cooperation, missing parties, or unrealistic time frames
2. *Cognitive frame-of-reference* barriers, associated with differences in language, values, etc.
3. *Knowledge-retention and procedural* barriers, such as lack of technical documentation, unclear roles, and diffused responsibilities
4. *Knowledge-acquisition* barriers resulting in lack of available knowledge

A connection between coordination mechanisms and the possibility of mitigating knowledge-development barriers is based on theory of organizational information processing (Galbraith 1974, Daft and Lengel 1986). This theory postulates that structural mechanisms for coordination must provide the means to handle the amount and richness of information processing required by the *uncertainty* and *equivocality* of an organization/team's task and environment. In other words, coordination mechanisms make a major difference in how well deliberations in nonroutine work incorporate the right information and knowledge and the right participants at the right time.

Specific mechanisms to permit coordination have been proposed using an information-processing view of organization design. However, more specific to global software projects, and most relevant for our study of R and D, Sabherwal (2003) condensed many classifications identified in the information systems literature into a typology of four major coordination mechanisms: (1) standards, (2) plans, (3) formal mutual adjustment, and (4) informal mutual adjustment.

Coordination through "standards" relies on prespecification of rules, routines, techniques, and targets. Coordination through "plans" is another approach that is mostly impersonal in nature once implemented. Both of these forms of coordination are often built into the structure of information systems. By contrast, in both forms of "mutual adjustment," coordination is made possible through interpersonal communication, feedback, and interaction. In formal mutual adjustment, coordination is "more structured" in design-review meetings and in supervisory or liaison roles versus informal mechanisms of impromptu or face-to-face communication. In addition to defining key modes of coordination, theory, and empirical research (Thompson 1967, Galbraith 1974; Kraut and Streeter 1995) have identified the level of task uncertainty and the degree of task equivocality (or ambiguity) as key determinants of the requirements for specific coordination mechanisms. In broad terms, the proposition has been that "more informal, communications-oriented" mechanisms are more suitable "when uncertainty is greater [for example] during the requirements analysis phase." On the other hand, "more formal, control-oriented" mechanisms are "most suitable when uncertainty is less [for example] during the design, implementation, and testing phases of a project" (Sabherwal 2003).

In summary, there is considerable prior literature suggesting that task uncertainty is an important factor influencing coordination mechanisms. The intent of this comparative case study has been to extend these findings to a virtual context, and over a wider range of the innovation continuum, beyond product development to include fundamental research activity as well.

FINDINGS

THE LVG PROJECT
The Large Video Game project is a critically time-bound commercial-product-development process based in the United States with a virtual organization of contractors dispersed across the globe. There is limited

economic viability for face-to-face interaction among members of the virtual project teams. Production includes 3D animation art assets, systems engineering, website design, and quality assurance. In addition to LVG home-based staff, the virtual organization includes external art-asset vendors, as well as engineering and website development vendors.

Key deliberations at LVG often occur at the front end of the production process involving "choice points" such as vendor selection. Examples of other key deliberations are defining and estimating outsourced project work and specifying documentation and production requirements.

During the period of this case study, it appeared that knowledge-sharing and development barriers were less prevalent in virtual art production than for virtual organization of software engineering and web systems development, where barriers included unclear expectations, unrealistic time frames, and lack of documentation. Delayed data transfer resulted sometimes from incompatible IT systems and/or security issues. Intellectual-property issues could also prevent LVG core operations from sharing vital source code with vendors.

In the relatively routine and mature work processes of virtual art production for LVG, information systems have provided vital support for clear expectations about task deliverables. Agreements on acceptable output are coordinated using screen shots, visual targets, e-mails, extensive digital documentation, and in some cases, web-based project-management software.

For engineering and web/online game development, however, LVG staff will most often *not know* the fine details of *how* the outputs are to be achieved. For example, in-house staff may do preliminary design of new website features, but detailed technical design would be done by a vendor. However, the quick feedback that is possible in-house, standing over each other's computers and making "live" corrections to any misunderstandings has generally been unavailable with engineering vendors in a virtual organization. This results in delay and cost overruns, particularly for the first product version of game development observed in this study.

Fortunately, in the time period between the two product-development runs, LVG staff made important changes in their coordination mechanisms. Engineering projects are now "chunked" into phases, and vendors must provide schedules for specific deliverables. And, supplementing all of the regular project-management tools and systems, LVG made a structural role change to designate a single "product owner" contact person to resolve issues with each vendor for a specific engineering assignment. New technical arrangements have also helped overcome the intellectual-property issues that previously constrained the sharing of game source code—a "cloud-based desktop" solution provides vendors access to source code and the ability to integrate new code, while preserving LVG proprietary control. And selection of any vendor is now dependent on verification of IT compatibility and an on-site security check. To close yet another gap in knowledge coordination, quality-assurance staff in a remote test center can now videoconference into production meetings and "scrums" at LVG core operations and thereby increase their tacit knowledge of game architecture. The overall effect of such changes was that the second product run was completed on time, on spec with few quality issues, and within budget.

THE UDS PROJECT

The Uniform Data Set (UDS) is a longitudinal database of clinical and neuropathological information gathered from Alzheimer's patients in the United States. From 1984 to 1999, the initial development of this database (D1) was the Minimum Data Set that suffered a missing data rate of 20 to 30 percent. By 1999, the sponsor agency, the National Institute of Aging (NIA), recognized a need for a reliable, more robust data set as a resource for Alzheimer's research and established a National Alzheimer's Coordinating Center (NACC) at the University of Washington. The center's mandate was to support more effective collaboration among twenty-nine Alzheimer's Disease Centers across the United States in development (D2) and utilization of a Uniform Data Set. Since then, the NACC has worked with clinical task forces of Alzheimer's Disease Center directors and clinical core directors to develop and update the standardized content of the UDS.

Key deliberations in this project (conducted via videoconferences, teleconferences, e-mail, and sometimes in person) have selected the 725 data points to include in the data set—an important issue because it determines what longitudinal information will be available for researchers. Another key deliberation has revolved around how to collect the UDS data: as many as eighteen standardized forms developed by clinical task forces are now used to collect patient data on sociodemographics, family history, dementia history, neurological exam findings, functional status, neuropsychological test results, clinical diagnosis, and imaging tests. Data managers at each of the twenty-nine centers monitor the quality of the local data before submitting it electronically to the NACC each month, creating a reliable, large-scale pool of data for scientists to analyze.

The move to the UDS from the original data set raised a number of issues. Initially, many of the Alzheimer's Disease Centers resisted the concept of a coordinating center and viewed the requirement to use standardized data collection systems as an imposition on being able to collect data best suited to their particular research interests. This created major barriers to knowledge sharing in the early deliberations about what elements to include in the UDS. Other barriers arose from the different frames of reference associated with researchers' diverse disciplines.

The NACC was a purposefully designed coordinating mechanism to address the barriers. It has provided an infrastructure, a neutral "referent organization" (Trist 1983), guiding stakeholder participation for effective deliberations on the design and ongoing refinement of the UDS. This coordination mechanism is activated by the skill of specific individuals within the NIA and NACC in key "network builder" (Hargadon 2003) roles: they have built relationships across organizations and disciplines, often through multidisciplinary, multicenter, technical steering committees. The outcome has been that NACC is now instrumental in Alzheimer's research, and the UDS has received acclaim as an exemplar of research collaboration (Kolata 2010).

THE ORCHID PROJECT

The Orchid project was an international multiuniversity collaboration by a team of twenty physicists and graduate students led by faculty at the California Institute of Technology (Caltech) who partnered with scientists at other universities in Europe and North America. The research was theoretical and experimental with high interdependence among physically dispersed teams. Two teams were designing and building lab equipment and conducting the experimental research, while three other groups formed a team of theorists supporting experimentation. Together, these diverse research groups aimed to advance knowledge in a new field of science—optomechanics (i.e., the use of light to manipulate mechanical devices at nano scale).

Key deliberations within this project focused on the selection of experiments to run, the design of the actual experimentation, and the interpretation and refinement of the data gathered. Knowledge barriers associated with these deliberations were significant. Varied disciplinary roots of the research groups led them to use different language to describe the same data, and each group had its own unique problem-solving approach. A significant challenge was the wide geographic dispersion combined with the high degree of reciprocal and team interdependence among their laboratory facilities. There was a constant threat of failure to use knowledge if the diversity of scientific perspectives could not be accessed and integrated for creative problem solving in the experimental process. Another major barrier to the acquisition of knowledge resulted from some incompatibility in the equipment used by the different laboratories.

For coordination, Orchid project scientists made extensive use of shared databases and annotated document repositories. Whenever experiments picked up intensity, digital communication such as Skype conversations, sometimes with screen-sharing or use of electronic "whiteboards," texting, and e-mail could occur almost constantly during a long, multi-time-zone work day.

However, the project's greatest collaboration challenges were overcome quite serendipitously. The need to invent a methodology so that devices created at Caltech could run on different experimental equipment in Europe required a detailed understanding by each party of the other's technical capabilities and limitations. The mechanism in this virtual organization that helped bridge the different frames of reference most was what the scientists came to refer to as the role of an "embedded researcher." A European graduate student came to Caltech for a short visit by chance and was able to see differences in methods and technology between the two experimental groups and facilitated solutions to merge their approaches. Another graduate student, from the theoretical school, was also unexpectedly sent to Caltech—he was able to give real-time suggestions to help interpret data for the experimentalists. This liaison or "straddler" role was an ongoing help to coordinate knowledge exchange between project theorists and experimentalists.

Both of these temporary roles proved to be vital coordination mechanisms for this project that, over a period of four years, yielded a series of internationally recognized publications (Safavi-Naeini et al., 2013) and produced a "milestone" demonstration of optomechanical capabilities.

CONCLUSIONS

All of the virtual R-and-D project teams in this comparative case study encountered substantial knowledge-development barriers and used coordination mechanisms to overcome barriers, partly by chance in the case of the Orchid project, by astute leadership and participative design in the UDS project, and through effective organizational learning in the Large Video Game project.

Of the four main categories of coordination defined earlier (standards, plans, formal mutual adjustment, and informal mutual adjustment), all were used *to some degree* in specific examples developed by teams within each of the three R-and-D projects in our study sample (see table 7.1).

Coordination Category	Specific Examples	
Coordination by standards	• Output standardization prototype, screen shots, visual targets • Skills standardization/training	• Standardization of processes • Diagnostic instruments • Data formats • Error-tracking procedures
Coordination by plans	• Delivery schedules • Project milestones • Requirement specifications	• Sign-off • Financial incentives • Compelling 'mission'/goal
Coordination by formal mutual adjustment	• Site inspections/verification • Hierarchy/vertical communication • Shared database/repository • Formal meetings/ status review	• Steering committees/task force • Referent organization • Facilitator/"network builder" role • Liaison/"straddle" role
Coordination by informal mutual adjustment	• Impromptu communication • Informal meetings • Conferences, workshops	• Site visits • Temporary colocation

Table 7.1 Specific Examples within Four Categories
of Coordination Mechanisms

Moreover, the type of mechanisms that proved to be *most significant* in mitigating knowledge barriers and improving R-and-D performance in the context of virtual organization varied according to the nature of the project task. Thus, the findings extend previous theory about the correlation between types of coordination mechanisms and levels of task uncertainty across the full continuum of innovation (see fig. 7.2).

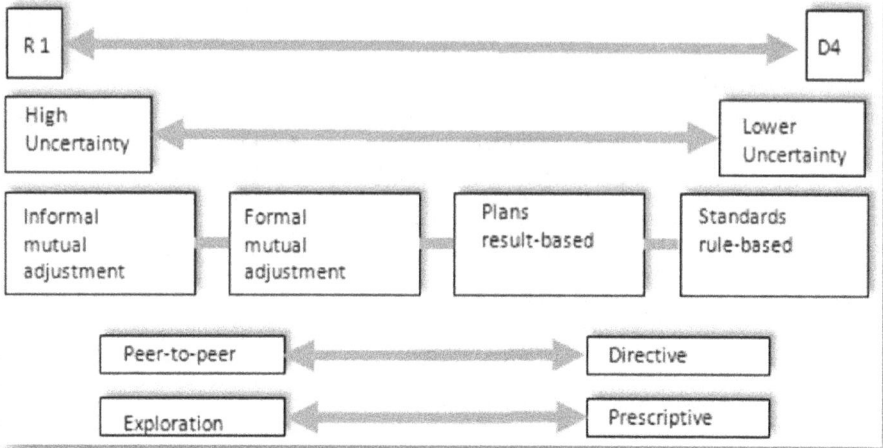

Figure 7.2 Coordination Mechanisms and Task Uncertainty on the Innovation Continuum

For those activities and projects with the lower degree of uncertainty, the more impactful were technical and structural—for example, the screen shots, visual targets, and project-management software that provided "standards" and "plans" to coordinate expectations between LVG and its art-production vendors. However, the social or mutual-adjustment coordinating mechanisms had more impact in mitigating barriers in those activities and projects in which there was higher uncertainty about outcomes and process: for example, the "embedded researchers" who contributed vital liaison across disciplines and institutions in the Orchid project functioned much like the "straddler" role described as a conduit for "transfer of tacit knowledge" in global software engineering projects (Heeks et al. 2001, Lai et al. 2003).

Indeed, there appears to be a complementarity between the "technical" and "socio" dimensions of coordination. Neither is entirely sufficient for overall coordination, but each tends to be more impactful, depending on the stage of innovation or nature of knowledge work (see fig. 7.3).

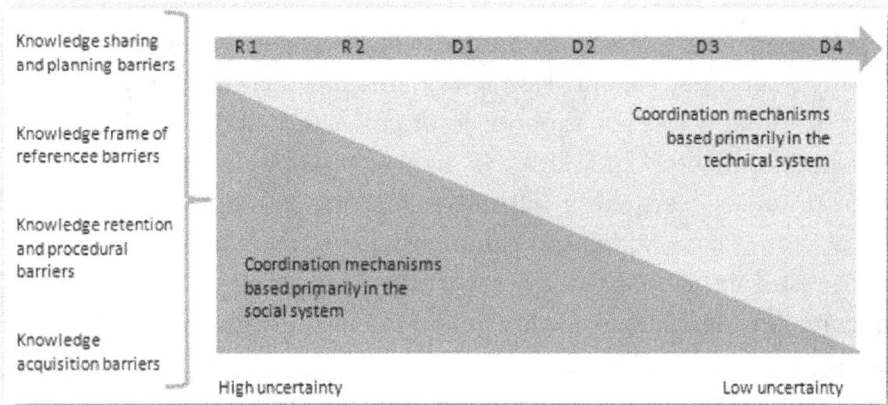

Figure 7.3 Differing Impact of 'Technical' and 'Socio' Forms of Coordination in Innovation

This complementarity of different types of coordination mechanisms is exemplified by the experience in the LVG project for systems engineering and website development. At this (D3) stage of innovation, effective coordination required a combination of important "technical" elements of web-based project-management software and short-time-frame "chunking" of project plans, along with a formal mutual-adjustment mechanism in the form of a new "product owner" role within the social system of relations between LVG and its vendors.

Another form of interaction between the "socio" and "technical" dimensions of coordination is the significance of how these mechanisms are used, aside from the process of their design or selection. For example, as suggested by prior studies (Malhotra and Majchrzak 2014), frequent annotation of documents in web-based repositories made the sharing of information and the interpretation of experimental data much more meaningful and productive for the theorists and experimentalists scattered across continents in dispersed scientific project teams. Conversely, what made the informal mutual-adjustment mechanism of their very infrequent face-to-face discussions most effective was the extensive planning done prior to their meetings.

Many of these effects often occur in colocated teamwork as much as in virtual organizations. However, participants in this study reported that, compared to their experience of colocated teamwork, barriers to the development of knowledge (e.g., intellectual-property issues, divergent priorities) were more difficult to manage in the virtual context of collaborative innovation. And although scientists and their graduate students used virtual workspace IT tools for task coordination, the difficulties of communicating tacit knowledge and the data-interpretation challenge of "sense making" (Boland and Tenkasi 1995) were accentuated in these case-study projects of fundamental research and advanced development.

Even so, there is "a common notion that collaboration technology and bandwidth will allow a virtual team to perform as if colocated...evidence shows this notion to be a naïve myth" (Moser and Halpin 2009). One implication for practitioners, from this comparative study of virtual teamwork, is that modern STS methodology (updated for nonroutine work in a virtual context) provides a way to assess and overcome "coordination costs."

As an indication, a recent trial application of these research findings in a major North American research laboratory was viewed very favorably by scientists and staff challenged with coordination of teamwork across time, space, and changing environments in the laboratory and its network of related universities and private-sector stakeholders. The work of these scientific teams covered a wide variety of topics at differing stages across the innovation continuum.

Workshops were held periodically over several months at the laboratory to share the findings of this research study. During and between workshops, scientists and their fellow team members applied the concepts to analyze the process of their teamwork and then to select or develop and evaluate new coordination mechanisms using a four-step STS design methodology:

1. Locate the project or specific knowledge work on the innovation continuum. Awareness of the positioning of a team's work on the continuum (and this positioning may well move during the life of a project) helps anticipate the types of "technical"

and/or "socio" mechanisms that are likely to be most significant in mitigating knowledge-development barriers (see figs. 2 and 3).

2. Identify the key deliberations or "choice points" that are essential to move the team's work forward. Deliberations are defined by a topic (e.g., what experiment to run, what software feature to develop), and they require specific information and knowledge, with the involvement of specific participants with differing perspectives and interests.

3. Analyze the most significant knowledge-development barriers that potentially or actually impede the quality of these key deliberations. To help maintain alertness to such barriers, use the typology of (1) knowledge-sharing and planning barriers, (2) cognitive frame-of-reference barriers, (3) knowledge-retention and procedural barriers, and (4) knowledge-acquisition barriers.

4. Select, design, and/or use appropriately the specific coordination mechanism(s) that seem most capable of mitigating the identified knowledge-development barriers. This aspect of "designing" (Boland et al. 2008) for effective collaboration needs to be understood and practiced as a continual, unfolding process to address both evolution in the type or stage of innovation/knowledge work and the ever-changing context of virtual teamwork.

At the conclusion of the trial application, more than 90 percent of the scientists and staff reported in a feedback survey that these concepts and methodology "will improve how we work together" and "address [distributed teamwork] issues we were trying to solve." These scientific teams, all challenged by some degree of "virtual distance," successfully designed or selected new coordination mechanisms for their work, including a range of standards and procedures, new systems for information sharing and storage, and new team roles.

In summary, the findings of the research reported here and the recent trial-application experience suggest that STS analysis and design can provide valuable support for modern teamwork. In this digital age, "virtuality" is a characteristic of almost all knowledge-based teamwork (Dixon and Panteli 2010; Lojeski 2009). Varying degrees of innovation is a desired feature of almost all knowledge work.

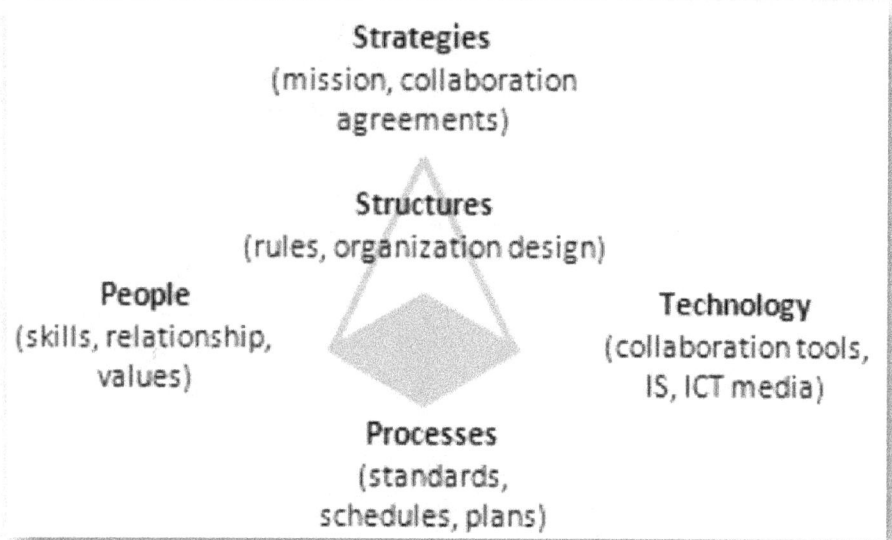

Strategies
(mission, collaboration agreements)

Structures
(rules, organization design)

People
(skills, relationship, values)

Technology
(collaboration tools, IS, ICT media)

Processes
(standards, schedules, plans)

Figure 7.4 Sociotechnical Systems Framework
for Coordination of Virtual Teamwork

Now, with proper planning and budgetary provision for collaboration, multiuniversity research teams or global technology consortia should be able to mix and match from the palette of characteristics of a socio-technical systems (STS) framework (fig. 7.4) to select and design the right combination of "socio" and "technical" ingredients for effective coordination of their virtual teamwork.

REFERENCES

Binder, J. 2007. *Global Project Management: Communication, Collaboration, and Management across Borders.* Hampshire, UK: Gower Publishing Ltd.

Boland, R. J., F. Collopy, K. Lyytinen, and Youngjin Yoo. 2008. "Managing as Designing: Lessons for Organization Leaders from the Design Practices of Frank O. Gehry." *Design Issues* 24 (1): 10–25.

Boland, R. J., and R. V. Tenkasi. 1995. "Perspective Making and Perspective Taking in Communities of Knowing." *Organization Science* 6 (4): 350–372.

Chudoba, K. M., E. Wynn, E., M. Lu, and M. B. Watson-Manheim. 2005. "How Virtual Are We? Measuring Virtuality and Understanding Its Impact in a Global Organization." *Information Systems Journal* 15: 279–306.

Cummings, J. N., and S. Kiesler. 2007. "Coordination Costs and Project Outcomes in Multiuniversity Collaborations." *Research Policy* 36: 1620–34.

Daft, R. L., and R. H. Lengel. 1986. "Organizational Information Requirements: Media Richness and Structural Design." *Management Science* 32 (4): 554–71.

Dixon, K. R., and N. Panteli. 2010. "From Virtual Teams to Virtuality in Teams." *Human Relations* 63 (8): 1177–97.

Galbraith, J. 1974. "Organization Design: An Information Processing View." *Interfaces* 4 (3): 28–36.

Gibson, C. B., and J. L. Gibbs. 2006. "Unpacking the Concept of Virtuality." *Administrative Science Quarterly* 51: 451–95.

Hargadon, A. 2003. *How Breakthroughs Happen: The Surprising Truth about How Companies Innovate.* Boston: Harvard Business School Publishing Corp.

Heeks, R.B., S. Krishna, B. Nicholson, and S. Sahay. 2001. "Synching or Sinking: Global Software Outsourcing Relationships." *IEEE Software* 18 (2): 54–61.

Herbsleb, J. D. 2007. "Global Software Engineering: The Future of Socio-technical Coordination." *Proceedings of FOSE '07 2007 Future of Software Engineering*, IEEE Computer Society, Washington, DC. 188–98.

Kolata, G. August 2010. "Sharing of Data Leads to Progress on Alzheimer's." *New York Times* 12: A1.

Kraut, R., and L. Streeter, L. 1995. "Coordination in Software Development." *Communications of the ACM* 38 (3): 69–81.

Lai, S., R. Heeks, and B. Nicholson. 2003. *Uncertainty and Coordination in Global Software Projects: A UK/India-Centered Case Study.* Institute for Development Policy and Management, University of Manchester, Manchester, UK.

Lojeski, K., and R. Reilly. 2008. *Uniting the Virtual Workforce: Transforming Leadership and Innovation in the Globally Integrated Enterprise.* New York: John Wiley and Sons.

Malhotra, A., and A. Majchrzak. 2014. "Enhancing Performance of Geographically Distributed Teams through Targeted Use of

Information and Communication Technologies." *Human Relations 67* (4): 389–411.

Malone, T., and K. Crowston, K. 1994. "Interdisciplinary Study of Coordination." *ACM Computing Surveys* 26 (1): 87–119.

Moser, B., and J. Halpin, J. 2009. "Virtual Teams: The Design of Architecture and Coordination for Realistic Performance and Shared Awareness." *PMI 2009 Global Congress Proceedings, Orlando, Forida, October 10–13, 2009.* Project Management Institute, Newton Square, PA.

Nobelius, D. 2004. "Toward the Sixth Generation of R&D Management." *International Journal of Project Management* 22: 369–75.

Pasmore, W., and K. Gurley. 1991. "Enhancing R&D across Functional Areas," in R. Kilmann (ed.), *Making Organizations More Competitive.* San Francisco: San Francisco: Jossey-Bass. 368–96.

Pava, C. 1983. *Managing New Office Technology.* New York: Free Press.

Pava, C. 1986. "Redesigning Socio-technical Systems Design." *Journal of Applied Behavioral Science* 22 (3): 201–21.

Purser, R. E, W. A. Pasmore, and R. V. Tenkasi. 1992. "The Influence of Deliberations on Learning in New Product Development Teams." *Journal of Engineering and Technology Management* 9: 1–28.

Revkin, A. December 12, 2008. "Dot Earth: 'R2-D2' and Other Lessons from Bell Labs." *New York Times* Blog.

Sabherwal, R. 2003. "The Evolution of Coordination in Outsourced Software Development Projects: A Comparison of Client and Vendor Perspectives." *Information and Organization* 13 (3) 153–202.

Safavi-Naeini, A., et al. 2013. "Squeezed Light from a Silicon Micromechanical Resonator." *Nature* 500: 185–89.

Shani, A. B., J. A. Sena, and T. Olin. 2003. "Knowledge Management and New Product Development: A Study of Two Companies." *European Journal of Innovation Management* 6 (3): 137–49.

Thompson, J. 1967. *Organizations in Action*. New York: McGraw-Hill.

Trist, E. 1981. "The Evolution of Socio-technical Systems," in A. H. Van de Ven and W. F. Joyce (eds.), *Perspectives on Organization Design and Behavior*. New York: John Wiley.

Trist, E. 1983. "Referent Organizations and the Development of Interorganizational Domains." *Human Relations* 36: 269–84.

Eight

STS Designing for a Networked World

CAROLYN ORDOWICH AND DOUGLAS AUSTROM

INTRODUCTION

The fact that the future will be characterized by networks of interconnected people and information is no longer debatable. Traditional
ways of organizing, such as hierarchies and market forms, are ill-suited
to a hyperturbulent, iVUCA (interdependent, volatile, uncertain, complex, and ambiguous) environment. *Hierarchies* are organized through
densely interconnected relationships bound by shared traditions and
institutional loyalty, clear roles, consistent opportunity for advancement,
job security, and benefits. The combination of loyalty and bureaucratic
structure allows such organizations to reach unprecedented scale but
makes them inflexible and slow to innovate. *Market or free-agent models*
of organizing, by comparison, tend to be more innovative and flexible,
and they foster individualism. They forgo rules, procedures, and deferen-
tial relations in favor of individual effort and reward. Loyalties are based
on affection for charismatic leaders. This model is effective for modular
projects, but weak organizational ties make it difficult to build the extensive interrelationships that are needed for new knowledge-based work
(Powell 1990).

On the other hand, *network models* of organizing have been shown
to excel at interdependent knowledge-based work. They emerge around
a sense of shared purpose and are coordinated through collaboratively
developed, carefully chosen procedures suited to the context of work

to be done. People work both in teams and as independent individuals (nodes) who come together to solve a problem and who are motivated to come up with solutions without being asked to. They do so out of a deep sense of devotion to the cause and a desire to contribute. Network organizations are strongest when you give people the freedom to use their skills and talent for the greater good. The diversity of capability stimulates innovation and coproduction. Network organizing is the only effective response to the information flows of complex problems, embodying all the interdependencies within and outside the system, in real time (Bar-Yam 2015).

All three organizing models reflect the underlying value as to whether they result in humane, healthy, and innovative high-performing organizations or design patterns that are harmful to people. Hierarchies can be designed to be relatively flat, fluid energizing entities or designed with so many rules that they end up as bureaucratic dead weight. Market forms can be designed to produce challenging, creative, well-paying "freelance work" or to produce "contract work" with low pay and little opportunity to exercise talent. Network design can generate tremendous learning and co-creaion of knowledge or be designed for control through contracts that undermine the very trust needed for co-creaion. Most of the previous chapters of this book deal with designing at the level of a single organization.

We propose that in every organizing model, STS design generates a quality of roles and organizing that is healthy and humane and elicits the highest potential of all individuals, both for their benefit and for the good of the whole. We believe STS design is well suited to addressing the complexity of working with diverse parties across multiple boundaries, uncertain conversion processes, and problematic interfaces with a system's environment. In this chapter, we explore the heritage of STS theory and practice as it relates to network design. We show how the unique approach of STS design can achieve healthy, humane, and innovative network and ecosystem (networks of networks) design.

STS NETWORK-DESIGN THEORY AND PRACTICE

STS network organizing is a transparent, open, and decentralized way of connecting *nodes* (such as a person or organization) through a set of relationships. These nodes connect because of a common interest in an issue of deep concern to all. While networks as a form are not new, their present-day scale is amplified by digital, information, and communication technologies (ICT) producing new media for social interaction such as blogs, wikis, Facebook, and Twitter, thus creating a "complex socio-technical organizing form" in contrast to the simple hub-and-spoke, face-to-face network models of the predigital past. Some of the key elements of network-design theory are shown in figure 8.1.

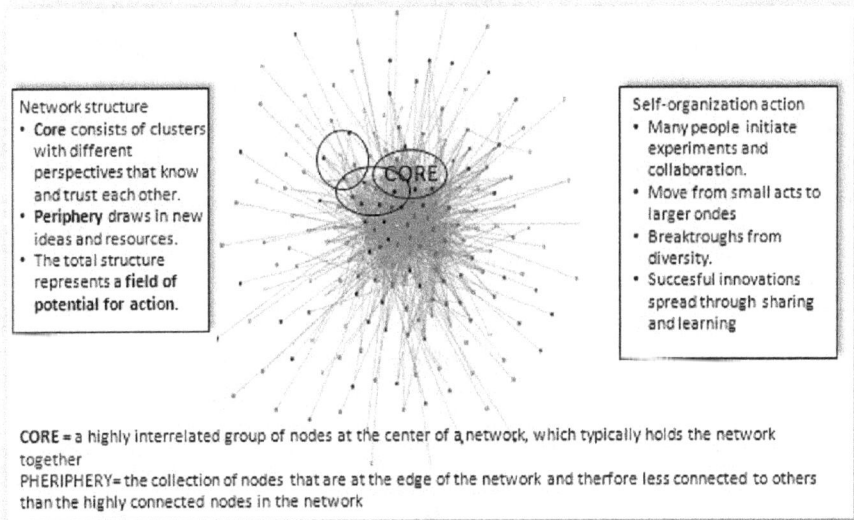

Network structure
- **Core** consists of clusters with different perspectives that know and trust each other.
- **Periphery** draws in new ideas and resources.
- The total structure represents a **field of potential for action.**

Self-organization action
- Many people initiate experiments and collaboration.
- Move from small acts to larger ondes
- Breakthroughs from diversity.
- Succesful innovations spread through sharing and learning

CORE = a highly interrelated group of nodes at the center of a network, which typically holds the network together
PHERIPHERY= the collection of nodes that are at the edge of the network and therfore less connected to others than the highly connected nodes in the network

Figure 8.1 Networkstructure and Self-Organizing Action (Adapted from Holley 2010)

Complex network theory has evolved independently of STS design theory, but the two are similar in many respects and if considered together, could significantly improve the design of networks. One of the key similarities is that both theories are based on a purposeful systems paradigm (Ackoff and Emery 1972). Also alike is the axiom that networks evolve or adapt (Emery and Trist 1965). The self-organizing foundation of network theory is analogous to the STS notions of participation and pluralistic democracy as found in the Emery-Trist systems paradigm for the redesign of workplaces (Emery and Trist 1973). One of the major differences is that in complex network theory, social phenomena should be conceived and investigated primarily through the properties of relations between and within units, instead of the properties of these units themselves. Thus, it is often criticized for ignoring individual agency. In classical socio-technical theory, we focus on both individual structures such as that of job or role design (social psychological) and collective structures (socio-technical) for team and unit design within an integrated open-system (socioecological) design. Pava's model for the STS design of nonroutine work systems[5] also provides a road map for the design of roles and discretionary coalitions for deliberations in the same fashion. And like networks, these structures are always changing to fit the context of work. STS network design also pays attention to relations among structural elements, especially as they relate to authority within an organization (Emery 1967) and to "fit" with the work system's environment.

EARLY WORK ON STS NETWORK DESIGN

In the evolution of socio-technical systems thinking, Trist and Emery shifted their primary focus in the 1970s from redesigning single firms to applying STS thinking and principles to address complex problems—also referred to as messes, problematiques, and metaproblems—at the domain or social ecosystem level. In the Ontario QWL Center monograph titled *The Evolution of Socio-technical Systems*, Trist (1981) provided the following definition of a *social-ecological system*, which was based on his earlier work with Emery:

> The terms social and organizational ecology are not used in Aldrich's (1979) sense, which is close to biological usage and

---

5 See chapter 4 for a more detailed discussion of Pava's model.

emphasizes determinism, but as in Emery and Trist in a systems sense where an ecological system is taken as a set of interdependencies in which no entity can control the others. Nor can it succeed apart from them. It constitutes a nonhierarchical field with open-systems characteristics in relation to its environment. It is combined of purposeful systems (organizations) that have to align their purposes with each other and with those of their members, since they are directively correlated with both (Sommerhoff 1950, 1969).

In his John Madge Memorial Lecture delivered at Glasgow University in 1978, Trist spoke about the increasing dysfunctionality of traditional bureaucratic and hierarchical responses to the social issues that have emerged in the turbulent and hyperturbulent sociopolitical environment. He noted that the "interdependencies, complexities, and uncertainties of the contemporary environment" had become too great for it to be effectively and exclusively managed by the traditional centers of power and resources, whether they be political, industrial, or urban. What he observed—and what gave him hope for the future—were "an increasing number of self-initiating, self-regulating innovative organizations" that provided an effective alternative either to overcentralization on the one hand or chaos on the other.

In his lecture at Glasgow University, Trist provided several examples of novel approaches that emerged from the "intimate experience" of the people who "live with the problem year in and year out." Trist's examples of innovative ecosystems included industry-level action-learning projects such as the Norwegian shipping industry, community-based sociotechnical endeavors such as the Jamestown Area Labor Management Committee, and both formal and informal networks such as the National Center for Productivity.

While not presented as design principles per se, Trist (1979) identified four primary "new directions for hope" and social innovations at the ecosystem level that were common to all of the cases he discussed:

1. These social innovations tend to emerge *outside*—that is, on the periphery or the fringes, not the center of the social system.
2. They emerge from *below*. They tend to be bottom up and not top down.
3. They occur in the *middle*, at the community level between the firm and the national level.
4. They typically operate *across*, leveraging networks of local actors rather than relying solely on the more traditional formal channels. These observations are similar to the axioms in complex network theory.

In addition to these four directions for innovative social problem solving, Trist also identified the common characteristics possessed by these innovative issues-based ecosystems that serve as *de facto* design considerations or guidelines for ecosystem interventions. First, he noted that there must exist a chronic *critical situation* that is not being addressed satisfactorily by traditional means. The problem being addressed tends to be a microcosm of a *major societal problem*, so local solutions have symbolic as well as actual impact. Even so, the version of the "mess" or metaproblem is *local* and requires direct knowledge of the issues, as well as the passion to find a solution best suited to those who are directly impacted. Further, the concerned communities or ecosystems have a *negative image* that is both ascribed externally and often accepted locally. These innovative networks also tended to be *independent* of the formal institutions that have not been able to resolve the "mess" and may actually be part of the problem. To undertake effective responses to the mess, the network of shared interest needs to *secure resources* and the support and collaboration of *key interest groups* who may otherwise have had conflicting interests. Finally, the wide base of resources will provide these networks with the *complementary power* needed to deliver unique solutions to otherwise intractable social issues.

In examining STS's historic contributions relative to the challenges of the new millennium, Pasmore (1995) noted that we needed to shift our thinking from organizations being viewed as independent actors in competition for survival to organizations being viewed as increasingly interlinked through alliances and networks, where collaboration for survival is the underlying truth. But despite the foundation that Trist and Emery provided for multiorganizational, multisector responses to environmental turbulence, and even though networks and ecosystems have garnered considerable attention in both academic and practitioner literature, relatively little of this work has been explicitly informed by the field of socio-technical systems.

STS FIRST PRINCIPLES FOR A NETWORKED WORLD

The enduring contribution of socio-technical systems theory and practice has been the design of humane, innovative, and collaborative enterprises that optimize the fit of both the social and the technical subsystems. The foundation of this contribution can be found in the core principles and design principles upon which STS theory and practice are based. STS design has unique first principles that we contend scale across organizing contexts or domains (teams, organizations, networks, and ecosystems), industries, sectors (for-profit, not-for-profit, government), and business models.

First principles are defined as *the fundamental concepts or assumptions on which a theory, system, or method is based* (Oxford Dictionaries 2014). STS first principles fit the dynamism and complexity of an iVUCA world and the context-specific nature of networks and ecosystems. Networks and ecosystems and the hyperturbulence we are currently experiencing make a rule-bound orthodoxy largely impractical and unworkable, and most certainly unpopular. It also violates one of STS's most cherished design principles, *minimum critical specifications*, that no more should be specified than is absolutely necessary.

We have attempted to articulate what we believe[6] to be the essence of STS core values and design principles in three first principles:

1. Profound respect for people
2. Self-regulation and mutual adaptation
3. Reciprocity and mutual benefit

Profound Respect for People

There is an extensive body of literature from multiple disciplines—philosophy, humanistic psychology, management theory, leadership practice, and motivation theory—that speaks to the fundamental importance of profound respect for human dignity. It is, we believe, the defining distinction between traditional approaches to workplace design such as Taylorism and scientific management and more humane approaches such as socio-technical design.

In his book *I-Thou*, Martin Buber (1937) described this distinction as the difference between instrumental I-It relationships and symbiotic I-Thou relationships. More recently, the Arbinger Institute popularized Buber's thesis in *Leadership and Self-Deception*. Writing the book as a novel, they demonstrated the profound impact on an hypothetical organization's culture of viewing *people as objects* literally to be used, managed, manipulated, controlled, or overcome (consider for example, the concept of "resistance") versus viewing *people as people* and affording them the basic respect they deserve as such. In essence, it is as simple—and as difficult, apparently—as viewing and treating people as people rather than as objects to be manipulated or as "subordinates" such as "slower, smaller, better-smelling horses," to quote Daniel Pink (2009). In the management classic *The Human Side of Enterprise*, Douglas McGregor (1967) cogently articulated a set of implicit Theory X assumptions about human nature

---

6 We offer these STS first principles not as a finished product but as an invitation for consideration and further elaboration.

that are foundational to the design of highly centralized, command, and control structures—namely, that the average person is indolent and not very bright, works as little as possible, lacks ambition, dislikes responsibility, and prefers to be led. The theory also postulates that without active intervention of management, people will be passive, even resistant, to organizational needs. Management's role then is to persuade, reward, punish, and control people. In contrast, McGregor's Theory Y assumptions about people embody a high degree of respect for human nature. People are not presumed to be lazy, resistant to organizational needs, or passive by nature; they have become so as a result of their experience in organizations. Creativity, ingenuity, and imagination are widely distributed. The motivation and the desire for development and self-direction are present in all people. Management's role is to trust workers and give them the freedom so they can be independent, make a difference, and strive for success. When people make implicit I-It and Theory X assumptions about people, they typically design organizations that rely on bureaucratic, centralized, and hierarchical "command and control" means of coordination and integration. When we design from a place of profound respect for people and Theory Y assumptions, then self-management and self-determination are natural outcomes. Similarly, this first principle promotes a much more effective balance of lateral and hierarchical coordination and integration. Finally, codesign and the freedom to participate in decisions directly affecting one's work and life become natural ways to work.

The design implications of profound respect for people are also consistent with Fred Emery's (1967) Design Principle 2, or DP2. To emphasize this point, de Guerre, Emery, Aughton, and Trull (2008), in describing DP2, state that people *"do not appreciate being treated as children and denied responsibility for decision-making about their own work."* Further, *responsibility for coordination and control is located with the people performing the task.*

SELF-REGULATION AND MUTUAL ADAPTATION

The next STS first principle, self-regulation and mutual adaptation is a natural extension of profound respect for people. It too is consistent with Emery's DP2 insofar as the responsibility for the design and coordination of activities is located with the people and stakeholders who comprise the network or ecosystem. In the article "The Environment and System Response Capability," Trist (1980) cogently argues that we must co-creae the future: *We cannot do this alone or against others—only with others as coproducers, with those who compose our interdependence system.*

Trist's notion of *self-regulation within an interdependent whole* corresponds well with the application of this first principle to network enterprises and ecosystems, which he described as a new logical type of organization, one that is better suited to operate in an iVUCA environment. In this new logical type, everyone in the network or ecosystem codesigns and self-organizes their specific work context to co-creae unique value. Also, all participants in the network or ecosystem are lifted up above their distinctive organizational identities and engage in a rich collaborative experience of continual learning and dynamic, mutual adaptation.

RECIPROCITY AND MUTUAL BENEFIT

Our increasingly interconnected and interdependent world necessitates the cooperation of interest groups and the identification of shared purpose and congruent values, continuous learning, and adaptive planning. As such, STS-designed networks and ecosystems require a shift from an ethos of conquest and competition to an ethos of collaboration. As Axelrod (1964) demonstrated, the emergence of cooperation and collaboration are predicated on reciprocity and mutually beneficial outcomes.

Furthermore, this perspective may better reflect our true human nature—arguably more so than the widespread notion of self-contained individualism—because humans are a social species and virtually unthinkable as solitary organisms (Wilson 2012, van den Berghe 1979). The logics of this emerging paradigm emphasize the fundamental interrelatedness and interdependence of open systems. And in an era of unprecedented interconnectedness, an ecological worldview provides a more appropriate lens for interpreting and thriving in our current reality. Rather than emphasizing the distinctions between phenomenon, both/and thinking provides a way to resolve apparent contradictions and dualities as interdependent paradoxes, such as doing well by doing good and the dual purposes of social businesses.

In applying these STS first principles to the building of robust networks, we would in all likelihood seek to optimize whole system outcomes that reflect the core values of people, prosperity, and planet; pursue symbiotic relationships and genuine partnerships based on shared purpose and mutual benefit; and achieve an optimal fit of the social and technical systems.

The determination of context-specific design principles needs to be an emergent process, activated by the designers themselves, that enables them to address the specific challenges they face while staying true to these STS first principles.

STS NETWORK DESIGNING APPROACH IN PRACTICE: PROCESS, METHODS, AND TOOLS

Although the practice of STS network designing is still evolving, a variety of methods and tools that can be applied to multiparty enterprises already exists. This is also where complex network theory may be useful in providing us with a framework for understanding how networks develop. For example, each phase of network evolution increases the network's structural complexity with the addition of more and more relationships and thus requires a distinct way of organizing, discrete cultures and different skill sets. Thus, we are *not* designing a network organization as a total entity but rather designing distinct structural phases of network evolution that are delivering to the same purpose, albeit each with its own specific tasks, people, culture, and enabling infrastructure (coordination, governance, information flows, collaborative technologies, learning loops, etc.) as a total system in its own right for a given phase.

The success of the network depends on the agility of the nodes to reconfigure for each phase. This is where Pava's (1983) design of deliberations and discretionary coalition becomes an especially relevant and robust design tool. The "work" of each phase is to resolve a set of equivocalities about achieving the purpose from idea to execution, and Pava's model demonstrates how to design for resolving these equivocalities. The evolution is not strictly linear but more like a spiral, with steps moving forward and backward, depending on the context. So deliberation design is useful in tracking the topics and hubs involved at any point in time.

While there is no universal pattern, most networks focused on achieving a goal—versus remaining a loose social group—tend to evolve according to the pattern or typical phases (Scearce 2011) outlined in table 8.1. The table also describes the structural rationale of each phase (Krebs and Holley 2002) and provides a nonexhaustive set of STS-related approaches that can be employed in the appropriate phase of development. While there are many work tools in the marketplace today to help people communicate and collaborate, they are typically nonsystemic and disconnected from a context-specific purpose. Even so, many of these tools could enrich the STS Toolkit, as long as they are aligned with STS first principles.

Phase	Structural rationale	Designing methods and tools
1. Know the network	*Scattered needs* require connection through different entry points (for diversity of interests) and engagement through mapping the issue, stakeholders, and constituents of the potential ecosystem	• Deliberation design (Pava 1983) • Search conference (Emery and Emery 1978; Weisbord 1995) • O.N.E. (Organization, Network & Ecosystem) System mapping (Austrom, de Guerre, Maupin, McGee, Mohr, Norton and Ordowich 2010) • Action research (Lewin 1948)
2. Connect the network	*Simple hub-and-spoke network* brings into focus the system, for the issue by formulating the purpose, designing the boundaries of the system and framing the learning question so they can go beyond symptoms to root causes and new evidence	• Deliberation design (Pava, 1983) • Positive participative innovation workshop (Mohr, Austrom, de Guerre 2014) • STS values and principles (Cherns 1976) • Visiting STS sites • STS technical and social system diagnostics (Lytle, 1991; Taylor and Felton 1993) • Lowland STS 'system' definition (De Sitter 1997) • Action research (Lewin 1948)
3. Organize the network	*Multihub "small world" network* establishes shared structures, processes, and norms to begin the work of prototyping, pilots, and trails and for ongoing learning and adaptation	• Deliberation design (Pava 1983) • Participative design workshops (Emery and Emery 1974) • Referent organization (Trist 1993) • Backbone organization (Turner 2012) • Adaptive work systems and networks (Winby 2011) • Action research (Lewin 1948)
4. Grow the network	*Core multi-hub 'large world' periphery network with 'fittest' nodes* grows and diversifies network participation, builds enduring trust and connectivity, decentralizes network functions, and spreads, deepens, and diversifies network strategies and ensure long-term financial stability	• Deliberation design (Pava 1983) • Positive participative innovation workshop (Mohr, Austrom, de Guerre 2014) • Participative design workshops (Emery and Emery 1974) • Lowlands STS (Van Amelsvoort 2015) • Referent organization (Trist 1993) • Backbone organization (Turner 2012) • Action research (Lewin 1948)

Table 8.1 Network Development Phases and STS Designing Methods

THE EQUITABLE FOOD INITIATIVE: AN EXAMPLE OF A STS-DESIGNED NETWORK

The Equitable Food Initiative (EFI) is a unique network of retailers and food-service providers, growers, nongovernment organizations (NGOs), and farmworker unions working together to ensure the supply of safer and healthier food to consumers. It is designed to be profitable for the farmers, retailers, and food-service providers while also improving labor relations and the standard of living for farm workers. The initiative has been a response to the deplorable working conditions for farmworkers and the limits of traditional oppositional check-and-balance of labor relations among farmworkers, unions, and farmers (see chapter 9). As stated on the EFI website (2015), "The EFI has developed a certification and verification system through which farms that comply with the EFI Standard will be issued a certificate and licensed to apply an EFI trustmark to their product. This trustmark will signal a new level of assurance that food-safety protocols are being observed, that pesticide use is carefully managed, and that workers are treated fairly. In order to help the farms achieve conformity with its standard, EFI has also created a Leadership Training Program to educate teams of farmworkers and farm managers regarding on-the-farm labor, pesticide and food-safety benchmarks, as well as how to engage the entire workforce in compliance. And what sets the EFI certification apart from other certification programs is the farmworker involvement in ongoing monitoring and verification."

The EFI was designed and developed through the participation of buyers, vendors, and farmworkers in lengthy deliberations. The participants in this initiative had to think differently and more broadly about the whole system end-to-end supply chain and adjust their attitudes toward the other players in this value-realization network. As a result of these new ways of working together, the stakeholders in this network have been able to identify and achieve tangible, mutually beneficial outcomes. For consumers, it is the assurance of safer food. For food retailers, it is reduced spoilage, which has significant cost benefits. For farmers, it is higher prices for their products, and for the farmworkers, safer working conditions and a greater voice in food safety, higher wages, and increased pride of craft.

The EFI is an excellent example of Trist's "New Directions for Hope" and shares most, if not all, of the same characteristics of the social innovations that Trist highlighted in this article (see table 8.2). The initiative emerged from outside and below in that it was initiated by farmworker unions and supported by a NGO, Oxfam, and not by government agencies or major corporate interests. In a similar way to how this social innovation emerged on the periphery or the fringes, the EFI operates at the community level between the firm and national levels—albeit in this instance, at the community of "shared interest" level. Similarly, it has engaged and leveraged networks of "local" actors or key stakeholders rather than relying solely on traditional formal channels.

THE LEGACY AND NEW FRONTIERS OF STS NETWORK DESIGNING

The legacy of STS network design is a story still in the making. Because of the basic tenet of designing for "best fit" of the environment, technology, and people, by definition STS methods and tools must be regenerated as the world changes; otherwise we are designing with yesterday's logic. But STS originated as a new paradigm for *humane, high-performing, and ethical organizing*, not solely as a methodology. As Enid Mumford (2006) reminded us, "The most important thing that socio-technical design can contribute is its value system. This tells us that although technology and organizational structures may change, the rights and needs of the employee must be given as high a priority as those of the nonhuman parts of the system" (p.338).

Bernard J. Mohr and Pierre van Amelsvoort

Common Characteristics of social innovation as identified by Trist	Characteristics of the equitable food initiative
Chronic critical situation that is being addressed satisfactorily by traditional means	The joint issue of food safety and working conditions for farmworker are chronic issues arguably have reached a critical state
Microcosm of a major societal problem so local solutions have symbolic as well as actual impact	Both issues -food safety and working conditions for farmworkers- are significant global challenges and the EFI can certainly serve as innovative and replicable model for other areas in the food industry.
Metaproblem is local and requires direct knowledge of the issues as well as the passion to find a solution	The EFI is founded on the notion that addressing the issue of food safety must be addressed at the point of production
Concerned communication have a negative images	Public opinion of migrant farm workers as low-skilled, 'illegal' immigrants
Independent of formal institutions	Initiative evolved independently of government regulatory agencies and most industry associations
Network of shared interests needs to secure resources and the support and collaboration of key interest groups	The success of the initiative relies on the full engagement of all stakeholders
Complementary power	The traditional power imbalances among food retailers, producers and farmworkers, while certainly not eliminated due the mutually beneficial outcomes realized via the EFI program

Table 8.2 EFI and the Characteristics of Social Innovation

To this end, we have attempted to articulate the first principles of STS—*profound respect for people, self-regulation and mutual adaptation, and reciprocity and mutual benefit*—as an expression of the fundamental values that underlie the new organizing paradigm and the pursuit of humane, high-performing, and ethical organizational forms. They also provide a much-needed alternative to the implicit logics of the technocratic imperative of ICT.

We now face the challenge of reinterpreting the STS paradigm for future work. But we have a rich body of work to draw on for this purpose. Self-directed and self-regulating work teams proved highly effective at generating high-performance workplaces. Marina Gorbis (2013), executive director of the Institute for the Future (IFTF), says this is really how work is now done, albeit at a different scale and without regard for traditional organizational boundaries. Today, people bypass established institutions and processes and instead work to create what they find missing in the world by communicating the need to their social networks, mobilizing whatever resources they have at their disposal, and pursuing solutions collaboratively—in short, creating self-directed and self-regulating networks.

Trist's concept of domain spoke to the need to design at multiple social system levels (micro, meso, and macro) through understanding the whole ecosystem and each organization's role in it. Open socio-technical systems theory proposes that a single entity's actions (at any level), to varying degrees, will affect the health of the whole system, which in turn will ultimately affect the entity's performance (for ill as well as for good) because ultimately it shares its fate with the network or ecosystem as a whole. Emery and Trist (1965) developed the notion of organizations as open systems in the context of environments with unique causal textures.

This speaks to the need to widen our systems lens of organizing to encompass organizations, networks, and ecosystems—abbreviated as ONE enterprises—to demonstrate how STS first principles scale to organizations that now increasingly are using network models internally and externally. This is an expanded notion of Cherns's design principle, *boundary location*, which the EFI case exemplifies. Designing for these three contexts—organizations, networks, and ecosystem—strengthens integration and enables greater impact on society's "wicked problems." This also speaks to both the legacy and the future of STS network designing: Trist and Emery were both involved with the creation of processes for bringing about change at the individual, group, organizational, and interorganizational levels that reflect the way networks and ecosystems are undergoing design today.

CONCLUSIONS

We live in a complexly interconnected and interdependent world—a truly networked world—in which mass collaboration and co-creation are needed more than ever. Socio-technical systems have provided significant theoretical contributions to our understanding of how to design at the interorganizational or domain levels. But as rich as the conceptual contributions STS has made to the field, there has not been a concomitant contribution to the world of practice. And in the world of practice, numerous collaborative responses to the turbulent environment have emerged—cf. collective impact, global solutions networks, public-private partnerships, and issues-management alliances, to name a few. But there has been no unifying theory or model that adequately reflects or encompasses these social innovations. We believe STS theory and first principles can provide the new logics and foundation for designing dynamic networks as well as designing approaches and tools for effective collaboration.

REFERENCES

Ackoff, R., and F. Emery. 1972. *On Purposeful Systems*. Chicago: Aldine.

Austrom, D., D. de Guerre, H. Maupin, C. McGee, B. Mohr, J. Norton, and C. Ordowich, C. 2010. *ONE (Organization, Network, and Ecosystem) Systems Mapping*. Unpublished manuscript.

Arbinger Institute. 2000. *Leadership and Self-Deception: Getting Out of the Box*. San Francisco: Berrett-Koehler.

Austrom, D. and C. Ordowich. *North American Approach to Design of Nonlinear Work Systems (1980s–'90s)*. In press.

Axelrod, R. 1964. *The Evolution of Cooperation*. Cambridge: Basic Books.

Bakan, D. 1966. The *Duality of Human Existence*. Chicago: Rand McNally.

Bar-Yam, Y. March 11, 2015. New England Complex Systems Institute http://www.necsi.edu/opportunities/salon/distributedorg.html

Bright and Fry, 2013. "Introduction: Building Ethical, Virtuous Organizations." *Journal of Applied Behavioral Science* 49: 17.

Buber, Martin. 1937. *I and* Thou. New York, NY: Charles Scribner's Sons.

Cherns, A. 1976. "The Principles of Socio-technical Design." *Human Relations,* 29: 783–92.

de Guerre, D., M. Emery, P. Aughton, and A. Trull. 2008. "Structure Underlies Other Organizational Determinants of Mental Health: Recent Results Confirm Early Socio-technical Systems Research." *Systemic Practice and Action Research* 21 (8): 359–79.

de Sitter, U. F. den Hertog, and B. Dankbaar, B. 1997. "From Complex Organizations with Simple Jobs to Simple Organizations with Complex Jobs." *Human Relations* 50 (5).

Emery, F. 1967. "The Next Thirty Years: Concepts, Methods, and Anticipations." *Human Relations* 20: 199–237.

Emery, F., and M. Emery. 1974. *Participative Design: Work and Community Life.* Canberra: Centre for Continuing Education, Australian National University.

Emery, F., and M. Emery, M. 1976. *A Choice of Futures.* Leiden, Netherlands: Martinus Nijhoff.

Emery, F. and M. Emery. 1978. "Searching: For New Directions in New Ways for New Times." *Management Handbook for Public Administration,* J. W. Sutherland (ed.), New York: Van Nostrand.

Emery, F. and E. Trist. 1965. *The Causal Texture of Organizational Environments.* International Psychology Congress, Washington, DC. *Human Relations* 18: 21–32.

Emery, F. and E. Trist. 1973. *Toward a Social Ecology: Contextual Appreciation of the Future in the Present.* New York: Plenum Press.

Emery, M. 1999. *Searching: The Theory and Practice of Making Cultural Change.* Amsterdam: John Benjamin Publishing.

Equitable Food Initiative. 2015. The Equitable Food Initiative Certification Requirements. January 1, 2015. http://media.wix.com/ugd/e9574b_0 84b036f528d465091a6e2aa97a3e8e8.pdf.

Gorbis, M. April 23, 2013. "The New Kind of Worker Every Business Needs." https://hbr.org/2013/04/the-new-kind-of-worker-every-business.

Holley, J. 2010. "Network Basics." www.networkweaver.com/wp-content/.../NetworksinaNetworkWorld.ppt.

Krebs, V. and Holley, K. 2006. *Building smart communities through network weaving.* http://www.orgnet.com/BuildingNetworks.pdf.

Lewin, K. 1948. *Resolving Social Conflicts: Selected Papers on Group Dynamics.* Gertrude W. Lewin (ed.). New York: Harper and Row.

Lytle, W. 1991. *Socio-technical Systems Analysis and Design Guide.* Plainfield, New Jersey: Block, Petrella, Weisbord.

Maenen, S., C. Ordowich, and D. Austrom. 2014. "Interorganization STS Design." Paper presented at the annual meeting of the Societechnical Systems Roundtable, Montreal.

McGregor, D. 1960. *The Human Side of Enterprise.* New York: McGraw-Hill.

Mohr, B., D. Austrom, and D. de Guerre. 2014. *Positive Participative Innovation Workshop.* Annual meeting of the STS Roundtable, Montreal.

Mumford, E. 2006. "The Story of Socio-technical Design: Reflections on Its Successes, Failures, and Potential." *Information Systems Journal* 16: 317–42.

Oxford Dictionaries Online. 2014. http://www.oxforddictionaries.com/us.

Pasmore, W. 1995. "Social Science Transformed: The Socio-technical Perspective." *Human Relations* 48 (1): 1–21.

Pava, C. 1983. *Managing New Office Technology: An Organizational Strategy.* New York: Free Press.

Pink, D. 2009. *Drive: The Surprising Truth about What Motivates Us.* New York: Riverhead Books.

Powell, W. 1990. "Neither Market Nor Hierarchy: Network Forms of Organization." *Organizational Behavior* 12: 295–336.

Scearce, D. 2011. *Catalyzing Networks for Social Change: A Funder's Guide.* http://community-wealth.org/content/catalyzing-networks-social-change-funders-guide.

Sommerhoff, G. 1950. *Analytical biology.* London: Oxford University Press.

Sommerhoff, G. 1969. "The Abstract Characteristics of Living Organisms," in F. Emery (ed.), *Systems Thinking.* 147–202. Harmondsworth, UK: Penguin.

Taylor, James C., and David F. Felten. 1993. *Performance by Design: Socio-technical Systems in North America.* Englewood Cliffs, New Jersey: Prentice Hall.

Trist, E. 1979. "New Directions of Hope." *Regional Studies* 13: 439–51.

Trist, E. April 1980. "The Environment and Systems Response Capability: A Futures Perspective." *Futures,* 113–27.

Trist, E. 1981. *The Evolution of Socio-technical Systems.* Occasional Paper no. 2, Ontario Quality of Working Life Centre.

Trist, E. 1983. "Referent Organizations and the Development of Interorganizational Domains." *Human Relations* 36: 269–84.

Turner, S., K. Merchant, J. Kania, and E. Martin. 2012. "Understanding the Value of Backbone Organizations in Collective Impact." *Stanford Social Innovation Review Blog*. July 20, 2012.

van Amelsvoort, P. 2000. *The Design of Work and Organization: The Modern Socio-technical Systems Approach*. Vlijmen, Netherlands: ST-Groep.

van den Bergh, P. 1979 *Human Family Systems: An Evolutionary View*. New York: Elsevier.

Weisbord, M. 1992. *Discovering Common Ground: How Future Search Conferences Bring People Together to Achieve Breakthrough Innovation, Empowerment, Shared Vision, and Collaborative Action*. San Francisco: Berrett-Koehler.

Wilson, E. O. 2012. *The Social Conquest of Earth*. New York: Liveright Publishing.

Winby, S. 2011a. "Adapting to New Realities: The Emergence of Network Organizations and Work Systems." http://www.slideshare.net/STSRoundtable/winby-adaptingto-newrealities.

Winby, S. 2011b. "Adaptive Work Systems: A Perspective on the Evolution of Socio-technical Systems." http://www.slideshare.net/STSRoundtable/winby-adaptive-worksystems-sts.

Nine

The Employee's Voice in the Design of Humane and Innovative work(places)

Kevin Boyle, Wim Sprenger, and Ike Overdiep

INTRODUCTION

In this chapter, we concentrate on worker voice in design processes via representation of trade unions.[7] Although this voice has been seen as an essential element of socio-technical design processes from the start, its relevance and presence seem to have declined in recent years.

Globalization, development of regional/national and international value chains, outsourcing and offshoring, and privatization processes have complicated and blurred the boundaries of "the system"—from the individual firms toward complex (eco)systems and from decision-making within the firm to shareholder value and hedge-fund dominance.

For trade unions, the articulation of employees' voices, mainly in single firms and workplaces, has moved into the challenge of designing worker voice from *an interorganization and networks/ecosystem design perspective* (Maenen et al. 2014).[8]

In this chapter, we argue that worker voice, as represented by trade unions, can be understood and activated as an essential element of

---

7 Where we deal with "trade unions," we include work councils (worker representations at the company level), which exist in a number of countries. They (can) play an important role in representative participation at the workplace.

8 For more details and backgrounds of an extension toward the contexts of network and ecosystems, see chapter 8.

design processes only by integrating and facilitating the unions as eco-systems of their own.

WORKER VOICE IN 2015—LEVELS AND STRATEGIES

Fred Emery saw "a world that is consciously designed by people and for the people." He believed in the need "to develop a conceptual framework of integrated theory and practice where the practice involves important human concerns, societal and organizational" (Emery 2000).

Emery's perspective is not easy to bring into one model or design principle. Actual practices show at least four degrees and levels of involvement and integration of worker voice in change processes:

1. *No active involvement by employees*, changes decided and implemented by management or owners—employee's voice not heard or taken into account. This might be the dominant praxis for many employees, in particular those in Asian, African, and South American countries.
2. *"Direct participation,"* involvement of employees at workplace or organizational level—worker voice heard at individual levels.
3. *"Representative participation"* via the trade union and/or works councils, involvement of worker representatives at workplace, company and interorganizational level—worker voice heard at collective and representative levels;
4. *"Indirect participation"* by employees' representation; involvement at national, regional, or sectorial levels (in regional or national structures, facilitating activities by trade union representatives)—policies and initiatives facilitating worker voice and its quality and influence.

Worker voice is seldom restricted to just one of these levels. It may also include two or even three levels, although managers often see direct and representative or indirect participation as excluding each other. Emery's perspective, however, suggests that direct participation, representative participation, and indirect participation would go hand in hand and reinforce each other to help employees play their essential role in design processes. This is the systemic approach to worker voice and participation. This is not the case in many situations nowadays. In particular for trade unions, representing employees or indirectly participating in the conditions for designing humane and innovative workplaces, the dilemmas for fruitful participation have grown.

DILEMMAS OF WORKER VOICE AND WORKPLACE DESIGN

A variety of factors makes explicitly hearing and integrating worker voice in design processes more complex than thirty years ago.

DECLINING DENSITY RATES

There is a worldwide downturn of the position of labor organizations. Between 1999 and 2013, density rate in the OECD countries went down from one in five employees (20.8) to one in six employees (16.7). Relatively high density rates can still be found in Scandinavian countries and Belgium. Canada, Italy, Norway, and Belgium show a rather stable rate. The same is true for Spain and France, but already on a (very) low level.

CHANGING LABOR MARKETS—UNIONS STRUGGLING FOR SURVIVAL AND MERGING

Against this background and due to the global changes in work processes, the union movement is struggling for its survival and position, also in relation to employers and public institutions. Unions are particularly weak or absent in "new industries" and with "new groups in the labor markets." In general, they are stronger in the public sector and within bigger companies.

The labor-market share of the traditional stronghold for the unions— the skilled worker with a permanent contract in industry and services— is gradually diminishing. Nowadays, two of every three employees in the European Union are employed in a small or medium-sized company (Bussat,

Triomphe, and Körper 2013). Many of them work for or are connected to bigger corporations, which can "decide" on price, quality, and quantity of production or services to be delivered by contracts. A majority of employees nowadays are in unstable, precarious, informal forms of employment and are often unemployed for parts of their working lives. Migrant labor is a global issue, with varied responses by unions nationally/locally.

A growing number of unions understand it is time to move beyond narrow definitions of interests of existing membership and representation. They recognize the necessity of moving to a more global response through new-organization strategies and forms.

CHANGING UNION STRATEGIES, COOPERATION, OR CONFRONTATION?

Confronted with declining density rates, huge inequalities, and growing complexities, unions are choosing to abandon strategies based on "equal', trustful, and cooperative relations with employers." Union strategies focusing on conflicts and confrontation at workplaces, to be more visible, attractive, and inspiring for frontline employees and those with vulnerable contracts, have gained popularity since 2000. These models were developed by unions like SEIU (Service Employees International Union) to get entrance into the many nonunionized companies and outsourced/marginal service providers. These approaches have gained popularity in European countries (the UK, the Netherlands, Germany, and Italy), Australia, and New Zealand.

It would be too simple to position such strategies as the negation of cooperation. Trade-union organizers also invest in skill building, higher activity, and involvement at work and improvement of work organization and quality of working life. Big organizing campaigns in cleaning ("Justice for Janitors") have been exemplary in many countries, focused not only on pay and more secure jobs but also on "respect" for the worker and the work done. Activation and empowerment are main elements from these union strategies, similar to what we see in more cooperative STS design projects.

For a union, activated and empowered employees provide a power base and at the same time a threat for the general union strategy and goals (Savage 2006, van Klaveren and Sprenger 2009).

WHAT'S THE BENEFIT OF WORK INNOVATION FOR EMPLOYEES AND UNIONS?

Work innovation (typically in the form of team-based work) has become a more complex issue for unions. Over the past forty years, many examples of team-based work have been documented. However, the sustainability of the successes often was weak. The German Metal Union promoted "qualified group work" (team-based workplaces providing chances for employees to upskill and make their work more challenging and autonomous). Around 2000, the union observed that most group work had been turned into conveyor-belt-driven work, reflecting the developing global labor market in the car industry. The union decided to cut its program (Salm 2001).

To this day, Scandinavia provides many interesting projects. But disappointing developments like the elimination of the famous Arbetslivet Institute in 2006 (an important facilitator in Sweden) and the closure of socio-technical flagship Volvo Uddevalla years before (a market-driven Multinational) made the trade unions more critical about investments and results of codesign (Sandberg et al. 2013).

German researchers, though finding positive examples of team-based work, point at a "role conflict" for work councils. Within the company, they can lose support from the employees they represent, as "traditionally the promotion of innovation is more a management task, while the works council is traditionally responsible for employees interests" (Nerdinger et al. 2011).

Max Ogden, an Australian proponent of union involvement in workplace innovation, sees the unions captured in confronting forces: "Recent experience presents the real possibility that improved performance may lead to fewer jobs, so why should the union help?" (Ogden, 2012). Ogden's observation is not new. For decennia, there have been doubts about the involvement of the employee's voice in workplace innovation. Severe and fundamental critique came and comes from the labor process theory, which stresses *control by management* and in return the *resistance power* of employees at workplaces as major change factors, not cooperation for joint optimization in design processes (Thomson and Smith 2010).

We can conclude that joint optimization has turned into a multilevel challenge. Besides quality of work and innovation, employers focus on economic performance and productivity. Industrial democracy no longer seems to be the main driver of participative approaches. Support through public programs has declined. Productivity-oriented approaches can contribute to the competition between production sites in the same value chain or multinational company (Telljohan 2015). Here, trade unions need to develop coordinated strategies at a global level. Because the advantages for the companies are quite clear (increased productivity, competitiveness, better quality, etc.), unions should rethink the conceivable advantages for employees in the whole (eco)system and how to achieve them.

UNIONS AS (PARTS OF) ECOSYSTEMS AND PARTNERS IN INTERORGANIZATION DESIGN

Trade unions can be seen as (parts of) ecosystems, producing more than better workplaces and collaborating and negotiating in various networks and systems. However, they have to consider a complex product mix: survival (attracting new members); contracts and job protection; collective agreements at various levels directed at pay, working times, and job qualities; services to members; social plans; training facilities; and transition to other jobs.

Trade unions will have to play double and triple roles if they are serious about creating meaningful work for employee's across a network or ecosystem. Special leadership and new skills will have to be developed to make this possible (Telljohan 2010). Managing diversity within their own ecosystem in combination with interorganizational design with outside partners/stakeholders is a complicated but necessary condition.

Choices will have to be made about the reach and the moments of worker voice articulation. Unions have a choice and can do either of the following:

- Concentrate on input for the change process and output/results: here the employee's, the union, the works council stay out of the development process, but can be engaged in formulating general goals, conditions ("no loss of employment") and decision-making of the change process
- Cover the whole process of change: the day-to-day steps from an early stage until the new "end situation"

A combination of both types of involvement is possible. However both unions and managers often opt for the first option, as it reflects better the antagonisms in labor relations today. Process involvement implicates "dancing" strategies and new competencies of both management and employee's, the first option can more easily be part of "boxing" strategies,[9] but can this option deliver the outcomes for today's worker reality.

WORKER VOICE IN PRACTICE—RECENT EXPERIENCES

EQUITABLE FOOD INITIATIVE AND THE US FARM EMPLOYEES' UNION STRATEGY

In 2008, the United Farmworkers, Oxfam America, Farmworker Justice and a number of food safety, pesticide, and animal rights organizations began a discussion based on the *Decent Work Initiative Baseline Study*

---

9 Boxing and dancing are used as metaphors for various strategic choices, denoting adversarial and cooperative modes of industrial relations engagement, respectively. Boxing: winner-loser, distrust, negotiations and conflicts, clear outcomes. Dancing: partnerships, trust, win-win, outcomes insecure at the start of the process (Gregory et al. 2004, Van Klaveren and Sprenger 2005).

commissioned by Oxfam America, Inc. The intent of the study was to accomplish the following:

- Develop and implement new approaches to addressing farm worker living conditions and farm worker rights.
- Identify an approach that "certifies" produce as having been grown on farms that engage their employee's to the highest levels of food-safety awareness, pay employee's a living wage, and support viable working and living conditions.

Consumers and retailers would have to pay a small premium for this certified produce; that premium would go directly to the growers and the farm workers to meet the objectives and to improve the lives farmworkers. This was the start of the Equitable Food Initiative (EFI).

From 2010 EFI has participated in a process and structure creating a farm based standard with certification in labor rights, food-safety, and sustainable environment through responsible pesticide use. The core of this certification and the key value to retailers and food providers is the training and knowledge of farm workers and an on-farm process for ongoing assessment, problem solving and solution implementation led by farm workers and supervisors in the field.[10]

The union's knowledge base for work design of work in agriculture covers at least 4 knowledge fields:

- The formation of global alliances—bringing together growing and distribution across multiple borders with multiple organizations involved in supply chain.
- Operating in interorganizational design with communities of co-operating growers and co-operating unions able to fill a retailers supply chain.

---

10 For a more comprehensive description of the benefits for the various network-partners, see chapter 7.

- Farm networking within a certain geographic area, sharing capital, tools and work force
- Raising labor productivity at the individual farm, producing one or more products.

Important design criteria for unions coming from the EFI experience include the following:

- Development of optimal variety in work and the organization (people are not doing the same thing day after day, hour after hour).
- Meaningful work and meaningful outcomes (people are a part of designing their work and the outcomes of this work, aligned with the end product).
- Decision-making autonomy (people doing the work, are the best people to make decisions on improving the work)
- Mutual support and respect (Both are built into the design of the organization; people doing the work will design what and how this is developed.)
- Making sure the end product/service meets consumers' expectations (This could be the food-buying consumer or the worker/member of the UFW.)
- An opportunity for a self-defined desirable future (Work or organizations are designed for people to see opportunities.)
- Opportunity for continuous learning.

How can a union broaden its traditional often confrontational activities into working with growers to help expand their market and enhance their operations, with the end result of impacting the lives of hundreds of thousands of farm workers globally? The UFW development shows that alternative strategies, broadening the union's strategic potentials, can be more promising and effective than only a strategy of confrontation. But it is a long and intense movement and not free of confrontation, but disagreements are integrated as part of the dynamic design process within the ecosystem.

BOMBARDIER BELGIUM AND THE POSITION OF BELGIAN UNIONS

Bombardier Inc. is headquartered in Montréal, Canada, and is structured around two businesses—aerospace and transportation—with seventy-six production and engineering sites in more than sixty countries, with 65,400 employees. To survive in the global market, the Belgian site decided to innovate its organization. Beginning in 2002, Bombardier management in Bruges initiated a program of workplace innovation (Maenen and De Hauw 2013) featuring the following:

- *Improving process efficiency and product quality* Changes came from Bombardier Operations System (BOS), inspired by Lean management and Six Sigma. BOS aims to guarantee high production standards and to remove as much organizational slack as possible from the process.
- *Introduction of teamwork.* Blue-collar employees and their supervisors ("team coordinators") were given more responsibility and more latitude in taking decisions, which was assumed to enhance job satisfaction as well.

Belgian unions were involved at a distance. Historically, the union position was "work organization is a management responsibility." Recent trade-union initiatives tend to question this position. The three main Belgian Trade Unions sought cooperation with a university in Antwerp. A strategy called "innovation of organizations" (IAO) was developed for involving employees. Focus groups with shop stewards of various public and private organizations explored changes in tasks and responsibilities of employees to stimulate the performance of companies and the workability of employees. The implementation of this strategy is still in its early stages; however, not many employers express the need to invest in representative participation about these topics: "Employers ready to extensively discuss their plans about the innovative work organization in the regular social platform ('overleg') are exceptions rather than the rule" (Gryp, Delissen-Jacobs, and Peirsman 2014).

Leaders in the Belgian unions remain skeptical about the possibilities for "democratic as well as workable work," despite sometimes enthusiastic shop stewards.[11]

SIPTU AND ITS INSTITUTE; PARTICIPATION IN IRELAND

The Institute for the Development of Employees Advancement Services (IDEAS) was established in February 2001 by SIPTU, Ireland's largest trade union. One of its aims is "to improve workplace performance and working lives and to stimulate positive organizational change through inclusive dialogue by releasing the creativity of employees." In cooperation with IDEAS, the manufacturing sector in SIPTU has developed and successfully "road-tested" a robust yet flexible model of a joint union-management approach in manufacturing companies, a pragmatic response to strengthen, and grow, the Irish manufacturing sector (SIPTU 2013).

The union will always consult its members first. It is only with members' approval that the management team is spoken to. From then, the initial meeting with management is especially critical. Senior managers need to be convinced that the union can bring a new and creative energy to the table and that worker voice should not be viewed as the traditional "part of the problem" but as a critical "part of the solution."

If both sides agree to proceed, a Joint Union Management Steering Group (JUMSG) is established and selected for the overall strategic direction to be taken. The unions sees the makeup of the JUMSG as "critical to future success...This requires the involvement of visionary shop stewards, as well as committed senior managers, together leaders of the change process." The union uses the metaphor of the scrum in rugby: "If either side will not agree to fully engage, then the process cannot begin...Both sides need to: "Crouch"—get ready and consider the process and potential outcomes, "touch"—make meaningful and constructive contact with the opposition, "pause"—take time to evaluate and consider response and

11 More information can be obtained with Saar Vandenbroucke (svandenbroucke@vlaams.abvv.be), Dries Delissen-Jacobs (u08ddj@acv-csc.be), Katrien Allaert (katrien.allaert@aclvb.be) and Dominique Kiekens (dominique.kiekens@uantwerpen.be)

align thinking, "engage"—both sides must stick their respective necks out and strive to keep the scrum from collapsing."

The JUMSG (managers and shop stewards together) train for these scrums during a six-day teamwork training course.

A DANISH TRADE UNION CATALOG FOR GREEN, INNOVATIVE WORKPLACES

LO, the Danish Confederation of Trade Unions, recently published a catalog of good examples for the creation of green workplaces and green jobs (LO 2015). The union presents itself as part of interorganizational design, combining initiatives for workplace innovation ("more green craftsmen needed to make the shift") and an invitation for widespread deliberations with employers and other stakeholders—in particular, municipalities.

LO sums up thirteen pieces of good advice on "green" employee involvement:

1. Use the detailed knowledge of the employees.
2. Keep an eye on the informal skills.
3. Give the employees ownership.
4. Use specialists to develop the green ideas further.
5. Create channels for the free flow of ideas.
6. Make it easier to be greener.
7. Define clear, specific, and local targets.
8. Give individuals specific responsibilities.
9. Acknowledge good ideas.
10. Draw attention to the good experiences.
11. Add a competitive element to green efforts.
12. Encourage joint efforts.
13. Seek funds for the green transition.

This is an example of indirect participation within an interorganizational context. It uses experiences from managers, municipalities, and employees to foster green workplace innovation.

INDUSTRIAL POLICY DOCUMENT 2014

In the spring of 2014, Europe's trade union for the industrial sector published a manifesto on the future of manufacturing. One of the chapters is a plea for a process of gradual transition toward an innovative new industrial paradigm based on the existing industrial structures in Europe. The manifesto calls for "promoting the development of a human-oriented manufacturing organization that stimulates employees to develop innovative behavior, is open and adaptive, while at the same time supporting and increasing human safety, health, and well-being. It should also have the capacity to cooperate in a supply chain and collaborate with knowledge institutions."

Conclusions: Worker Voice in the Twenty-First Century

Here are some recommendations for involving trade unions as representatives of worker voice in workplace-innovation projects:

- It will be necessary to extend the design process toward unions as (parts of) ecosystems of cooperating and partly conflicting organizations, sharing partly common goals with employers and management, and having to deal with internal diversities.
- New strategies and tools for and within unions will have to be developed, combining co-creating and shared interorganizational goals with conflict-oriented interests and activities.
- The new tools and policies will have to extend design processes beyond the individual firm.

This is not a simple change, as the recent examples in this chapter illustrate. Unions opting for participation:

- Are either convinced that influencing design of humane and innovative organizations could and should be a main and sustainable part of the union strategies, even if this has negative employment or wage effects on the short run or

- They estimate that in the end the potential benefits will be higher than the losses.

In both cases, approaches and cooperative structures between and within unions will have to be built to optimize the strategic choice.

TOOLS AND PRINCIPLES

Optimizing the employee's voice in design processes through a series of principles and tools is essential. First of all, the principles of *interorganization design* should be taken into account:

- Formulate results not only for the organization but also for the trade union or work council involved. What's in it for them, and how can this be quantified and communicated as results? Design the process in a way that takes core elements of union activities into account: (un)employment protection (also of involved employees outside the organization), pay/wages, working times, job changes, quality of working life, skills, etc.
- Create trust between employees (representatives) and management by and during the process and its results, not by claiming it from the beginning.
- Develop new tools and policies at various levels of value chains, labor markets, and global playing fields.

Second, it is essential to foster an employee's voice using *three interdependent forms of involvement*:

- **Direct participation** of the workers/employees directly involved in one or more workplaces and their change processes
- **Representative participation** by the union or work council within the organization and outside—the union as an independent partner in interorganizational design

- **Indirect participation** (again, interorganizational design in the sense of anticipation and condition setting): providing facilities, relations with other external stakeholders, and examples and inspirations from elsewhere

Third, *transparency about the time frame*:

- If the union or works council does not (or is not able to) choose the position of an integrated employee's voice from start to finish, create opportunities and tools to make employees' voices heard at *crucial stages* of the process, and integrate these stages into the design process.
- Be as transparent as possible about time frames: how can an employee's voice be heard before major decisions for the design have already been taken?

And last but not least: the *trade unions should develop themselves as an ecosystem*, starting with these steps:

- Develop skills and facilities for officials and members to play a productive role in indirect participation. In particular, they need to extend their competencies to be able to develop alternative solutions in the course of consultation and participation processes (Telljohan 2012).
- Design for feedback to the organization and its employees, as well as to the representative participants from the union or works council.

REFERENCES

Boyle, K. 2010. "Contemporary Approach for Sustainable Representation of Farmworkers in Global Market: UFW." Paper presented to UFW Board.

Boyle, K., and S. Pisha. 1995. *Building the Future through Quality Unions in Telecommunications, Unions, Management, and Quality:*

Opportunities for Innovation and Excellence. Ed Cohen-Rosenthal (ed.). Richard Irwin Publishing, Inc. Burr Ridge, IL.

Bussat, V., C. E. Triomphe, and B. Körper (eds.) 2013. *Crisis, Social Dialogue and Renewals in Restructuring: Restructuring in SMEs.* A project funded by the EU DG Employment, social affairs and inclusion

Eurofound, European Monitoring Centre on Change. 2013. "How Did the Job Structure Change During the Great Recession in the EU?"

EUWIN. 2013. "The Dublin Declaration, Social Partners as Knowledgeable Participants in Workplace Innovation." http://www.ksu.lt/!downloads/2014/04/SIPTU-manufacturing-conference-launches-declaration-on-workplace-innovation.pdf.

Gamble, D., N. Gregg, and P. Lazes. 2002. *Worker Voice, Unions, and Economic Development.*

Gregory, D., T. Huzzard, and R. Scott. 2004. *Strategic Unionism and Partnership: Boxing or Dancing?* Palgrave MacMillan, St. Martins Press. Houndmills, Hampshire, UK and 175 Fifth Avenue, NY, NY, USA

Gryp, S., D. Delissen-Jacobs, and S. Peirsman. 2014. "De Innovatieve Arbeidsorganisatie: Tussen (Syndicale) Droom en Daad (oP de Werkvloer)" ("The Innovative Work Organization: Between (Trade Union) Dream and Reality (On the Work Floor)."

Hirschhorn, L. 1984. *Beyond Mechanization.* Cambridge: MIT Press.

IndustriAll. 2014. "Manifesto to Put Industry Back to Work."

LO. 2015 "More Green Jobs: An Inspiration Catalogue on Green Transition and More Jobs through Employee Involvement and Local Cooperation." http://portal.ukwon.eu/pdfs/Green-Jobs-report.pdf.

Kriegesmann B., T. Kley, and S. Kublik. 2010. *Innovationstreiber Betriebliche Mitbestimmung?* WSI Mitteilungen 2, Francoforte.

Maenen, S., and Y. de Hauw. 2013. *Work Organisation and Innovation Case Study: Bombardier.* Belgium: Eurofound.

Maenen, S., C. Ordowich, and D. Austrom. 2014. "Interorganization STS Design." Paper presented at the annual meeting of the Socio-technical Systems Roundtable, Montreal.

Nerdinger, F.W., P. Wilke, S. Stracke, and R. Röhrig. 2010." Innovation und Beteiligung in der Betrieblichen Praxis: Strategien, Modelle, und Erfahrungen in de Umsetzung von Innovationsprojekten" ("Innovation and Participation in Company Praxis: Stages, Models, and Experiences in the Transition of Innovation Projects").

Nerdinger, F. W., E. Martins, and A. Pundt. 2011. "Betriebsrate und Mitarbeiter in Innovationsprozessen: Ergebnisse aus dem Projekt BMInno" ("Works Councils and Employees in Innovation Processes: Results of the BMInno Project").

Ogden, M. 2012. "Unions and High-Performance Work Systems—A Strategy." Paper presented STS Roundtable, New Orleans, LA

Salm, R. (I. G. Metall 2001). "Abschied vom Leitbild humaner Gruppenarbeit? Wie antworten die Gewerkschaften auf Tendenzen der Re-Taylorisierung der Arbeit?" ("Farewell to the Model of Humane

Group Work? How do Unions Reply To Tendencies of Re-Taylorization of Work?").

Sandberg, A. 2013. *Nordic Lights. Work Management and Welfare in Scandinavia.*

Savage, L. 2006. *Justice for Janitors: Scales of Organizing and Representing Workers.*

Schnabel, C., and J. Wagner. 1994. *Industrial Relations and Trade Union Effects on Innovation in Germany.* Labour.

Schwarz-Kocher, M., J. Dispan, U. Richter, and B. Seibold. 2010. *Betriebsratshandeln im Modus Arbeitsorientierter Innovationsprozesse.* WSI Mitteilungen 2, Francoforte.

SIPTU, press release. May 3, 2013. "SIPTU Manufacturing Conference Launches Declaration on Workplace Innovation." http://www.siptu.ie/ media/pressreleases2013/fullstory_17280_en.html.

Sprenger, W. 2010. "Innovation, Trade Unions, and Works Councils in a European Perspective: Experiences from Selected EU Member States," in Nerdinger et al. 2010.

Stracke, S., and F. W. Nerdinger. 2010. "Mitbestimmung und Innovation aus Betriebsratsperspektive, Ergebnisse Qualitativer Studien" ("Employee Participation and Innovation from Works Council Perspective: Results of Qualitative Studies"). *Industrielle Beziehungen* 17: 30–53.

Telljohann, V. 2010. "Employee-Driven Innovation in the Context of Italian Industrial Relations: The Case of a Public Hospital." *Transfer* 16 (2).

Telljohann, V. 2012. "Revitalising Participatory Democratic Practices in Workplaces," in F. Garibaldo, M. Baglioni, C. Casey, and V. Telljohann (eds.), *Workers, Citizens, Governance: Sociocultural Innovation at Work*. Frankfurt: Peter Lang, 169–85.

Telljohann, V. 2015. "Coordinated Interest Representation along the Automotive Value Chain as a Response to Social Dumping Practices," in M. Bernaciak M. (ed.) *Market Expansion and Social Dumping in Europe*. London: Routledge (forthcoming).

Thompson, P., and C. Smith (eds.). 2010. "Working Life, Renewing Labour Process Analysis."

Twix, A. 2010." Democratizing Work and Unions." New Unionism blog.

van Gyes, G. 2003. "Industrial Relations as a Key to Strengthening Innovation in Europe." Innovation paper no. 36. European Commission, Fifth Framework Programme, Innovation Policy Studies.

van Klaveren, M., and W. Sprenger. 2005. "Boxing and Dancing: Dutch Trade Unions and Works Councils Experiences Revisited."

van Klaveren, M., and W. Sprenger. 2009. "Organising Binnen de Nederlandse Arbeidsverhoudingen" ("Organizing within Dutch Labor Relations").

Ten

Democratic Dialogue

BJORN GUSTAVSEN

INTRODUCTION

When the notion of socio-technical design first emerged, emphasis was on the design principles. Implementation of design-principle demands, however, communication among all concerned. Throughout the 1970s and '80s, focus came to an increasing degree to turn toward the communicative processes as such. This is the context in which democratic dialogue made its appearance, initially as a negation of negotiations between parties in opposition to each other and eventually as a more broadly defined set of principles to guide collaborative efforts between the labor-market parties centrally as well as locally. This chapter traces the points of origin of the concept and follows its evolution up until the present.

There are two aspects of the notion of socio-technical design: the characteristics of the workplace and the process through which the characteristics are created. Both have generally been considered, but in the early period, the main emphasis was on characteristics. From the 1970s, with the appearance of notions like participative design and user-driven change, there has been a growing focus on process. If a process is to make people learn how to create participative work roles, they need to participate in the learning process. What this implies can vary within broad limits.

This is the area in which the notion of democratic dialogue belongs. Using this notion as the point of departure, it is possible to perform a broader analysis of the role of communication in design processes. Why is there a need for considering communication as an issue in its own right? What challenges appear in creating adequate forms of communication? What solutions can be brought to bear on these challenges?

CHANGE AND VISIBILITY

When socio-technical perspectives on work and work relationships first gained broad attention, their link to field experiments was a decisive factor. Contrary to pure texts, a field experiment represents an intervention into reality and an illustration in practical terms of the meaning of concepts and ideas. In the early phase, the experiments were largely thought to demonstrate the validity of psychological job requirements, such as the need for autonomy, learning, and social contacts in work, and how work roles should be shaped to meet these requirements. There were, however, more issues involved:

In Scandinavia, the field experiments appeared against a background of what can be called "centralized constructivism" (Gustavsen 2011). When the social democrats came into power in the period between the World Wars, one of their major goals was to reduce the level of conflict and increase the level of productivity in working life. This was not to be done through waiting for one or the other of the major worldviews competing for attention at the time—market liberalism and more or less radical socialism—to make itself true through some kind of historical process, but rather through a series of active interventions in society and working life. After inviting the labor-market parties to participate, the outcome was a descending order of agreements and other regulatory mechanisms. Under this umbrella, a period of active implementation of motion, time and measurement (MTM) systems and similar approaches—"Taylorism"—occurred, with Sweden in the leading role (Johansson 1989). This led, in turn, to a rising level of problems and discontent among those who were at the receiving end of the process. There emerged a need to counteract this development. But how could this be done without losing the tripartite cooperation inherent in the central initiatives? A major point of demonstration in the Scandinavian experiments was that this kind of coalition could be created locally and that it could actually work out solutions to the challenges emerging out of centralized constructivism. This perspective was at least as important as the more scientific content of the initiatives.

As other countries are concerned, there may have been other aspects of the experiments that generated attention. In, for instance, Germany, there is a strong tradition of focusing on competence in work, and the Peiner project (Fricke 1975) may have appeared as a demonstration of the potential of learning in work as a major source of competence development. In the United States, it may have been the labor-union cooperation as such that emerged as an innovation. The point is that all initiatives emerged within specific, and different, contexts and gained much of their visibility through their ability to concretize issues of critical importance within each of these contexts.

This point is of major importance in understanding what happened after the field-experiment period. Social visibility cannot be gained once and for all but has to be continuously renewed, and what came to represent an adequate renewal was dependent on the context. Employers as well as unions are membership organizations under the obligation to create solutions that pertain to all members, or at least are open to all members. The acid test of the value of the experiments was, consequently, not what scientific conclusions they gave rise to but the degree to which they generated processes that reached other workplaces. Did they function as sources of broad movements in working life, or were they splendid but isolated events? This was the challenge that came to put its mark on all later developments, including the emergence of the notion of democratic dialogue.

THE CHALLENGE OF DIFFUSION

The experiments in Norway were supervised by a bipartite committee. In the early 1970s, this committee was replaced by a permanent cooperation council. A major task for this council was to launch measures that could function in support of the diffusion of impulses from the experiments, such as information, conferences, and training programs. This notwithstanding, diffusion was slow, and the council was not satisfied with the achievements. Around 1980, the labor-market parties started, within the context of the regular renegotiations of their main agreement, to discuss an alternative approach. This resulted in a new agreement on development that went into force in 1983.

This agreement did not focus on design principles but on the processes needed to work out and implement alternatives to Taylorism. In line with such notions as participative design and user-driven change, what was seen as the key issue was to create a broad interest in exploring alternative forms of work organization and help the interested parties develop fruitful processes during which they, themselves, could decide on design issues. The basic idea was to organize a new wave of encounters that could bring workers and managers together in new contexts and create new processes. But how to do this? Since Burns and Stalker (1961) specified the characteristics of innovative communication, there has been no lack of views on what characterizes good communication in organizations. Generally, however, these views have been developed by research through starting with general theoretical sources (e.g., Bohm, Buber, or Habermas) and then deducting operationals from these premises. Contrary to this, the notion of democratic dialogue emanated with the labor-marker parties and initially took the form of a negation of the characteristics of negotiations.

Negotiations are generally performed through representatives, in an adversarial way, and concern quantifiable issues, mainly time and money. What the parties did was to reverse these characteristics and replace them with the notion of direct participation in a constructivist setting in which all topics of interest to the participants can be brought up. In developing this idea, there was a cooperation with research, and research came to play an active role when the new communicative notions were to be put into operation.

DEMOCRATIC DIALOGUE

Given the point of departure sketched above, many of the joint efforts of research and the labor-market parties during the 1980s were a further development of the notion of democratic dialogue, eventually resulting in a set specific criteria:

- Dialogue is based on a principle of give and take, not one-way communication.
- All concerned by the issues under discussion should have the possibility of participating.
- All participants have the same status on the dialogue arenas.
- Work experience is the point of departure for participation (experience that everybody has).
- Participants are under the obligation to help other participants be active in the dialogue.
- It must be possible for all participants to gain an understanding of the topics under discussion.
- An argument can be rejected only after an investigation (and not, for instance, on the grounds that it emanates from a source with little legitimacy).
- All arguments that are to enter the dialogue must be represented by actors present.
- All participants are obliged to accept that other participants may have arguments that are better than their own.
- The dialogue should be able to overcome a growing degree of disagreement.
- The dialogue should continuously generate decisions that provide platforms for joint action.

In addition to the dialogue criteria, a set of perspectives was worked out concerning the design of the encounters. Although encounters could be organized in many different shapes and forms, the typical dialogue conference had an ideal number of participants around forty, allowing for work in four parallel groups. In single enterprises, these were selected to represent an inverted T, with all levels of the formal organization present, plus a fairly broad representation from the shop floor.

Most work was performed in groups; plenaries were used for summarizing. All tasks were subject to rotation. Duration could range between one and three full working days. The most common pattern was lunch to lunch at a conference center, with an evening for social purposes. The topics were what their workplace would be like two to three years ahead, what challenges had to be overcome to get there, what ideas did they have concerning how meet the challenges, and finally, what joint action plans could be worked out. While the topics were conventional, the setting was new. (For more detailed presentations, see Gustavsen 1992, 2001).

Throughout the 1980s, about three hundred conferences were organized under the umbrella of the Norwegian agreement on development, reaching about four hundred enterprises (Gustavsen 1993). To that number we can add the approximately one hundred conferences organized within the framework of the LOM program in Sweden (Gustavsen 1992, Naschold 1993). Researchers could not participate in all conferences but were able to cover a reasonable number.

ISSUES AND QUESTIONS
Given the pragmatic point of departure, the chief criterion for validating the various aspects of democratic dialogue was "what works." There was, in fact, a lot of experience in this area even before the agreement was made because all kinds of development projects in workplaces demand communication with those concerned. "The dialogic turn" was, in this sense, not something new but rather a change of the figure-ground relationship: from the topics of the conversations to the conversations as such. As the criteria emerged, they were continuously confronted with perspectives from theoretical discourse to see if these could enrich the points emanating from practical experience. An advantage of concepts at play in practical discourse is that they do not have to be fully settled in

advance on theoretical grounds but can be subject to continuous adjustment as the process unfolds.

In addition to ordering the field of discourse into a pattern, the notion of democratic dialogue made it possible to overcome a basic dilemma inherent in pure design approaches:

In the experimental period, it was common to argue that one-sided, highly specialized work drained people of the resources needed for participation, be it in society or in the workplace. If they lacked the resources needed for participation, the workers concerned had to stand outside the decision to launch an initiative to increase participation. Through making the communicative aspect into a dimension in its own right, the participatory potential of workers subject to heavy Taylorism could be assessed against criteria pertaining to their ability to communicate rather than against the socio-technical characteristics of their work role. This made it possible to give, say, membership in a free-union movement weight as a factor underpinning participation from workers even in the most narrow assembly-line jobs.

Democratic dialogue has been criticized for being an insufficient framework for organizational change (i. e. Marrewijk et al. 2010). This may be correct but is built on a misunderstanding of the purpose of the concept. Democratic dialogue is not intended to be a full package of measures and methods for change but frame conditions, set by the labor-market parties centrally, open to association with a number of different approaches on the project level, such as SWAT analyses; various concepts used in improving health services, such as patient-centered care; and in the promotion of the notion of best practices. Various versions tailored to fit other contexts than labor-management conversations have appeared, such as collective reflections among managers in innovation processes. To some extent, the notion of dialogue has invaded the established bodies for labor-management cooperation, such as works councils and work-environment committees. With the growing emphasis on interorganizational relationships, democratic dialogue has become associated with notions like innovation systems and (learning) regions. (A presentation of

Scandinavian developments in the borderland between innovation and work reform can be found in Ekman et al. 2011.)

Democratic dialogue has a number of characteristics overlapping with the notion of search conference, and a number of the characteristics of dialogue conferences were taken over from the idea of search conference. The notion of search conference is, however, founded on a theory with universalist claims, with a radical realist epistemology at the core. To Emery, the architect behind the notion of search conference, the world is not only massively present but subject to forces, or laws, that can be expressed in systems-theoretical terms (Emery 1981). This external reality is identical for all concerned—say, all members of an organization—and the purpose of the search conference is to make them discover this world together as a prerequisite for making them able to act together. Against this, democratic dialogue is based on more of a linguistic and constructivist perspective, where language is assigned a weight of its own and where the characteristics assigned to reality appear as constructions, not as pure mirroring. Because a given reality can be seen and interpreted in different ways, with no supreme court to decide which way is the right one, there is a need for a process that can make people, without the force of an unequivocal reality, adjust their concepts in relation to each other to a degree sufficient to make joint action possible. It may be worth noting that when dialogue conferences came to deviate from search conferences, the initial reason was not theoretical differences but the simple fact that the labor-market parties found that search conferences, in spite of their democratic structure, tended to favor management because of their generally superior knowledge about the environment of the enterprise.

Assigning the work "democratic" to the notion of dialogue can be seen as unnecessary because all dialogues by definition are democratic. When this was nonetheless done, it was to emphasize the link between dialogue and the institutional conditions of society, such as the relationships between the labor-market parties and, through this, to issues like the right to organize and the freedom of speech.

The idea of dialogue conference appeared successful in the first decade of its existence. The conferences represented a notable break with traditional forms of communication in organizations. Not only did workers and unions find that this form of communication served their interests; so did a substantial amount of managers. As the latter were concerned, it seems clear that they often found the traditional hierarchical forms, supplemented by more or less adversarial negotiations, to constitute too narrow a framework for the relationships to their employees that they felt that they needed.

When the labor-market parties in Norway made, in the context of a renewal of their agreements around 1990, an assessment of the advances made during the 1980s, they concluded that the agreement had reached out well in working life but that the actual changes achieved were too limited. Of the four hundred or so enterprises that had participated in at least one conference, about 10 percent had gone into depth as real changes were concerned. When Naschold (1993) assessed the LOM program in Sweden, he found that of the approximately 150 organizations that had related to the program, about half had developed processes that implied improved employee participation. Of these, however, only about 10 percent had moved from increased participation to deeper changes in other respects. While the notion of democratic dialogue seemed able to attract participants and to trigger processes of change, much remained concerning the depth of the processes. This became the core issue in the following revisions of the agreement.

TOWARD A NEW VIEW ON DIFFUSION AND SCALE

With the advent of notions like participative design and user-driven and dialogue-driven change, the notion that change is an issue of simple diffusion of patterns from one, or a few, demonstration cases to working life in general had been strongly modified. Impulses from interesting or outstanding cases could be of importance, but together with other impulses they formed the kind of composite map of knowledge by Latour (1978) called "hybrid." In a hybrid approach, impulses can come from many different sources. In Norway, it was discovered, as early as in the 1970s, that organizations could learn from each other, even when none of them represented "a spearhead case." In this kind of setting, a number of organizations moved in parallel rather than in sequence.

When the labor-market parties looked for ways in which the stream of impulses to each organization involved in change could be strengthened, it was this notion of moving in parallel and exchanging impulses that came into focus. This was strengthened by the point that while Norway had, up until the late 1980s, seen only one network, or cluster, of coop- erating enterprises, a number started to appear in the late 1980s. Could cooperation between equal partners be used to promote broad change in work organization?

Considering several bases for clustering, ranging from belonging to the same union or employer organization to membership in the same local community, the labor-market parties' first choice was to go for the union-employer version. Although some branch or industry initiatives appeared, these units of change turned out to be too large and cumber- some, and during the 1990s, focus successively turned toward smaller clusters.

When a new research-based support program was launched in 1994— the Enterprise Development 2000 program (Gustavsen, et al. 2001)— the main focus was on the relationships between enterprises and the building and strengthening of networks and clusters.

With the growing emphasis on interorganizational relationships, there emerged a need for a new type of encounter. While most of the encoun- ters during the 1980s took the form of conversations between labor and management in single enterprises, conversations between bipartite proj- ect groups from several enterprises became a common pattern during the 1990s.

Around 2000, the agreement was again renegotiated. At this time, there were some new elements in the situation, in particular the estab- lishment, upon government initiative, of partnerships for the promotion of economic development in all the administrative regions into which

Norway is divided. With the labor-market parties represented in all the partnerships, the door was open for a link between the cluster policy of the parties and the partnership policy of the government. Because many of the emerging clusters were regional, it was thought that there would be advantages associated with a regional policy level that could, among other things, not only promote new clusters but also links between clusters and closer links between enterprises on the one hand and regional as well as national policies on the other. In this context, the notion of democratic dialogue came to serve an even more complex set of actors and relationships.

These developments reflect a policy whereby the challenge of diffusion is met through a continuous widening of the circle of actors involved in democratic dialogue, rather than through, say, campaigns in which a central authority "tells" the workplace actors what they should do. If people can relate democratically to each other, they are expected to shape their material and organizational structures in a way that reflects democratic values.

DEVELOPMENTS AFTER THE TURN OF THE CENTURY

After the turn of the century, the development of the notion of democratic dialogue has been influenced by two main factors: the growing importance of innovation and the mainstreaming of the notion of dialogue.

It has been about five decades since the first major work on innovation and enterprise organization appeared (Burns and Stalker 1961). Although the authors were very familiar with the Tavistock Institute and its work on socio-technical design and systems perspectives, they chose to place their main emphasis on communication and associated relations in the organization. When the issue is transcendence, existing and potential socio-technical frameworks are pushed into the background, in favor of an emphasis on the elements that promote freedom and openness, such as open communication, multiple relationships, and trust.

This perspective has continued to be valid, and it has implied that with a growing focus on innovation there has been a growth in the focus on dialogue and similar concepts that can be used to identify processes of open communication between equal partners, where a strong element of trust replaces formal and material steering mechanisms.

While an emphasis on innovation functions toward lifting notions like dialogue higher in the discourses of society, there are also forces that function toward robbing the concept of its radical content and sharp edges. By 2010, the estimate of the joint labor-employer secretariat in charge of promoting the workplace development agreement was that over the years, approximately two thousand enterprises had used the agreement and, at least as a point of departure, promoted the notion of democratic dialogue as well. When originally launched, the concept represented a break with the established forms of communication in organizations. It had a distinctive profile and could be promoted through specific initiatives. During the past ten years or so, dialogue has become the most common form of communication in general—at least according to the claims that are put forth. Actors who used to "tell," "inform," or "communicate" today perform dialogue. In this sense, the concept has moved from exceptionalism to mainstream. This pertains not only to working life but to society as a whole, and not only to Norway. Today there is a dialogic turn of global proportions. In the vast sea of dialogues characterizing present-day society, it is no longer possible to gain any overview of the criteria associated with the concept or of what it achieves.

CONCLUSIONS

The strong focus on socio-technical design in a narrow sense characterizing the 1960s and '70s gave rise to a basic problem: If workers in highly specialized roles are drained of their resources for participation, what are the grounds for having them participate in projects aimed at doing away with the high degree of specialization? The notion of democratic dialogue lifted the issue of resources for participation out of a pure job-design sphere and made it possible to consider such assets as membership in a free union movement.

While the 1960s and '70s saw the emergence of a number of examples of alternative design principles, diffusion was limited. How could working life in general be reached? Through associating democratic dialogue with strategies for the building of continuously expanding networks of social relationships, the diffusion of democratic forms of work organization was transformed from centrally designed enlightenment to broad involvement in democratic processes of communication.

For broad and long-term processes of democratization in working life to become possible, there is a need to ensure the stable and long-term commitment of major actors in society, in particular the labor-market parties. Through linking democratic dialogue to the institutionally granted human rights in democratic society—such as the freedom of association, the freedom of speech, and the right to be heard—a link was forged between tools in workplace development and the institutional order of society.

If we look at the comparative European studies of working conditions, Norway appears, along with the other Scandinavian countries, with relatively high scores on autonomy and learning in work (Lorenz and Lundvall 2011). None of the other Scandinavian countries (Denmark, Finland, and Sweden) can show a "dialogic turn" directly comparable to that of Norway. There are, however, a series of parallel initiatives and developments that contributes to much the same results (Gustavsen 2011).

As other countries are concerned, the same is likely to be the case, in particular with respect to the Netherlands because the Netherlands follow the Scandinavian countries as freedom and learning in work is concerned. Elements of a communicative mechanism that can ensure mobilization around such ideas as autonomy and learning in work are probably present in a number of other countries as well. What this implies will vary among countries, or even regions, but the notion of democratic dialogue can be used as a background against which to map out the characteristics of the communicative patterns in working life.

REFERENCES

Burns, T., and G. M. Stalker. 1961. *Management of Innovations.* London: Tavistock Publications.

Ekman, M., B. Gustavsen, B. T. Asheim, and O Palshaugen (eds.). 2011. *Learning Regional Innovation.* London: Palgrave-MacMillan: 104–19.

Emery, F. E. (ed.) 1981. *Systems Thinking.* Harmondsworth: Penguin.

Fricke, W. 1975. "Arbeitsorganisation und Qualifikation" ("Work Organization and Qualification"). *Schriftenreihe des Forschungsinstitut der Friedrich Ebert Stiftung.* Bonn: Nue Gesellschaft.

Gustavsen, B. 1992. *Dialogue and Development.* Assen: van Gorcum.

Gustavsen, B. 1993. "Creating Productive Structures: The Role of R&D" in F. Nascholdet al., *Creating the New Industrial Society.* Amsterdam: John Benjamins.

Gustavsen, B. 2001. "Theory and Practice: The Mediating Discourse." In P. Reason and H. Bradbury (eds.), *Handbook of Action Research*, first ed. London: Sage: 17–26.

Gustavsen, B. 2011. "The Nordic Model of Work Organization." *Journal of the Knowledge Economy* 2: 463–80.

Gustavsen, B., H. Finne, and B. Oscarsson. (eds.) 2001. *Creating Connectedness: The Role of Social Research in Innovation Policy.* Amsterdam: John Benjamins.

Johansson, A. L. 1989. *Tillvaxt Och Klassamarbete: En Studie Av Den Svenska Modellens Uppkomst (Economic Growth and Class*

Cooperation: A Study of the Emergence of the Swedish Model).
Stockholm: Tiden.

Latour, B. 1987. *Science in Action*. Cambridge: Harvard University Press.

Lorenz, E., and B.-A. Lundvall. 2011. "The Organization of Work and
Systems of Labor-Market Regulation and Social Protection," in M.
Ekman, B. Gustavsen, B. T. Asheim, and O Palshaugen (eds.), in
Learning Regional Innovation. London: Palgrave-MacMillan.

Marrewijk, A., M. Veenswijk, and S. Clegg. 2010. "Organizing Reflexivity
in Designing Change: The Ethnoventionist Approach." *Journal of
Organizational Change Management* 23 (3): 212–29.

Naschold, F. 1993. "Organization Development: National Programmes
in the Context of International Competition," in F. Naschold, R. E.
Cole, B. Gustavsen, and H. van Beinum (eds.), *Constructing the New
Industrial Society*. Assen: van Gorcum. 3–120.

Eleven

Workplace Innovation

FRANK POT AND STEVEN DHONDT

INTRODUCTION

Workplace Innovation, as it developed from the beginning of this
century, is a member of the STS-D family and shares its roots with
many of the approaches in this book, going back to the restructuring
of Europe after the Second World War, when campaigns were started
for productivity and industrial democracy (chapter 5). It is first of all a
policy concept. In the application for the European Workplace Innovation
Network (EUWIN) that started in 2013, it is described as follows:

> Workplace innovations designate new and combined inter-
> ventions in work organization, human resource management,
> labor relations, and supportive technologies. It is important to
> recognize both process and outcomes. The term "workplace
> innovation" describes the participatory and inclusive nature of
> innovations that embed workplace practices grounded in con-
> tinuing reflection, learning, and improvements in the way orga-
> nizations manage their employees, organize work, and deploy
> technologies. It champions workplace cultures and processes
> in which productive reflection is a part of everyday working life.
> It builds bridges among the strategic knowledge of the leader-
> ship, the professional and tacit knowledge of frontline employ-
> ees, and the organizational design knowledge of experts. It seeks

to engage all stakeholders in dialogue in which the force of the better argument prevails. It works toward "win-win" outcomes in which a creative convergence (rather than a trade-off) is forged between enhanced organizational performance and enhanced quality of working life.

The concept refers to the organizational level (workplace as an establishment or virtual organization) and not to individual workplaces.

Compared to other approaches in the STS-D family, a special circumstance is that the European STS-D community succeeded in getting the concept of workplace innovation adopted in 2012 as part of the policy of the European Commission. The European Commission commissioned a European Workplace Innovation Network (2013–2017) to disseminate this policy and best practices and to build workplace-innovation alliances among employers' associations, trade unions, governments, and knowledge institutes in all parts of Europe. A few European bodies use the concept as well (EESC 2011, Eurofound 2012, EU OSHA 2013a and 2013b, European Parliament 2013; IndustriAll European Trade Union 2014). Other typical features of the concept are its connections to "innovation" (Totterdill et al. 2002, Ramstad 2008, Döös and Wilhelmson 2009), as well as to "well-being at work" (Eeckelaert et al. 2012, EU OSHA 2013a and 2013b) and its emphasis on capability development for productive reflection (Totterdill et al. 2012). Although consensus about the use of the concept is growing and its policy profile is getting stronger, other concepts are being used for more or less the same approach. Examples are "innovative workplaces" (e.g., OECD 2010a and 2010b and sometimes EESC 2011) and "sustainable work systems," a concept that up till now was used by the Swedish part of the STS-D family (Docherty et al. 2002). As can be expected, in national programs and initiatives (Totterdill et al. 2009, Pot et al. 2012b), concepts in the country's language are being used. "Workplace innovation" is also being used in the United States, Canada, and Australia, in addition to concepts such as "high-performance workplaces" and "relational coordination" (Gittell et al. 2010).

SOCIETAL CONTEXT

How can this emergence of interest in workplace innovation, this new élan, be understood? The broader context is that in the early 1990s, a significant shift in our economy and businesses could be observed, fueled by information technology. This shift reversed the historical pattern in which tangible capital was the main asset in companies. Around 1990, investments in intangible capital (percentage of adjusted GNP) became higher than investments in tangible capital (Corrado and Hulten 2010). Regarding innovation, the conviction grew in Europe that "social innovation" (work organization, competency development, employee participation, etc.) is probably more important than "technological innovation" to explain the company's performance (Bolwijn et al. 1986). Business models changed from products (Philips: lightbulbs) to services (Philips: city lighting). This context explains the need to develop and use the skills and competencies of the potential workforce to increase added value as part of a competitive and knowledge-based global economy (European Commission 2014). One more reason for "social innovation of work and employment" (nowadays called "workplace innovation") is that private and public organizations can fully benefit from technological innovation only if it is embedded in workplace innovation (making technology work by means of proper organization). Finally, there is a need to enhance labor productivity to maintain our level of welfare and social security in the near future, with fewer people in the workforce due to the aging population.

Referring to these kind of considerations, a number of European countries started national programs or initiatives in the first years of this century: Finland (workplace development/innovation), Germany (innovative Arbeitsgestaltung), the UK and Ireland (workplace innovation), the Netherlands and Flanders, Belgium (sociale innovatie), Denmark (employee-driven innovation), and Sweden (management and work-organization renewal) (Totterdill et al. 2009, Pot et al. 2012b) (chapter 9). Recent programs sometimes have new names—for example, in Finland "business, productivity, and joy at work," 2012–2018.

The governance models differ among countries. In some countries, government is leading; in other countries, social partners are leading. In all countries, knowledge institutes are supporting. A contextual condition for these programs seems to be the tradition of partnership of these stakeholder organizations. On the European level, it "started" with the publication of the "Green Paper on Partnership for a New Organisation of Work" (European Commission 1997). Contributions came from the European Work and Technology Consortium and from the European Work Organization Network (EWON), the latter hosted by DG Employment for a couple of years. DG Research funded the report of the Hi-Res project ("the High Road Concept as a Resource") (Totterdill et al. 2002). Later, facilitated by the Sixth Framework Program, the "Work in Net" (WIN) consortium was one of the networks continuing the work (Alasoini et al. 2005, WIN 2010). At the time of the Social Innovation Europe (SIE) initiative (launched in 2011), workplace innovation was connected to the broad European concept of social innovation (Pot et al. 2012a).

In the same period, the European Economic and Social Committee (employers' associations, trade unions, NGOs) published an opinion on "innovative workplaces," using the concept of "workplace innovation" as well (EESC 2011). Researchers from different networks organized seminars and developed the Dortmund/Brussels Position Paper[12] titled "Workplace Innovation as Social Innovation" (2012), which was discussed with members of the European Commission, politicians, and social partners. In October 2012, DG Enterprise and Industry adopted "workplace innovation" in its "industrial policy" and in its "innovation policy" and commissioned a European Workplace Innovation Network (EUWIN, 2013–2017) to disseminate the approach and to build regional "workplace innovation alliances."[13]

---

12 http://ec.europa.eu/enterprise/policies/innovation/files/dortmund-brussels-position-paper-workplace-innovation_en.pdf
13 http://ec.europa.eu/growth/industry/innovation/policy/workplace/index_en.htm.

DESIGN THEORY—WORK ORGANIZATION

In de Sitter's socio-technical systems design theory (chapters 5, 6, and 17) the central idea is the balance between "control requirements" (demands) and "control capacity" (job control). "It's not the problems and disturbances in the work that cause stress, but the hindrances to solve them" (De Sitter1981, 155). To maintain this balance, control capacity is required regarding the performance of a given job at the individual job level (internal control capacity), as well as regarding the division of labor, and in particular the reduction of organizational complexity on production group and plant level (external-control capacity): "From complex organizations with simple jobs to simple organizations with complex jobs" (De Sitteret al. 1997). So, besides internal control capacity, complex jobs also include participation in external-control activities at the production-group and plant levels (shop-floor consultation on processes, division of labor, targets, etc.). The aim of this socio-technical design is to result in simultaneously improved organizational performance, quality of working life, and better labor relations.

In 1981, De Sitterintegrated the "job demands control model" (Karasek 1979) in his theory. The Job Demand Control (JDC) model holds two predictions. First, high job demand and low job control individually represent risk factors that are detrimental to (mental) health outcomes such as work stress and coronary heart disease. Second, the model also predicts that high job demand and high job control foster motivation and learning. Central features of the JDC model are also the strain and learning hypotheses, referring to two interaction hypotheses on the balance between job demands and job control.

Jobs with high demands and low control can be called "high-strain jobs," which are a risk for work-related stress. Moreover, stress inhibits learning. Jobs with high demands and high control are called "active jobs," which offer opportunities for learning and coping with stressors (Karasek 1979, Karasek and Theorell 1990). Later, this model was extended with the social-support dimension and with innovative and productive work behavior (Karasek and Theorell 1990).

MANAGERIAL TECHNOLOGY THEORY—CAPABILITY MOBILIZATION

The proportional shift from tangible to intangible investments meant a lot for styles of management. Because "hard" technological innovations do not seem to explain persistent productivity differentials, Bloom and van Reenen present evidence on another possible explanation for persistent differences in productivity at the firm and the national level—namely, that such differences largely reflect variations in management practices (Bloom and van Reenen 2010). They stand in the tradition of the *resource-based view* as the framework of research into the conditions for acquiring and maintaining competitive advantage. The focus is not only on the competitiveness of products and services but on internal resources for competitive advantage as well, such as management skills, work organization, knowledge, and competencies. Competitive advantage can be achieved when these resources improve efficiency and efficacy and when they are rare or difficult to copy. The *dynamic resource-based view* of today, taking into account necessary adaptations to changes in the environment, is directed at *dynamic capabilities* (Eisenhardt and Martin 2000). So this is not only about management capabilities but about innovation capabilities at the organization level as well. One of these management capabilities is "managing human resources"—how to stimulate "employee voice" or develop "employee capabilities."

The most important fields of intervention or (re)design are work organization, competency development, and labor relations. Here, the discussion on "complex jobs" can be continued because that concept can also be found in two other theories: the action regulation theory—although in the wording of "complete jobs," - which Hacker (2003) and Volpert (1989) developed, and the double-loop learning theory by Argyris and Schön (1978). Hacker distinguishes three stages of action regulation: action preparation, implementation, and evaluation. Complete jobs cover all these stages. "Decision latitude (or autonomy) is the most important feature of complete activities. Complete activities offer the decision latitude that is necessary for setting one's goals. These are prerequisites of comprehensive cognitive requirements of a task and determine the intrinsic task motivation (i.e., being motivated by a challenging job content). These aspects serve as a well-known buffer against negative consequences of high workload" (Hacker 2003, 112).

In the learning theory by Argyris and Schön (1978), two levels of control can be recognized. "Ordinary repetitive acting corresponds with the 'given order with prescribed procedures' method. Innovative acting includes the characteristics of ordinary repetitive acting but is also aiming for improvement of procedures, working conditions, and results in order to enhance effectiveness or efficiency" (Argyris and Schön 1978, 117). In other words: job autonomy (internal control capacity) relates to "single-loop learning" (doing things better), and complex or complete jobs with external-control capacity facilitate "double-loop learning" (e.g., "Are we doing the right things?"). Another way of conceptualizing learning at the organizational level is the use of the concept of "productive reflection," covering jointly "the role that organizational structures have in articulating employee voice together with the active use of employees' formal and tacit skills and competencies in the process of improvement, innovation, and change" (Cressey et al. 2013, 221). However, job control is not a sufficient condition, and productive reflection is not only a matter of good intentions. Akerlof contends from an economic perspective that participation needs to take the form of gift exchange or reciprocity to be effective (Akerlof 1982). Gustavsen emphasizes the need for democratic relations to optimize the outcomes for management and employees alike (Gustavsen 1992).

INTEGRATED APPROACH

The socio-technical design theory is a systems approach, integrating technological and social innovation. For the foundation of explanatory theories and design theories, it can be related to the "configurational approach of strategic human resource management" (SHRM). "In general, configurational theories are concerned with how the pattern of multiple independent variables is related to a dependent variable rather than with how individual independent variables are related to the dependent variable" (Delery and Doty 1996, 804). From a design point of view, this means that "HR-bundles" are more effective than separate interventions (Sheehan 2014).

EVIDENCE DISSEMINATION

Data from the European Working Conditions Survey (employees) demonstrates marked differences between countries in the control that employees can exercise over their work tasks, their participation in wider organizational decision making, and the likelihood that they work in a high-involvement organization. The Nordic countries (Denmark, Finland, and Sweden) and the Netherlands had the highest levels of involvement, while the Southern countries (Greece, Italy, Portugal, and Spain) and the East-South countries (Bulgaria and Romania) had particularly low levels.

Job autonomy has not risen in the past decade, and stimulating work did not increase during the past twenty years. The frequency of repetitive tasks has remained the same, and the level of monotonous work has gone up. Only 47 percent of European workers are involved in improving work organization or work processes in their department or enterprise (Eurofound 2012).

Data from the European Company Survey (managers) show a different picture. Of the managers interviewed, 85 percent says that the establishment uses regular meetings between employees and their immediate managers to involve employees in how work is organized (Eurofound 2013). So, at least from the point of view of the employees, there is room for improvement in the social dialogue and direct participation.

EVIDENCE CLAIMS ORGANIZATIONAL PERFORMANCE AND QUALITY OF WORKING LIFE
There is empirical evidence for the JDCS model. Reviews of longitudinal studies lend some support to these strain and learning interaction hypotheses (de Lange et al. 2003). The main effects of job demands

and job control on health and well-being are more often found than demand-control-interaction effects (Hausser et al. 2010, Dhondt et al. 2014). However, empirical findings with the model also suggest that the presence of high job demands, more than a lack of job control, results in work stress and work-related health problems. Conversely, especially the presence of job control is associated with positive outcomes such as learning, job engagement, well-being, and organizational commitment (Demerouti et al. 2001, Lyness et al. 2012, Stansfeld et al. 2013, Dhondt et al. 2014).

Investigating the relationship between workplace innovation and organizational performance in surveys is not easy. Every case is different, and quite a number of methodological and practical pitfalls exist (Armbruster et al. 2008). However, there seems to be some evidence for this relationship with labor productivity and innovation capability (and sometimes more) in a number of studies (Pot 2011). In a research project on the effects of the early Finnish workplace-innovation program on the quality of working life, it appeared that the positive effects (increased discretion, improved job security, enhanced job satisfaction) were much more likely to occur than negative effects (job intensity and mental strain) (Kalmi and Kauhanen 2008). Only a few surveys investigate organizational performance as well as quality of work. A large-scale investigation of Eurofound and an evaluation of the early Finnish workplace-innovation program show that both positive effects can be achieved simultaneously, in particular when development of plans and implementation of changes have been done from the beginning with the involvement of employees and their supervisors (Eurofound 1997, Ramstad 2009). Some studies in the United States (mainly case studies) support that as well (Appelbaum et al. 2011), as do the more than one hundred case studies that Totterdill et al. examined (2002).

DESIGN PRINCIPLES

Regarding both process and outcomes of workplace innovation the following design principles should be taken into account

- Integrated design:
  - ← Integration of technological innovation and social innovation
  - ← Integration of work organization, human resources mobilization, labor relations
  - ← Process of productive reflection of all stakeholders
- Work organization:
  - ← Balance of job demands and job control (job autonomy, functional support, organizational-level decision latitude)
  - ← Complete jobs (action preparation, implementation, and evaluation)
- Human resources mobilization:
  - ← Developing competencies
  - ← Developing capabilities
- Labor relations:
  - ← Direct participation, democratic dialogue, reciprocity

TOOL: WEBA (WELL-BEING AT WORK)

Based on these theories (JDCS model, socio-technical systems design theory, action regulation theory, and double-loop learning), a practical expert tool has been developed in the Netherlands to assess the quality of jobs and to design high-quality jobs. The Dutch government funded the development of the instrument, which was—among other aims—supposed to help the Labor Inspectorate to enhance work-related well-being conditions. The instrument is called WEBA, a Dutch abbreviation of well-being at work (Pot et al. 1994, Dhondt and Vaas 2001). The WEBA distinguishes seven dimensions: Completeness of the job, sort-cycle tasks, cognitive complexity, job autonomy, contact opportunities (social contacts and opportunities for assistance or functional support), organizational-level decision latitude, and information. Job control is covered by the three dimensions of autonomy (internal control capacity), contact opportunities, and organizational-level decision latitude (the last two dimensions cover external-control capacity). The instrument is being used mainly in the Netherlands and Flanders.

Tool: The Resilience Diagnostic Tool and Action Resource Kit

The Resilience Action Resource Kit (ARK) was developed by an expert team from UKWON, the Confederation of British Industry, and their network of European partners. It is designed to help organizations assess their ability and that of their employees to survive—and thrive—in an environment in which radical change and uncertainty have become commonplace. Resilience grows from established workplace practices as well as from the way in which change is handled. ARK invites both managers and employees to assess ten dimensions of the way their organization works through an online questionnaire. Results from this consultation then guide people toward resources and support that can lead to effective and sustainable change. ARK measures an organization's working practices and cultures against ten key dimensions: communicative competence, preparedness for change through partnership, organizational orientation, transferrable competencies, reflexivity, health and well-being, orientation toward learning and development, team orientation, work relationships, and creative thinking [14] (chapter 14).

TOOL: THE WORKPLACE INNOVATION CAPABILITY MATURITY FRAMEWORK (WI-CMF)

TNO developed the WI-CMF using the ideas of Bloom and van Reenen (2010) and is targeted at improving business value from organizational change. It translates the generic concepts of modern socio-technical thinking into an actionable and measurable set of capabilities and of capability levels necessary for creating sustainable organizations, good work, and active jobs. It consists of four major strategies at the management and shop-floor levels (managing strategy, human resources, production processes, and communication); twenty-three capabilities, of which fourteen are critical capabilities, four are maturity levels (initial, intermediate, optimizing, and high-level); and assessment and benchmark tools. The assessment possibilities are executive assessment of areas for further focus and investigation from over- and underinvestment, single-process

---

14 http://www.goodworkplaces.net/.

assessment (deep dive), cluster assessment, comparison with goals, comparison management, and shop floor. The instrument helps identify the organization's current and desired WI position and addresses the road map and practices to improve the maturity level of WI. This kind of instrument is often only used top down. However, workplace innovation requires management and the shop floor working together to get these capabilities "into shape" (Dhondt et al. 2013).

DSM SINOCHEM PHARMACEUTICALS, THE FORMER DSM ANTI-INFECTIVES, DELFT, THE NETHERLANDS

Self-organization improves innovation capacity at DSM Sinochem Pharmaceuticals DSM. In 2000, DSM anti-infectives built a new plant for the production of antibiotics. This plant had to be the most efficient plant in the world due to technological innovations (new enzymatic processes) and self-steering teams. Up until now, new processes and workplace innovations have been implemented to make a difference in global competition.

In two units (ZOR-F and the Enzyme Plant), operators produce enzymes needed for the production of antibiotics. The ten production teams, each consisting of five operators, manage themselves and ensure that the two units produce 7 x 24 hours. Two operation experts and four process engineers work close to the process. The team also includes one operations manager, a maintenance manager, and a plant manager. The operations manager communicates directly with the operators. There is no management layer in between. In the beginning, the self-steering teams did not function very well; however, the management did not drop the concept but, on the contrary, improved it by organizational innovations. They used socio-technical theory, in particular the concept of delegated tasks (van Amelsvoort et al. 2003). The "delegated task" is a role for an operator in one of the supporting processes (quality, logistics, technique, personnel). The operator with a delegated task stays in contact with all other teams and with staff members and management on the topic of his concern and brings the information back to his teammates. Four operators were kept out of the schedules; these "operation experts" get a role in coaching the operators and controlling the planning, safety, and hygiene (they got the nickname "oilman," the man who is walking around to oil the machine). The process engineers work in the room opposite the control room, and they take part in the daily morning consultation. The plant manager and operations manager state that their part in the success is trusting the operators. The two units are managed by three to five men each. In the nights, only these men are there. The production teams function without a team leader. The operators are supported in their daily work by the operation expert. The process engineers are part of the Operations Department; they collaborate intensively with the operators while optimizing or innovating the processes. Operators and engineers report directly to the operations manager. This manager is responsible for the two units.

The success is to be seen from the fact that in 2011, the plant in Delft still produces enzymes better and cheaper than any other plant in the world. In 2007, it was shown that the plant produced one and a half times as much volume with half the staffing compared to what was planned at the time the plant was built in 2000. (This case was taken from Schuiling 2008.)

CONCLUSION

Although there are enough reasons to develop workplaces from the point of view of quality of working life and performance, it is not an easy job to do. There are many obstacles that must be overcome (chapter 18). Company managements, workers, trade unions, the social partners, and governments all have a role to play in the process. Obstacles are an inevitable part of change—and are perhaps integral to the process of organizational learning. Most organizations experience unforeseen difficulties and setbacks when trying to implement new forms of work organization. Organizational culture and resistance to change underlie many of these problems. The failure of previous change initiatives, insufficient resources, and failure to keep employees properly informed can all cause problems.

Changes in the economic climate, market demands, trends, legislation, or public policy frameworks can also have adverse impacts on the success and sustainability of workplace innovation (Totterdill et al. 2002, iv).

Employees and their representatives are facing a number of dilemmas with respect to their involvement in and commitment to workplace development. These include the long- and short-term effects (e.g., employment) and getting more responsibility but no more authority. It also includes situations in which organizational commitment leads to working harder instead of working smarter, as happens in those varieties of Lean that do not stand in the participatory tradition (chapter 17). The employer/management side also faces dilemmas—for example, the benefits of workplace development appear later than the results of short-term budget cuts; bonuses stimulate short-term thinking; social innovation is more complex than technological innovation; and sharing knowledge and power is not easy. However, the argument of many executives, who claim to be imprisoned by iron economic laws dictating them to match employment practices offered by their lowest-cost competitors, is contradicted by research findings (O'Toole 2008).

In spite of the obstacles, the evidence is growing from surveys and case studies that workplace innovation contributes to better jobs and performance. To cope with the dilemmas, a good starting point in a number of countries (such as Finland, Germany, and the Netherlands) is that unions and employers' organizations have a tradition of cooperation and mutual consultation. It is clear that in countries where the government supports workplace innovation politically (campaigns) and financially (e.g., by using ESF funding), the attention for and dissemination of workplace innovation increases. Finland, Germany, and Flanders, Belgium have recently decided to continue and refresh their programs. A big challenge is now to spread the ideas and the practices to Southern and Eastern European countries.

The European Workplace Innovation Network (EUWIN) that was commissioned by the European Commission and the programs of EU OSHA and Eurofound will certainly appear to be helpful.

MORE INFORMATION

EUWIN:

http://ec.europa.eu/growth/industry/innovation/policy/workplace/index_en.htm

http://www.linkedin.com/groups/EUWIN-European-Workplace-Innovation-Network

https://twitter.com/euwinEU

http://www.facebook.com/#!/euwinEU

To become an "ambassador" of EUWIN or to get information: http://portal.ukwon.eu

Case descriptions:
http://www.kennisbanksocialeinnovatie.nl/nl/over-de-kennisbank

http://portal.ukwon.eu/euwin-knowledge-bank-menu-new

REFERENCES

Akerlof, G. A. 1982. "Labor Contracts as Partial Gift Exchange." *Quarterly Journal of Economics* 97 (4): 543–69.

Alasoini, T., E. Ramstad, T. Hanhike, and M. Lahtonen. 2005. *European Programmes on Work and Labour Innovation—A Benchmarking Approach.* WORK-IN-NET, Helsinki/Bonn.

Appelbaum, E., J. Hoffer Gittell, and C. Leana. March 20, 2011. *High-Performance Work Practices and Sustainable Economic Growth.* Washington: CEPR (Center for Economic and Policy Research).

Argyris, C., and D. Schön. 1978. *Organizational Learning.* Massachusetts: Addison-Wesley.

Armbruster, H., A. Bikfalvi, S. Kinkel, and G. Lay. 2008. "Organizational Innovation: The Challenge of Measuring Nontechnical Innovation in Large-Scale Surveys." *Technovation* 28: 644–57.

Bloom, N., and J. van Reenen. 2010. "Why Do Management Practices Differ across Firms and Countries?" *Journal of Economic Perspectives* 24 (1): 203–24.

Bolwijn, P. T., Q. H. Breukelen, S. van Brinkman, and T. Kumpe. 1986. *Flexible Manufacturing: Integrating Technological and Social Innovation.* Amsterdam: Elsevier.

Corrado, C., and C. Charles Hulten. 2010. "How Do You Measure a Technological Revolution?" *American Economic Review* 100 (5): 99–104.

Cressey, P., P. Totterdill, and R. Exton. 2013. "Workplace Social Dialogue as a Form of 'Productive Reflection.'" *International Journal of Action Research* 9 (2): 209–45.

de Lange, A. H., T. W. Taris, M. A. J. Kompier, I. L. D. Houtman, and P. M. Bongers. 2003. "The Very Best of the Millennium: Longitudinal Research and the Demand-Control (Support) Model." *Journal of Occupational Health Psychology* 8 (4): 282–305.

Delery, J. E. and D. H. Doty. (1996). "Modes of Theorizing in Strategic Human Resources Management: Tests of Universalistic, Contingency, and Configurational Performance Predictions." *The Academy of Management Journal* 39 (4): 802–35.

Demerouti, E., A. B. Bakker, F. Nachreiner, and W. B. Schaufeli. 2001. "The Job-Demands-Resources Model of Burnout." *Journal of Applied Psychology* 86 (3): 499–512.

de Sitter, L. U. 1981. *Op Weg Naar Nieuwe Fabrieken en Kantoren (Heading for New Factories and Offices)*. Deventer: Kluwer.

de Sitter, L. U., J. F. den Hertog, and B. Dankbaar. 1997. "From Complex Organizations with Simple Jobs to Simple Organizations with Complex Jobs." *Human Relations* 50 (5): 497–534.

Dhondt, S., and F. Vaas. 2001. *WEBA Analysis Manual*. Hoofddorp: TNO Work and Employment.

Dhondt, S., P. Oeij, F. van der Meulen, T. Preenen, R. Vergeer, R. van der Kleij, and M. Steen. 2013. *Platform Workplace Innovation: Workplace Innovation in a Capability Maturity Framework*. Hoofddorp: TNO Work and Employment.(Confidential; open publication was expected in 2015.)

Dhondt, S., F. Pot, and K. Kraan. 2014. "The Importance of Organizational-Level Decision Latitude for Subjective Well-Being and Organizational Commitment." *Team Performance Management: An International Journal* 20 (7/8): 307–27.

Docherty, P., J. Forslin, and A. B. Dhani (eds.). 2002. *Creating Sustainable Work Systems: Emerging Perspectives and Practice*. London/New York: Routledge.

Döös, M., and L. Wilhelmson (eds.). 2009. *Organising Work for Innovation and Growth: Experiences and Efforts in Ten Companies*. Stockholm: Vinnova.

Dortmund/Brussels Position Paper. "Workplace Innovation as Social Innovation."

Eeckelaert, L., S. Dhondt, P. Oeij, F. Pot, G. I. Nicolescu, J. Webster, and D. Elsler. 2012. *Review of Workplace Innovation and Its Relation with Occupational Safety and Health.* Bilbao: European Agency for Safety and Health at Work.

Eisenhardt, K. M., and J. A. Martin. 2000. "Dynamic Capabilities: What Are They?" *Strategic Management Journal* 21: 1105–21.

European Commission. 1997. *Green Paper on Partnership for a New Organisation of Work.* Luxembourg.

EESC (European Economic and Social Committee). 2011. *Innovative Workplaces as a Source of Productivity and Quality Jobs.* Brussels: EESC.

Eurofound (European Foundation for the Improvement of Living and Working Conditions). 1997. "Employee Participation and Organisational Change." EPOC survey of six thousand workplaces in Europe. Dublin: European Foundation.

Eurofound. 2012. *Fifth European Working Conditions Survey.* Luxembourg: Publications Office of the European Union.

Eurofound. 2013. *Third European Company Survey: First findings.* Dublin.

EU OSHA (European Agency for Safety and Health at Work). 2013a. *Priorities for Occupational Safety and Health Research in Europe: 2013–20.* Bilbao: EU OSHA.

EU OSHA (European Agency for Safety and Health at Work). 2013b. *Well-Being at Work—Creating a Positive Work Environment*. Bilbao: EU OSHA.

European Commission (2014). "Advancing Manufacturing—Advancing Europe: Report of the Task Force on Advanced Manufacturing for Clean Production." Brussels: Commission staff working document (SWD[2014] 120 final).

European Parliament. 2013. *Report on Reindustrializing Europe to Promote Competitiveness and Sustainability*. (2013/2006[INI]).

Gitell, J. H., R. Seidner, and J. Wimbush. 2010. "A Relational Model of How High-Performance Work Systems Work." *Organization Science* 21 (2): 490–506.

Gustavsen, B. 1992. *Dialogue and Development: Theory of Communication, Action Research, and the Restructuring of Working Life*. Assen: Van Gorcum.

Hacker, W. 2003. "Action Regulation Theory: A Practical Tool for the Design of Modern Work. *European Journal of Work and Organizational Psychology* 12 (2): 105–30.

Hausser, J. A., A. Mojzisch, M. Niesel, and S. Schulz-Hardt. 2010. "Ten Years On: A Review of Recent Research on the Job-Demand-Control (Support) Model and Psychological Well-Being." *Work and Stress*, 24 (1), 1–35.

IndustriAll European Trade Union. 2014. *Manifesto to Put Industry Back to Work*. Brussels.

Kalmi, P., and A. Kauhanen. 2008. "Workplace Innovations and Employee Outcomes: Evidence from Finland." *Industrial Relations* 47 (3): 430–59.

Karasek, R. A. 1979. "Job Demands, Job Decision Latitude, and Mental Strain: Implications for Job Redesign." *Administrative Science Quarterly* 24 (2): 285–308.

Karasek, R. A., and T. Theorell. 1990. *Healthy Work: Stress, Productivity, and the Reconstruction of Working Life.* New York: Basic Books.

Lyness, K. S., J. C. Gornick, P. Stone, and A. R. Grotto. 2012. "It's All about Control: Worker Control over Schedule and Hours in Cross-National Context." *American Sociological Review* 77 (6): 1023–49.

OECD (2010a). "The OECD Innovation Strategy: Getting a Head Start on Tomorrow." OECD, Paris.

OECD (2010b). "Innovative Workplaces: Making Better Use of Skills within Organizations." OECD, Paris.

O'Toole J. 2008. "Free to Choose—How Managers Can Create Globally Competitive and Healthy Workplaces (an American Perspective)," in: V. Weber (ed.), *Achieving Business Excellence—Health, Well-Being, and Performance.* Essen Germany: Bertelsmann Stiftung/BKK; 2008. 24–39.

Pot, F. D., M. H. H. Peeters, F. Vaas, and S. Dhondt. 1994. "Assessment of Stress Risks and Learning Opportunities in the Work Organisation." *European Work and Organizational Psychologist* 4 (1): 21–37.

Pot, F. D. 2011. "Workplace Innovation for Better Jobs and Performance." *International Journal of Productivity and Performance Management* 64 (4): 405–15.

Pot, F., S. Dhondt, and P. Oeij. 2012a. "Social Innovation of Work and Employment," in H.-W. Franz, J. Hochgerner, and J. Howaldt (eds.). *Challenge Social Innovation: Potential for Business, Social Entrepreneurship, Welfare, and Civil Society.* Berlin: Springer. 261–74.

Pot, F., S. Dhondt, E. de Korte, P. Oeij, and F. Vaas. 2012b. "Workplace Innovation in the Netherlands," in I. Houtman (ed.), *Work Life in the Netherlands.* Hoofddorp: TNO Work and Employment. 173–90.

Ramstad, E. 2008. *Innovation-Generating Model—Simultaneous Development of Work Organization and Knowledge Infrastructure.* Helsinki: Tekes.

Ramstad, E. 2009. "Promoting Performance and the Quality of Working Life Simultaneously." *Internal Journal of Productivity and Performance Management* 58 (5): 423–36.

Schuiling, G. J. 2008. Zelfsturend: "Let Op de Spatie!" ("Self-Steering: Watch the Interspace!") *M&O, Tijdschrift Voor Management en Organisatie* 62 (3/4): 113–36.

Sheehan, M. 2014. "Human Resource Management and Performance: Evidence from Small and Medium-Sized Firms." *International Small Business Journal* 32 (5): 545-70.

Stansfeld, S. A., M. J. Shipley, J. Head, R. Fuhrer, and M. Kivimaki. 2013. "Work Characteristics and Personal Social Support as Determinants of Subjective Well-Being." *Plos One* 8 (11): 1–8.

Totterdill, P., S. Dhondt, and S. Milsome. 2002. *Partners at Work? A Report to Europe's Policymakers and Social Partners.* Nottingham: The Work Institute.

Totterdill, P., O. Exton, R. Exton, and J. Sherrin. 2009. *Workplace Innovation Policies in European Countries.* Nottingham: UKWON.

Totterdill, P., P. Cressey, and R. Exton. 2012. "Social Innovation at Work: Workplace Innovation as a Social Process," in H.-W. Franz, J. Hochgerner, and J. Howaldt (eds.), *Challenge Social Innovation. Potential for Business, Social Entrepreneurship, Welfare, and Civil Society.* Berlin: Springer. 241–60.

van Amelsfoort, P., B. Seinen, H. Kommers, and G. Scholtes. 2003. *Zelfsturende Teams—Ontwerpen, Invoeren, Begeleiden (Self-Steering Teams—Designing, Implementing, Supporting).* Oss: ST-Groep.

Volpert, W., W. Kötter, H.-E. Gohde, and W. G. Weber. 1989. Psychological Evaluation and Design of Work tasks: two examples. *Ergonomics,* 32 (7), 881–90.

WIN (WorkInNet). 2010. "The Grand Societal Challenge: Sustainable European work to Withstand Global Economic Change and Crisis." Declaration. March 11–12, WIN, Berlin.

Twelve

Purpose and Power in the Evolution of Socio-technical Systems Design

INTRODUCTION

As a management trainee in BOAC (British Overseas Airways Corporation), I thought organization was like the English weather: "bloody awful, but there is little you can do about it." That was until, in a brief and primitive management-training course, I read J. A. C. Brown's *The Social Psychology of Industry* as part of a requirement to write a paper on the effect of management theory on management practice. The book gave a review of the early attempts to bring science and psychology to the workplace. The idea that you could do something about organizations—make them more effective while improving the pay and quality of the work life of employees—opened my eyes and started a new career.

The shift in attitude had a dramatic effect on my first posttraining position as a liaison officer for BOAC's airport operations in Fiumincino, Rome's international airport at the time. Within six months, without spending extra funds and without control of local staff (they were managed by a local agent.), Rome became the best-performing airport in BOAC's network of agency-run airports. Being trained in work-study, I examined all the relevant work-flow patterns and found nothing had changed. I had no idea what had happened, and the few steps I had taken seemed inadequate to explain the difference (e.g., start a local newspaper to share results of performance and have little celebrations to mark improvements). Clearly, I needed to understand more about organizations. My searches within BOAC prompted little interest, so I took a leave of absence and left England to pursue an MBA with an emphasis on organizational behavior at Indiana University. James D. Thomson became my mentor and supervised my master's thesis, in which I attempted to find reasons for the rapid increase in performance in Rome.

We studied all of the BOAC staff who had similar liaison positions to see if their pattern of work could give some insights. The research found none: Any changes in performance came from the local agent, not the BOAC liaison officer. The research did lead to policy changes. In the case of poor performance at any agency station, BOAC changed the agent rather than attempting difficult and costly improvements. This, however, didn't help my own search because, in some way, my presence improved performance and fell back to normal levels when I left. Thompson was preparing his now-renowned book *Organizations in Action* (1967). Inspired by this work, I developed the insight that organizations must be driven more by norms of *power* than norms of *rationality*. I took this idea with me into my subsequent jobs in consulting and to the International Division of G. D. Searle, a pharmaceutical company. Again we achieved similar success to Rome, producing significant improvements in our international subsidiaries. However, I could still not explain or offer to others the means by which they could replicate the results. I sensed that in some way we were using power differently and that we were bringing a broader perspective to what we were doing.

I joined with other innovative colleagues—working in such companies as DuPont and General Motors—to share and make sense of our experiences. We, for example, invited Eric Trist to join us and explore his latest thinking in socio-technical systems design. I adapted some of his ideas for use in the management-planning work I was evolving. My experience, however, confirmed his conclusions about why socio-technical design had not advanced as much as warranted. His significant and critical contribution to war-time productivity in coal production had not spread to the rest of industry. Trist concluded that management was much more interested in maintaining its control over workers than in productivity, and union leaders were much more interested in maintaining their independence than improving productivity. In other words, he confirmed what I had deduced from James D. Thompson's work *Organizations in Action* (1967): *Organizations are run more on norms of power than on norms of rationality.*

POWER IN THE DESIGN OF SOCIO-TECHNICAL SYSTEMS

How, then, were we to deal with power in the design of socio-technical systems? I decided to pursue a PhD in social systems sciences, and Trist became my advisor. I hoped to find new ways to design more effective sociopolitical-technical systems. By that time, Trist's thinking had evolved from his emphasis on socio-tech, through a phase of emphasis on improving the quality of work life to one of organization ecology (i.e., viewing the organizational field created by a number of organizations as a whole field with its own properties). Through this perspective, Trist advised me to never look for the answers to organizational effectiveness within the boundaries of the single organization. For my thesis, I decided to study multiorganizational fields and their impact on performance. I had the great fortune to find Francis Lethem at the World Bank. He was in Policy Advisory Services and recognized that the bank was acting on the edge of known organization theory. He asked me to take a look at project performance through that lens. I spent a summer reviewing evaluation reports of a whole range of bank projects.

At that time, the World Bank's project-planning process—called an "appraisal process," which was developed primarily from large physical infrastructure-planning and economic-planning projects—was regarded as one of its prime assets. They promoted it as one of the most thorough and professional in use anywhere in the world. When applied to the design of the newer, more social-oriented projects that McNamara emphasized in his focus on poverty, the results were problematic. They caused conflict between the new, more socially oriented staff and the traditional infrastructure-oriented staff.

My overall impression was that while the bank's approach was very professional and thorough, it was too narrowly focused. I used Fred Emery and Trist's (1965) concept of three organizational environments: internal, transactional, and contextual—to show that their projects focused too much on their internal environment and failed to pay sufficient attention to the other two. As a result, more than two-thirds of all newer projects were failing to meet their goals.[15]

I then took insight from the overall review and focused on the design of six rural development projects. From these, I made recommendations for improvement in the bank's planning/appraisal process. The recommendations focused on the following:

1. Assessing purpose, power, and commitment of the project's participants as a basis for organizational design
2. Designing interorganizational relationships (i.e., organizing the environment itself toward the project purposes), as well as relationships within the organization
3. Building a learning process (i.e., monitoring and evaluation) into the organizing process

PURPOSE IN THE DESIGN OF SOCIO-TECHNICAL SYSTEMS

During this development process, I discovered that power became not only a factor that had to be optimized jointly with the social and technical systems but one that transcended those systems. The environment was that which the projects, organization, or any system did not control. Therefore, environmental relationships were power relationships. Emery and Trist's three environments described three different power relationships:

---

15 Later, I found that this project failure rate of at least two thirds appears to be general. Almost all areas of any degree of complexity seemed to incur failures at the rate of two-thirds or more (e.g., in mergers and acquisitions, new-product launches, large IT and software development, and cultural change).

Their internal environment became the one that the system or project could control.

The transactional environment became the environment they could influence.

Finding a name for the third power in the contextual environment proved much more difficult. It took three or four months before I drew on Sir Geoffrey Vickers's work, *The Art of Judgment: A Study of Policy Making* (1965), and borrowed his term "appreciation." He in turn had borrowed the term from the British military, which would carry out appreciations of both allies' and enemies' entire thinking and how it might affect their campaigns. We were asking the World Bank's leadership to appreciate all those factors that affected the performance of their projects but which they could not influence or control.

During the research, another major conceptual breakthrough occurred. When viewing a chart showing the three nested environments—internal, transactional, and contextual—as power relationships, I asked, "If control, influence, and appreciation are power relationships, where does the power come from?" The answer came back immediately: from *purpose*! The idea was so important that I spent a great deal of time researching the concept of purpose in religion, philosophy, and science and reported my findings in the book *The Creative Power* (Smith 2009). Basically, I concurred with the philosophers following Kant who saw purpose as part of the essence of all things. Through science, I saw that purpose is organized in at least five space-time dimensions, and I summarized my view in the following chart:

Purpose	Essence	Dimensions of space-time	Manifest power	Prototypical expressions
Open	Emergent Whole Possible	Infinite Transcendent Beyond space-time Fifth dimension	Appreciation	Potential Ideals Meaning
Permeable	Dynamic Relative Probable	The ever-present now Transformative Cyclical Fourth dimension	Influence	Intents Values Relations
Closed	Statis Real Certain	Past, present, future Formative Duration Third dimension	Control	Ends Goals Means

Table 12.1 The essence and manifestation of purpose (adapted from chapter 5, "The Creative Power")

I was surprised, though, that no one had actually said or written that *purpose is the source of power*. Dr. Martin Luther King Jr. came the closest when he said, "Power properly understood is nothing but the ability to achieve purpose." In dealing with poverty and rural development, this idea was huge. Ultimately, power does come from people. *Anyone, no matter how poor or rich, who has a purpose has power—the bigger the purpose, the bigger the power.*

Design is the process of converting purpose into power. Having *control* over resources is the most traditional view of the power or capacity to achieve purpose. *Influence* is a less certain but more extensive form of power. *Appreciation* is the lightest form of power but is practically limitless in its availability. It is the power that comes from understanding the situation in all its aspects. In 1980, the World Bank published a paper covering the diagnosis, recommendations, and new framework based on the three power relationships, appreciation, influence ad control (AIC); it was titled "The Design of Organizations for Rural Development," Staff Working Paper 375. It was regarded as a breakthrough in thinking by the three major Global Centers of Rural Development[2] and sold more copies than any of the bank's previous 374 in the series. There was clearly a latent need for concepts and practices that could deal with the possibilities, realities, and tensions between purpose and power. The ideas proved very attractive and useful in practice and spread rapidly through specially designed workshops. We used role-playing in which we simulated the three environments of a project. We gave participants roles, for example, of peasants, business owners, government departments, priests, NGOs, political parties, and radical social groups. We tried to represent all the values and powers—not just the economic ones—that influenced or needed to be appreciated by project planners.

We took what we learned from these simulations and began to apply it directly to bank work. The work advanced through ever-increasing levels: from project to sector to country to region and eventually to the global level. The AIC power approach was used to evaluate the role of the World Bank and the three other Regional Development Banks, generating the global conference "New Paradigm for Development."[3] The first full-scale project using the AIC approach was carried out at the sector level to solve the problems of the economic collapse of the electricity sector in Colombia. During the 1980s, the Colombian electricity sector was buffeted by adversity: worldwide recession, devaluation of the peso, and a lower rate of demand than forecast. The sector was spending an unsustainable 40 percent of GDP to the detriment of all other sectors. The paper, "Planning for the Electricity Sector in Colombia" (Smith 1985), describes the use of the AIC power concepts to tackle the issue from a higher level of purpose and to create new flows of power. Implementation resolved the key issues, and a ten-year program that extended to the entire energy sector was launched. In addition, it influenced the progress in other key sectors. In brief, we accomplished this by taking the following steps.

1. *Raising the Level of Purpose*
   We deliberately elevated the level of purpose in the conference by visualizing the electricity sector's problems as those of the whole Colombian economy. In an idealization, exercise participants were asked to play the role of concerned Colombian citizens rather than their normal sector roles. The electricity sector was figuratively destroyed, and the participants were asked to produce the best design possible for the future of their country within the next twenty-four hours.

2. *Using All Levels of Power*
   Some sixty participants attended the workshop, drawn from a bipartisan list to represent all three system levels. From the national policy level came the sponsoring agencies: Mines and Energy, Planning, Finance, and academics from local universities specializing in energy policy (appreciated environment). From the influence level, we drew heads and key staff of energy subsectors like coal and oil (influenced environment). Key power-sector institutions represented the subordinate level: major cities and regional utilities (controlled environment). Several congressmen and senators represented consumers. In addition, academics and consultants with knowledge of the sector were invited. Three World Bank and Inter-American Development Bank staff attended as observers.

3. *Creating a Horizontal Balance of Power*
   The workshop paid equal attention to appreciation, influence, and control means in each phase of the process—that is, to discovery (a), diplomacy (i), and policy (c) in the appreciative phase; to social (a), political (i), and technical (c) in the influence phase; and to learning (a), politics (i), and planning (c) in the control phase. (Note how social, political, and technical values are central to the whole process of design.) (Smith 1985).

The largest application involved an entire country: Thailand. The paper, "Building Partnerships between Government and Civil Society"

(Furugganan and Lopez 2002), showed how the usage of the overlapping influence and appreciated environments of projects can meet ever-larger purposes. It demonstrated that the creation of rapid, low-cost, self-organizing development that spreads from rural development to urban development, health, forestry, education, and even constitutional change is possible. The process used was very simple:

1. The principal activities in this project were village-level workshops, district-level synthesis workshops, and a training of trainers. These master trainers then carried out an initial round of workshops in sixteen villages to test and refine the workshop process into a standard process for use in the remaining villages. Each workshop lasted two and a half days. This process was subsequently compiled and published as a handbook for community-development workers. Two or three facilitators conducted each workshop, while one researcher observed, gathered data, and evaluated outcomes. The specific content of the workshops was divided into three sessions:

   a. *Village development experiences*: Villagers, particularly elders, describe their experience with village development, milestone events, and changing social and environmental conditions over the years. The workshop then divides into focus groups (women, men, youth) to describe in words and drawings the development and conditions of the village in the past and then in the present.

   b. *The ideal, or "developed," village*: The focus groups then discuss the ideal state of their developed village and the problems that need to be overcome to achieve this ideal state. They then sketch their individual pictures of the ideal village, share the pictures with the group, and sketch a common-vision picture that incorporates the ideal visions of each participant. Each participant then proposes several development activities or projects that would lead the village toward the ideal state. The large group then discusses, negotiates, and prioritizes the activities.

c. *Action planning*: The workshop participants review and agree on the common vision and the prioritized activities and break into groups to develop action plans for particular activities that the group will be responsible for (MacNeil 1999).

The research effort came full circle when the team decided to look at the whole of the international development system. Those in Japan, Europe, Africa, Latin America, the United States, and Scandinavia had evaluated the results of four decades of development assistance. They agreed that the current system, having accumulated some $1.5 trillion in debt, had not produced results commensurate with the resources expended. More needed to be done with a lot less. The Norwegians took the lead in providing the initial funding for the project; they had been most affected by Trist's work. They knew about self-help, reliance, quality of work life, and empowerment. For example, through the Volvo experiments, autonomous work groups replaced the assembly line; and through action research with the Merchant Navy, they created a more democratic organization for the navy. The effort brought together ten developing countries. Their efforts were focused on three strategic clusters of questions aimed at how to accomplish the following:

1. Design learning institutions and processes that can change the attitudes and mind-sets of those still caught in the old paradigm.
2. Ensure the necessary shifts in priorities, roles, and responsibilities that will produce more holistic, sustainable development.
3. Procure financial support for the use of democratic processes for full involvement.

The chart in figure 12.1, taken from the New Paradigm project, illustrates how the concept of power enlarged the socio-technical perspective that guided the discussions. The process and results are presented in the paper "The New Development Paradigm" (2002).

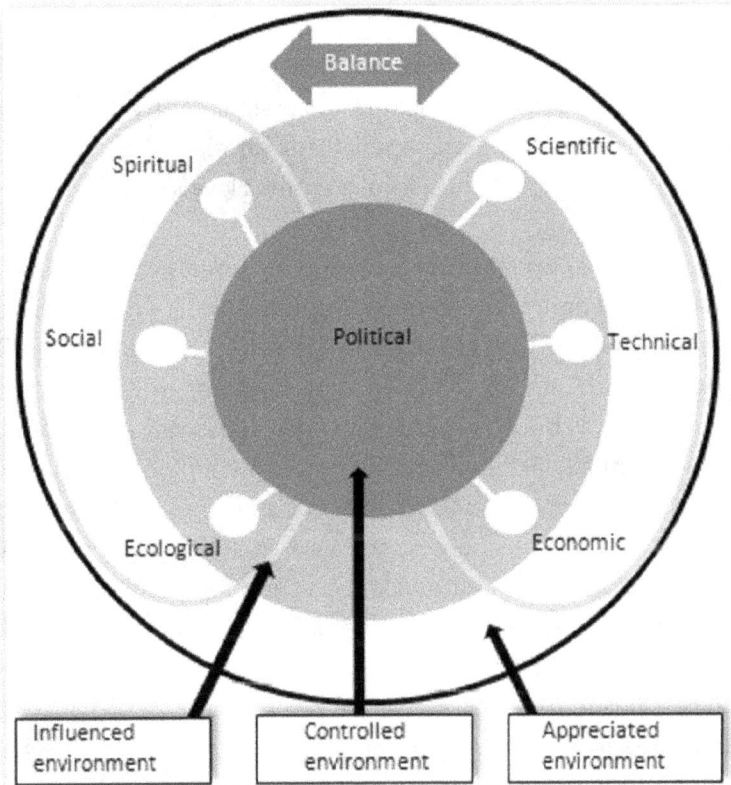

Figure 12.1 The New Development paradigm

THEORETICAL ROOTS

The roots of the AIC approach go deep into the origin of the social sciences, beginning with Kurt Lewin's famous equation B=f(P, E)—*Behavior is a function of the person and the environment.* At that time, Lewin was emphasizing the role of the present situation as opposed to the past in determining behavior. AIC, building on Emery and Trist's notion of three environments, shows that the person/environment relationships are power relationships derived from purpose. So B=f (P (A+I+C))—*the behavior of individuals, organizations, or communities is a function of their purpose manifested as their capacity for appreciation, influence, and control.* This treatment of the individual, the organization, and the community as a single system goes back to Talcott Parsons's specific insight in *Structure and Process in Modern Society* (1960): Organizations consist of a hierarchical or vertical dimension of nested technical (*control*), managerial (*influence*), and institutional levels (*appreciative*). In AIC, this vertical level becomes levels of purpose:

1. *Appreciative* purposes are open ends, *ideals*, that serve all people everywhere for all time (institutional level). They are future oriented. The concept of ideals, in this sense, is derived from Russell Ackoff and Emery's *On Purposeful Systems* (1972), in which they see ideals as purposes that we can successively approximate but never actually achieve and so are permanently open.
2. *Influence* purposes are relative ends, *values*, that are shared by interest groups and are conditional in space and time (managerial—mediating institutional, social, and technical concerns). They operate in the present and mediate between future possibilities and the realities of the past.
3. *Control* purposes are closed ends, *goals* that apply to specific individuals in fixed space and time (technical level). They rely more on learning from past experience.

AIC theory extends our understanding of nested levels of hierarchy by adding the concept of dimensions. Each level becomes a new dimension with an exponential increase in power:

1. The outcome, or *end*, of a purpose is the first dimension. In practice, it is our simplest form of organization: making a list—a one-dimensional line of things to do.
2. The second dimension is the *means* we use to obtain the outcome. We can now make a matrix consisting of the things we want and the different means we can use to acquire them.

3. To select from the matrix of ends and means that we will actually do, we need a *goal* perspective—a third dimension—to help us deal with our limits of time, space, and available resources.
4. Many goals we pursue are too large and complex for us to achieve on our own, so we need a yet higher level of purpose to harmonize our different goals. We use our *values*—a fourth dimension—that allow us to change and modify our choice of goals as time, conditions, and interests change.
5. To overcome value differences, we need purposes that all people can espouse—that is, *ideals* that appeal to everyone, everywhere, regardless of time or space. These provide our fifth dimension. They give us meaning that transcends differences of value, goals. or available means.

The Colombia case mentioned earlier shows quite dramatically how seemingly intractable problems were overcome by designing a process that consciously moved upward through these levels of purpose. Together these purpose and power insights give us a new definition of systems that has its design principles built in: *A system is the set of all relationships that affect or are affected by the pursuit of purpose. The boundaries of the system are determined by what the system can control, influence, and appreciate within the space and time constraints in which the purpose is conceived.*

In practice, we center our design process in influence. From current tensions, we create conditions in which we can examine future possibilities safely without fear of ridicule or pressure to meet current constraints. We spend equal time and give equal priority to the process for doing the following:

1. Appreciating future possibilities and reinterpreting the past in the light of those possibilities. We coax out latent needs primed for full expression. We appreciate by not allowing influence or control.
2. Exploring the primary sources of influence that would advance or constrain achievement of our purpose. We appreciate and influence, but we don't control. We evaluate (i.e., draw value out of the exploration of many paths) but do not yet choose one.

3. Allowing those with responsibility to make the best use of the information they have gained though appreciation and influence. In effect, they complete the process in reverse. Using all three powers, they decide what they will control or commit to. They identify whom they need to influence and what they believe others need to appreciate about their situation.

4. Using this information to return to the center of engagement and beginning the process all over again. Improvement of the engagement process provides the center of the organizing process.

In practice, the process not only reverses the problem of two-thirds of such projects failing, but it causes such projects to create benefits that are at least three times those planned. It achieves this in three ways:

1. It prevents the implementation of projects that don't have the power to succeed. It uses a process of increasing circles of influence to move toward a desired purpose. For example, it can begin with a few people who have an idea. They go through a mini-AIC process to identify those who might be able to advance the project. Before assembling the next circle of influence, they ensure that the cost of convening the next circle of influence is covered at least three times over by the benefits the participants will receive from their engagement. For example, this might be an introduction to new ways of thinking or practice, opportunities to participate professionally in a project, or forming or strengthening valued relationships. The process stops at any iteration in which it becomes obvious that the group does not have the influence to engage the required stakeholders. It can also end when those invited cannot say that the cost of their participation is covered at least three times by the benefits they obtain from participation.

2. The overlapping circles of influence and appreciation that are created during the project implementation become leveraged vehicles for unanticipated change and benefits. For example, the head of a large retail firm attending the Columbia Electricity

Sector workshop directly initiated the process for his own company, which was suffering economically for the same reasons the electricity sector was failing. His own employees ran the process to devise a way to deal with a downsizing that would save the company and look after those employees who would lose their jobs in a better way, more tailored to their unique needs.

3. The evaluation process does not wait until the end of the project but is built *into* the process so that it improves as it goes along or determines that the conditions no longer support the project's purpose. If so, it enables leadership to find a way either to repurpose the project or bring it to an end.

CONCLUSION

AIC grew from the constructive forces released by reactions of the post-WWII world. We can do better, and we have all the fruits of burgeoning science and technology to help us. In particular, we became aware, for the first time, that the way we design the human and social part of our systems is at least equal to the technical.

This was the time when the collapse of the Soviet Union brought an end to the belief in the efficacy of centrally organized and controlled five-year plans. You could no longer plan *for* people. You had to plan *with* them, and people had to plan also *for* themselves.

AIC grew from the realization that we needed new concepts of power to fulfill these dreams and chose to make its contribution in the area most needed: solving problems of poverty through rural development. Much of our world has learned to add influence to control to leverage its ability to achieve its purposes. However, we have not yet learned, on a large scale, how to add appreciation to influence and control. The result is that most of the great problems of our time stem from an excess of influence for control. We have learned to use our influence to hide information, distort it, and lie about it in the attempt to control through influence. We can see the result in the widening income gap in almost all countries, and gridlock in our political systems, endemic abuse of power and corruption in our institutions and corporations. The good news, in spite of all this, is that we are making progress. In spite of the two-thirds failure rate in projects, things still get done. We do get better. We do so because all of us as individuals try in some way to make the best of the situations we find ourselves in. We are the *Wisdom of the Crowds* (Surowiecki 2002). It is through each of us that things improve.

Successful appreciation is based on the inclusion of the whole—all of us. The biggest issues of our time—poverty, health, energy, abuse of power—cannot be addressed unless we all do our part. We can do this if we, in our own worlds, use appreciation, influence, and control equally. After all, appreciation costs nothing, is infinitely available, and nobody can stop us from doing it.

So how do we add the appreciative level? We acknowledge that appreciation is required for every purpose at every level. For example, we add appreciation as follows:

1. At the practical, operational level by understanding the effects of implementation on all those affected by what we implement
2. At the strategic, influence level by examining the positive and negative effects of all options before limiting ourselves to those options we act on
3. At the design or appreciative level when we extend the current space-time frame beyond that which we can control or influence and are guided by our ideals during that process

Although writing about these changes and ideas is helpful, we will not leverage change until we can demonstrate the results in a large enough setting that has global connections. The ideal project to provide this leverage and show the possibilities for such an evolution of power is what I call "Project 300." It should engage a region of at least one million people in tackling the major issues it faces:

1. It will engage 100 percent of the people, at least at the appreciative level, who affect or are affected by the project's purpose.

2. It will draw on 100 percent of all the power created by those purposes—what each purpose controls, what it influences, and what it needs to appreciate.
3. It will use 100 percent of the leadership capacity available by engaging with everyone affected as a leader operating within her or his own center of influence.

In summary, the addition of power to the design of socio-technical systems led not only to a means for the resolution of differences of value between social and technical actors but also a vertical resolution of difference in levels of purpose—between long-term, open-system, appreciative purposes (ideals and short-term, closed-system purposes [goals]).

REFERENCES:

Brown, J. A. C. 1954. *The Social Psychology of Industry: Human Relations in the Factory.* Harmondsworth, Middlesex, England: Penguin Books.

Emery, F. E., and E. L. Trist. 1965. "The Causal Texture of Organizational Environments." *Human Relations* 1 (1): 21–32). London: Tavistock Publications.

Furugganan, B., and M. Lopez. 2002. *Building Partnerships between Government and Civil Society: The Role of ODII and AIC.* Asian Institute of Management and Synergos Institute. Makati City, Philippines, and New York. http://aic-3.com/papers/Building_Partnerships_AIC_in_Thailand.pdf.

King, M. L. 1968. "Sermon: The Drum-Major Instinct." Ebenezer Baptist Church, Atlanta.

MacNeil, D. J. 1999. *The AIC Process: Generating Shared Visions for Community Development in Southeast Asia. Center for International Education.* djmacnei@educ.umass.edu.

Parsons, T. 1960. *Structure and Process in Modern Societies.* Glencoe: The Free Press.

Sato, T., and Smith, W. E. 1993. "The New Development Paradigm: Organizing for Implementation," in *New Paradigms and Principles for the Twenty-First Century* Jo Marie Griesgraber and B. J. Gunter (eds.). 1996._http://aic-3.com/papers/Development_paradigm.pdf.

Smith, W. E. 2009. *The Creative Power: Transforming Ourselves, Our Organizations, and Our World.* London and New York: Routledge.

Smith, W. E. 1985. "Planning for the Electricity Sector in Colombia," chapter 17 in *Discovering Common Ground: How Future Search Conferences Bring People Together to Achieve Breakthrough Innovation, Empowerment, Shared Vision, and Collaboration.* Weisbord, M.R. (1992). San Francisco: Berrett-Koehler. http://aic-3.com/papers/Colombia_for_printing_in_color.pdf

Smith, W. E., F. Lethem, and B. A. Thoolen. 1980. *The Design of Organizations for Rural Development.* Staff Working Paper 375. World Bank. http://aic3.com/papers/Design_for_Organization_of_Rural_Development.pdf

Surowiecki, J. 2004. *The Wisdom of Crowds: Why the Many Are Smarter Than the Few and How Collective Wisdom Shapes Business, Economies, Societies, and Nations.* New York, NY: Anchor Books.

Thomson, J. D. 1967. *Organizations in Action.* . New York, NY: McGraw-Hill.

Vickers, G. 1965. *The Art of Judgment.* London: Chapman and Hall.

Thirteen

Evolving Socio-technical Perspectives on Human Factors and Safety

ERIC-HANS KRAMER AND MATTHIJS MOORKAMP

INTRODUCTION

Traditionally, safety science has been dominated by engineering disciplines. Even the study of "human factors" has predominantly been the concern of engineering psychology. Approaches that were focused on the influence of the organizational dynamics on safety issues have either lived a life on the fringes of safety science or have lived a life outside safety science altogether. However, during the past decade, attention for the dynamics in socio-technical systems has increased concurrently with interest in mainstream safety science. Currently, there are different approaches that focus on the relationship between organizational dynamics and safety. Therefore, "evolving socio-technical perspectives on human factors and safety" can be identified.

However, the landscape constituted by these perspectives is shattered and complicated. The perspectives sometimes explicitly claim to develop an understanding of socio-technical systems. However, notwithstanding the occasional reference to the earliest work of Emery and Trist, they sometimes seem unaware of a socio-technical tradition in the first place. Furthermore, rather than being aware of each other's existence, the perspectives sometimes contradict each other or talk at cross-purposes. The goal of this chapter is to develop insight in the landscape of evolving socio-technical perspectives on human factors and safety. This goal is achieved by describing five of these perspectives.

These perspectives—Normal Accidents Theory (NAT), High Reliability Theory (HRT), the Swiss Cheese Model, Resilience Engineering (RE), and Macroergonomics—are discussed next. First we specify the background of the current interest in "complex socio-technical systems." It should be noted that a short overview like this cannot do justice to the full complexity of the field of emerging approaches, and not every relevant theorist is discussed. Particularly, the works of Diana Vaughan, Mathilde Bourrier, and Gudela Grote are missing from this overview.

SAFETY AND THE RELEVANCE OF "COMPLEX SOCIO-TECHNICAL SYSTEMS"

After the realization that accidents predominantly do not result from the failure of single (technical) components or a straightforward "human error" but instead occur in "complex systems," attention for "socio-technical systems" in safety science has been developing. This makes the analysis of accidents much more complicated and has led to attention for the influence of organizational contexts. This particular way of thinking has become part of the mainstream within safety science after Rasmussen (1997) raised a number of important issues. Rasmussen explicitly claimed that the object of study within safety science should be "complex socio-technical systems" as opposed to static systems.

According to Rasmussen (1997 p.186), a problem in understanding systems is this: "Compared to the stable conditions of the past, the present dynamic society brings with it some dramatic changes in the conditions of industrial risk management." So far, attempts at modeling socio-technical systems have come up short, according to Rasmussen, because they failed to capture the dynamic characteristics of such systems (Rasmussen 1997, 187): "While a system traditionally is modeled by decomposition into structural elements, the dynamic behavior of systems and actors is modeled by decomposition of the behavioral flow into events....The problem is that all work situations leave many degrees of freedom to the actors for choice of means and time for action, even when the objectives of work are fulfilled and a task instruction or standard operating procedure in terms of a sequence of acts cannot be used as a reference of judging behavior" (emphasis in original).

In other words, "socio-technical systems" are characterized by a specific dynamic: task descriptions are necessarily underspecified, never followed to the letter, and dynamic behavior is always under the influence of unpredictable contingencies. Rasmussen concludes that (1997, 190) "It is evident that a new approach to representation of system behavior is necessary, not focused on human errors and violations, but on the mechanisms generating behavior in the actual, dynamic work context."

Particularly, RE is an approach that contributes to these issues, as is also discussed in chapter 14 of this book. However, distinct from Rasmussen's theoretical elaborations, NAT and HRT already developed safety perspectives that aimed at understanding how accidents can happen in complex systems. Furthermore, in a technical discipline like ergonomics, socio-technical ideas had already been applied for more than fifteen years.

NORMAL ACCIDENTS THEORY

Perrow (1999) developed the Normal Accidents Theory (NAT) to make a specific point: Accidents can occur without major technical failure or human error. NAT aims to develop a theoretical logic that can explain how large "system accidents" can occur as a result of a cascade of smaller prosaic technical or human errors (Perrow 2004). According to NAT, characteristics of the system in which these prosaic errors occur determine whether a cascade will occur. According to NAT, certain systems are fundamentally uncontrollable. In such systems, accidents are "normal" in the sense that they are the inevitable result of the system's characteristics.

Central in NAT are two dimensions—"interaction" and "coupling"—that can be used to describe systems. *Interaction* refers to the way elements in a system influence each other. *Linear interaction* refers to a system functioning in the way it had been designed. In contrast, a system characterized by *complex interaction* is faced with unpredicted interactions among parts of the system. *Coupling* refers to the specific way parts of the system are interdependent. *Loose coupling* means that subsystems can operate relatively independently. *Tight coupling* refers to a situation in which each subsystem has a significant influence on others: a "failure" in one subsystem has a direct and major impact on the functioning of another subsystem. Tight coupling is a broadly defined concept and can refer to different phenomena. It can, for example, refer to minimal time lag between processes, to a fixed sequence in processing, and to little slack in systems (Shrivastava et.al 2011, 360).

According to Perrow (1999), systems that have to deal with complex interactions and are characterized by tight coupling suffer from a control dilemma. Complex interaction means that a system is faced with many unpredictable disturbances from the environment that can impact different organizational parts. Within such systems, decentralization is the most appropriate way of managing because local problem solving avoids the spread of disturbances. However, when a system is tightly coupled, NAT claims that centralization is most appropriate. After all, in this case, the dependencies among system elements are not clear at decentralized positions. A system characterized by both "complex interaction and tight coupling" suffers therefore from incompatible demands for control (Sagan 1993, 40). These incompatible demands for control cause such accidents in such systems to eventually become "normal." For example, Snook (2000) applied NAT by tracing a specific cause for a "friendly fire" incident in Iraq back to the complex network of organizational units that operated in an uncertain environment. NAT has been criticized for its loosely defined central concepts. In fact, Perrow (2004) himself has called NAT a "sensitizing concept." The academic discussion about NAT can best be described in relation to its counterpart, HRT.

HIGH RELIABILITY THEORY

High Reliability Theory (HRT) can be regarded as a response to NAT. When certain systems inevitably collapse at a given point, why aren't there more accidents? Could there perhaps be something that keeps systems afloat in spite of complex interaction and tight coupling? Organizations that maintain a high level of reliability, despite working with hazardous technology or in complex environments, are called High Reliability Organizations (HROs). The study of HROs is expected to reveal "sources of reliability" that keep systems afloat (la Porte and Rochlin 1994, 222). The kinds of organizations studied by HRT are aircraft carriers (Weick and Roberts 1993), submarines (Bierly and Spender 1995), air traffic control systems (la Porte 1988), and nuclear facilities (Perin 2006). These are organizations in which reliability is of utmost importance and in which accidents can have major consequences. The academic debate between NAT and HRT began around 1990 (Rijpma 1997, Shrivastava et.al. 2009).

Although HRT started with the study of remarkably reliable organizations—often in quite stable conditions—in a next phase of its development, HRT has sought theoretical underpinning in the organizational theory provided by Weick (Weick et al. 1999). Within this logic, organizations are confronted with "the unexpected" and need a "cognitive infrastructure" that enables them to deal with this. Important in this respect is the concept of "mindfulness": "By mindfulness we mean the combination of ongoing scrutiny of existing expectations, continuous refinement, and differentiation of expectations based on newer experiences, willingness and capability to invent new expectations that make sense of unexpected events, a more nuanced appreciation of context and ways to deal with it, and identification of new dimensions of context that improve foresight and current functioning" (Weick and Sutcliffe 2001, 42, emphasis in original). The well-known "HRO principles" are a further operationalization of the concept "mindfulness" (Weick et al. 1999). These are preoccupation with failure, reluctance to simplify, sensitivity to operations, commitment to resilience, and deference to expertise. HRT tends to focus on groups of operators at the lowest hierarchical level in organizations and is often related to subtle group dynamics related to mindfulness.

According to HRT, NAT has overlooked these "sources of reliability." Another critique voiced by HRT on NAT is that tight coupling is not a static property of systems. Certain dynamics can change the way parts of organizations are coupled. This makes the issue of "tight coupling" more complicated: What seems safe loosely coupled can suddenly become (unexpectedly) tightly coupled. A critique often voiced against HRT is that it is "too optimistic" (Sagan 1993) and that it is so focused on inter-actions within teams of operators that it overlooks the influence of struc-tural design on these interactions, which is a criticism on Weick's work in general (Taylor and Van Every 2000, 251). One reason this polemic has persisted might be that contrasting NAT and HRT is a useful rhetori-cal strategy to make a sketch of the academic field of the organizational approaches to safety.

SWISS CHEESE MODEL

The two approaches discussed above both originate in organizational science. The approach discussed here originates from psychology. James Reason is a psychologist who, after developing a theory on human error (Reason 1990), proceeded to develop a theory of systems in which these errors occur. The Swiss Cheese Model on organizational accidents dis-plays his thinking.

Reason explicates his system perspective as follows (2008 93): "For me, though not for all, a system perspective is any accident explana-tion that goes beyond the local events to find contributory factors in the workplace, the organization, and the system as a whole. The essence of such a view is that frontline personnel are not so much the instigators of a bad event; rather, they are the inheritors of latent conditions (or resident pathogens) that may have been accumulating for a long time previously." The Swiss Cheese Model captures this perspective: Barriers (slices of cheese) are supposed to prevent a hazard from developing into an accident. Due to "active failures" and "latent conditions," the slices of cheese have holes in them. If holes in different barriers "line up" (if different barriers fail to counter a certain hazard), an accident trajec-tory can pass through the system (Reason 2008, 101). These holes are not "fixed" but "dynamic"—they open, close, and shift around (Reason

1997, 9), making safety a "dynamic nonevent" (Reason 1997, 37): "What produces the stable outcome is constant change rather than continuous repetition."

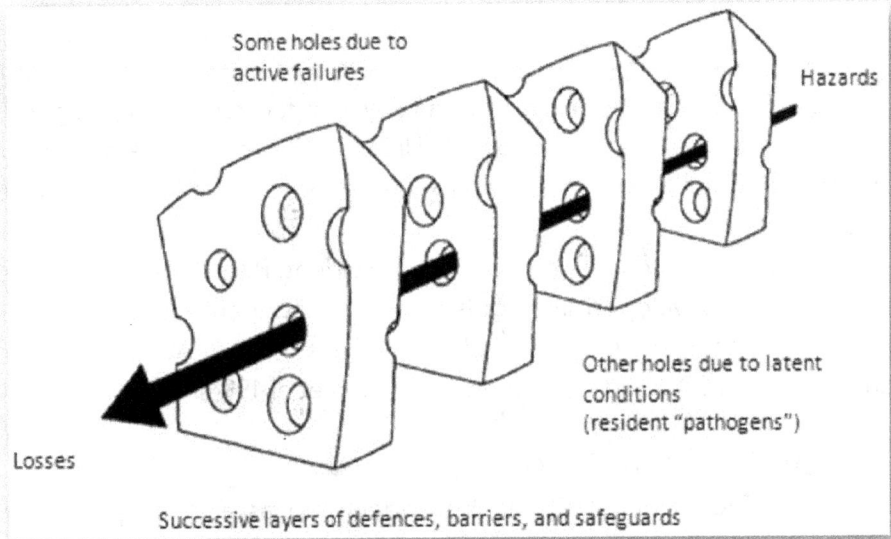

Figure 13.1. Swiss Cheese Model (from *Reason*, 2008, 102)

Active failures are "unsafe acts" performed by the personnel "at the sharp end" (Reason 1997, 10). Such acts can erode barriers and are likely to have a direct effect on safety. Reason recognizes fallibility as part of the human condition and his system perspective aims to move beyond referring only to the unsafe acts of operators. This is where the "latent conditions" come in to play (Reason 1997, 10):

Latent conditions are to technological organizations what resident pathogens are to the human body. Like pathogens, latent conditions—such as poor design, gaps in supervision, undetected manufacturing defects or maintenance failures, unworkable procedures, clumsy automation, shortfalls in training, and less than adequate tools and equipment—may be present for many years before they combine with local circumstances and active failures to penetrate the system's many layers of defense. They arise from strategic and other top-level decisions made by governments, regulators, manufacturers, designers, and organizational managers.

Reason's model therefore explains accidents by supposing an interplay among local hazards, active failures, and system failures (badly designed barriers or barriers that have eroded). Unlike HRT and NAT, Reason lacks an organizational theory. As such, Reason's model might be considered as an heuristic tool to think about how certain conditions, failures, and systemic issues can combine to cause an accident. Reason's way of thinking has been developed into tools to analyze accidents—for example, Human Factor Analysis and Classification System, or HFACS (Wiegman and Shappell 2003) and Tripod Delta (Hudson et al 1994).

RESILIENCE ENGINEERING

Resilience Engineering (RE) can be understood as a development of the issues raised by Rasmussen (1997). RE tries to develop a theoretical account of the dynamics in socio-technical systems and focuses on developing methods for modeling them. Furthermore, it tries to move away from a limited perspective on human error and technical malfunctions. According to RE, socio-technical systems need to "recognize, adapt to, and absorb variations, changes and disturbances, disruptions, and surprises—especially disruptions that fall outside of the set of disturbances the system is designed to handle" (Hollnagel et al. 2006, 3).

RE has developed a critique on Reason's Swiss Cheese Model. Although Reason's system perspective also aims at looking further than immediate failures, RE claims that operators are still implicitly blamed in his approach (Woods et al. 2010). This has to do with the way Reason perceives organizations.

Thinking in terms of barriers suggests that an organization needs to be protected from failing human beings (Hollnagel et al. 2006, 4). According to RE, this underestimates the true complexity of everyday work in organizations. Operators are frequently—and necessarily—confronted with a gap between procedures and a complex, uncertain reality (Dekker 2005, 133). Operators need to find ways to ensure reliability in spite of it (Dekker 2005, 141), which is the essence of "normal work." For maintaining reliability, it can be essential that operators do not follow rules to the letter. Reason's perspective suggests that either such operators commit "rule violations" or barriers are imperfect.

Neither is true for RE: The gap necessarily exists in a complex world, and specifically operators need to deal with it. This puts the generally accepted insight that 70 to 80 percent of accidents are caused by human error in a different perspective. Instead, 70 to 80 percent of the accidents might be caused by leaky organizational systems that operators kept afloat until the breaking point.

Another important theme in RE is the modeling of dynamics in sociotechnical systems. Functional Resonance Analysis Method (FRAM) represents such an attempt (Hollnagel 2012). Accidents are, in Hollnagel's view, "emergent" phenomena. This means that something happens that cannot be explained using the principles of decomposition and causality (2012, 25). This "intractability" is considered typical for complex sociotechnical systems. It is this dynamic of emergence that Hollnagel aims to capture with his FRAM model. What's typical of FRAM is a move away from analyzing "structures" in favor of analyzing "functions." A description on the basis of functions is supposed to lead to a description of what a system "does" instead of what it "is" (2012, 7). A function refers to the activities that are required to produce outcomes (Hollnagel 2012, 40). Typical of functions in socio-technical systems is their variability. "Functional resonance" refers to a phenomenon in which variability of different functions mutually influence or reinforce one another. If functions "resonate," they have become intertwined (possibly in an unpredictable way), and they can tumble each other over like domino stones. This explains for Hollnagel the way in which complex socio-technical systems can display behavior that is not "designed" and how accidents can emerge.

Quite clearly, FRAM resembles NAT: Unpredictable interactions between system elements (complex interactions) can lead to accidents if they influence each other (tight coupling). Nevertheless, FRAM has some distinctive features, which makes it different from NAT or STS-D. It seems that FRAM is based on an "either/or" idea regarding the description of systems: Either you study "structures" interpreted as fixed aspects of systems, or you study system dynamics. This differs fundamentally from the STS-D perspective: Indeed the dynamic aspects of system behavior are crucial for understanding organizations (and accidents), but the organizational structure influences "dynamic behavior." One of the goals of STS-D is to design organizations in a way that they are less vulnerable to "interference" or in a way that they can "attenuate" complexity (Achterbergh and Vriens 2010). Therefore, Moorkamp et al. (2014) conclude that "Due to this inconsistent application of systems-theoretical concepts and assumptions, resilience engineering theory is unable to address the relationship between organizational design strategy and safety." If Hollnagel advises researchers to turn their backs on organizational structures, he misses a crucial influence on the very behavior that he aims to understand.

MACROERGONOMICS

Macroergonomics is a subdiscipline of ergonomics with a focus on how organizational characteristics influence work-systems (Carayon and Smith 2000, 649–50). Macroergonomics is different from the approaches that have been discussed above. First, macroergonomics is independent from the approaches discussed above. Second, macroergonomics is not exclusively focused on safety but also on occupational health. Third, in contrast to the approaches discussed above, macroergonomics explicitly refers to the socio-technical tradition. In fact, socio-technical insights constitute its contribution to the field of ergonomics. The discussion here is specifically focused on reconstructing this socio-technical core, specifically brought forward by Hendrick (2007).

Within ergonomics, Hendrick (2007, 45–46) identifies a development from microergonomics via cognitive ergonomics to macroergonomics.

Microergnomics focuses on the design of human-machine interfaces and physical environmental factors affecting performance. It draws its insights from the traditional topics of engineering psychology (perception, learning, response time, etc.). Cognitive ergonomics came into focus after the development of information technology indicated different kinds of human-system interface problems. The emphasis of cognitive ergonomics is "on how humans think and process information and how to design software to dialogue with humans in the same manner" (Hendrick 2007, 46). Macroergonomics is a development that started at the end of the 1970s (Hendrick 2007, 46): "Ergonomists began to realize that they could effectively design human-machine, human-environment, and human-software interfaces and still have a poorly designed work system." Attention for wider influences from the organizational system as a whole seemed warranted. The subsequent development of macroergonomics is "soundly grounded in both empirically developed and validated socio-technical systems theory and general systems theory" (Hendrick 2007, 49).

Theoretically, the socio-technical theme of "joint optimization" is brought forward. Hendrick (2007, 52) signals three dysfunctional design practices for work systems:

1. Technology-centered design—Incorporating a technology in a piece of hardware before human factors/ergonomic aspects are considered
2. A "leftover" approach to function and task allocation. If a technology is designed without regard to the work system in which it will operate, to the characteristics of the workforce who need to operate it, and to the environmental factors impacting it, a badly designed work-system results, which does not make effective use of its workforce.
3. Failure to consider the system's socio-technical characteristics.

With this, Hendrick refers to the problem that four relevant elements of socio-technical systems are impacting each other: the technological subsystem, personnel subsystem, external environment, and organizational design of the work system. If only the technological subsystem is taken into account in the design of a work system, suboptimalization is often the result.

Designing work systems begins—top-down—by taking key organization design dimensions into account (Hendrick 2007, 54). Generally, Hendrick emphasizes how greater differentiation in the organizational structure creates a greater need for integration mechanisms, creating greater complexity of the organization structure. This limits discretion at the level of individual operators and has to be weighed against the potential advantages of specialization (Hendrick 2007, 55). Furthermore, Hendrick points to formalization as a relevant dimension of organization design. Hendrick (2007 p. 56) emphasizes that ergonomists can influence the degree of formalization by designing jobs, machines, and software in a way—for cases of low formalization—that work systems allow for considerably greater use of human resources, which in turn makes jobs intrinsically more motivating. Finally, Hendrick (2007) emphasizes centralization as a relevant design dimension, which affects the influence employees or lower-level supervisors have on decisions affecting their jobs. Given these essentials, Hendrick (2007) discusses a few methods to analyze work-systems—for example, Macroergonomic Analysis of Structure (MAS), Macroergonomic Analysis and Design (MEA), antropotechnology, Organizational Requirements Definition for Information Technology (ORDIT), and participatory ergonomics.

Quite clearly, familiar socio-technical themes return in macroergonomics. At its core lie ideas that are directly related to the earliest socio-technical insights, particularly "joint optimization" and "humanization." Later developments in STS-D, particularly the worked-out structural design theory, do not seem to be a part of macroergonomics. Macroergonomics shows that socio-technical ideas can be of value, even in the inner reaches of what is regarded as a technologically focused discipline.

CONCLUSION

Every organization can be regarded as a socio-technical system, but not every organization is studied using insights from the socio-technical tradition (Pasmore 1988). The evolving perspectives on human factors and safety that have been discussed indeed view organizations as socio-technical systems that display dynamics that explain the complicated ways in which accidents materialize. However, with the exception of macroergonomics, none of the approaches uses insights from the socio-technical tradition. At best, the insights are loosely related to the socio-technical tradition (NAT and HRT). Furthermore, the different perspectives discussed here conceptualize the dynamic that is typical of socio-technical systems in quite different ways, sometimes using different systems of theoretical underpinnings. For example, at the core of HRT lies a different conceptualization of systems compared to NAT. Instead of focusing on interactions and couplings—or "network characteristics" of systems—HRT theorists tend to focus on "interactions" and sense-making processes. RE uses insights from complexity science to explain the dynamics of emergence.

This is why discussions about the different approaches are sometimes more complicated than the dynamic they want to capture. As said, the landscape of evolving socio-technical perspectives on human factors and safety is scattered and complex. Perhaps the different perspectives each capture a relevant aspect of the dynamics in socio-technical systems. In some systems, different prosaic errors can lead to a cascade, causing "system accidents." Furthermore, interactions between operators are a crucial resource in dealing with "the unexpected," and the essence of "normal work" of operators might indeed be bridging the gap between organizational procedures and unexpected dynamics. However, combined, the different approaches do not constitute a coherent perspective. They differ too much in their theoretical underpinnings.

The fact that insights on organizational dynamics are unrelated to the socio-technical tradition is of course not a reason to disqualify them. However, a worked-out STS-D perspective on human factors and safety might help overcome the complicated scattering of insights on the topic. It is not the goal here to work out such a perspective, but the integral perspective on organizations that STS-D has developed offers possibilities. Such a perspective can be developed from a from a fully formed systems-theoretical underpinning. Furthermore, a cohesive theoretical perspective can account for the everyday problems of operators with routine and nonroutine disturbances, as well as the influences of organizational structures on the occurrence of such disturbances in the first place. An STS-D perspective would not predominantly emphasize the importance of structure or the importance of interactions but would emphasize how organization structure influences "interacting operators." Safety in such a perspective is something that is continuously created by operators who fight the forces of entropy (Moorkamp et al. 2014). After all, *emergence* refers to a situation in which "order develops out of chaos," while an *accident* refers to a situation in which an organized coherence is lost. At present, such an STS-D position does not exist, but it seems worthwhile to make the effort to create a cohesive and comprehensive theory.

REFERENCES

Achterbergh, J., and D. Vriens. 2010. *Organizations: Social Systems Conducting Experiments*, second revised ed. Heidelberg: Springer.

Bierly, P. E., and J. C. Spender. 1995. "Culture and High-Reliability organizations: The Case of the Nuclear Submarine." *Journal of Management* 21: 639–56.

Carayon, P., and M. Smith. 2000. "Work Organization and Ergonomics." *Applied Ergonomics* 31: 649–62.

Dekker, S. 2005. *Ten Questions about Human Error: A New View of Human Factors and System Safety.* : Mahwah, NJ: Lawrence Erlbaum Associates

Hendrick, H. 2007. "Macroergonomics: The Analysis and Design of Work Systems." *Reviews of Human Factors and Ergonomics* 3: 44.

Hollnagel, E. 2012. *Fram: The Functional Resonance Analysis Method: Modelling Complex Socio-technical Systems.* Farnham: Ashgate Publishing.

Hollnagel, E., D. D. Woods, and N. Leveson. 2006. *Resilience Engineering: Concepts and Precepts.* Aldershot, United Kingdom: Ashgate Publishing Company.

Hudson, P, M. J. Primrose, and C. Edwards. 1994. "Implementing Tripod-Delta in a Major Contractor" (SPE27302). *Proceedings of the SPE International Conference on Health, Safety, and Environment.* Jakarta, Indonesia. Richardson, Texas: Society of Petroleum Engineers.

la Porte, T. R., and G. Rochlin. 1994. "A Rejoinder to Perrow." *Journal of Contingencies and Crisis Management* 2: 221–7.

Moorkamp, M., E. H. Kramer, C. van Gulijk, and B. J. M. Ale. *Safety Management Theory and the Expeditionary Organization: A Critical Theoretical Reflection. Safety Science* (in press).

Perin, C. 2006. *Shouldering Risks: The Culture of Control in the Nuclear Power Industry.* Princeton, New Jersey: Princeton University Press.

Pasmore, W. A. 1988. *Designing Effective Organizations. The Socio-technical Systems Perspective.* New York: John Wiley and Sons.

Perrow, C. 1999. Normal Accidents. *Living with High-Risk Technologies,* second ed. Princeton, New Jersey: Princeton University Press. First published by Basic Books 1984.

Perrow, C. March 2004. "A Personal Note on Normal Accidents." *Organization and Environment* 17 (1).

Rasmussen, J. 1997. "Risk Management in a Dynamic Society: A Modelling Problem." *Safety Science* 27 (2–3): 183–213.

Reason, J. 1990. *Human Error.* New York: Cambridge University Press.

Reason, J. 1997. *Managing the Risks of Organizational Accidents.* Aldershot: Ashgate Publishing.

Reason, J. 2008. *The Human Contribution. Unsafe Acts, Accidents, and Heroic Recoveries.* Surrey, UK: Ashgate.

Rijpma, J. March 1997. "Complexity, Tight Coupling, and Reliability: Connecting Normal Accidents Theory and High Reliability Theory." *Journal of Contingencies and Crisis Management,* no. 1.

Sagan, S. 1993. *The Limits of Safety. Organizations, Accidents, and Nuclear Weapons.* Princeton, New Jersey: Princeton University Press.

Shrivastava, S., K. Sonpar, and F. Pazzaglia. 2009. "Normal Accident Theory versus High Reliability Theory: A Resolution and Call for an Open-Systems View of Accidents." *Human Relations* 62: 1357–90.

Snook, S. 2000. *Friendly Fire. The Accidental Shootdown of US Black Hawks over Northern Iraq.* Princeton: Princeton University Press.

Taylor, J., and E. van Every. 2000. *The Emergent Organization: Communication as Its Site and Surface.* New York: Psychology Press (Taylor and Francis Group).

Weick, K. E, and K. Roberts. 1993. "Collective Mind in Organizations: Heedful Interrelating on Flight Decks." *Administrative Science Quarterly* 38 (3).

Weick, K. W., K. Sutcliffe, and D. Obstfeld, . 1999. "Organizing for High Reliability: Processes of Collective Mindfulness," in B. Staw and R.I.Suttun (eds). *Research in Organizational Behavior* 21: 81–123). Greenwhich, Conn.: JAI.

Weick, K. E., and K. Sutcliffe. 2001. *Managing the Unexpected: Assuring High Performance in an Age of Complexity.* San Francisco: Jossey-Bass.

Wiegman, D., and S. Shappell. 2003. *A Human Error Approach to Aviation Accident Analysis: The Human Factors Analysis and Classification System.* Aldershot: Ashgate.

Woods, D., S. Dekker, and R. Cook. 2010. *Behind Human Error,* second ed. Farnham: Ashgate Publishing Limited.

Fourteen

Resilience-Centered Approaches for Training Design in an Electric Utility

Mohammed Alfayyoumi, Rocky Sease, and Pamela Ey

INTRODUCTION

High reliability is required in organizations in which high risk and high effectiveness need to coexist. Historically, reliability has often been accompanied by work practices centered on developing and following procedures, with the aim of standardizing work approaches. Also, there has been a work-design trend in North American utility organizations to create and use detailed task lists as a basis for work design. The types of tasks include, for example:

- Direct transmission switching
- Coordinate emergency dispatch of generation

According to a broad consensus in academic literature, this task-based approach does not go far enough toward ensuring safe operation and system reliability. Instead, the nature of the work is nonroutine, characterized mostly by making decisions—not merely by carrying out tasks that adhere to specifications within procedures. Approaches that focus merely on technical skills miss out on crucial dynamics that challenge reliability. We posit an emerging approach for work design in this utility-sector socio-technical-systems context that is informed by the principles of resilience engineering.

Resilience is the ability of systems to survive and return to normal operation despite challenges. Resilience engineering (Hollnagel, Woods, and Leveson 2006) comes primarily from the field of complexity study (Csete and Doyle 2002). Work approaches based on resilience engineering go about creating and maintaining systems—and supporting the people doing the work—to cope and adapt to complex, changing environments. The authors use the following guiding principles for resilience engineering work approaches:

- Job-performance conditions, such as the tasks identified by utilities, are always underspecified because of system complexity. Workers are continuously adapting and adjusting to current demands and resources. These adjustments will always be approximate.
- Some undesired events result from breakage or malfunction of system components. Other bad outcomes stem from unexpected combinations of performance variability. The authors understand performance variability as the ways in which individual and team performance is adjusted in real time to match current demands and resources with the aim of ensuring that things go right—ideally system reliability.
- Safety-focused work practices cannot be based exclusively on hindsight, calculation of failure probabilities, or counting and defending against individual errors.
- System reliability must be achieved by improvements, not just constraints.

Resilience engineering has its roots firmly planted in socio-technical systems (STS) design, which can be traced to the 1949 field studies of British coal miners, conducted by the Tavistock Institute of Human Relations. Based on the field studies, the Tavistock social scientists proposed that no longer would separate approaches to the social and technical dimensions of an organization be a viable solution. Later, in 1983, Calvin

Pava described a socio-technical framework for the dynamics involved in nonroutine work. Consistent with the literature on high-reliability organizations (e.g., Weick and Sutcliffe 1997), Pava emphasized the need for organizational learning. In 1993, Taylor and Fenten extended the work from the Tavistock studies with an examination of socio-technical systems in North American companies. The outcome was a set of principles that apply to both routine and nonroutine work, involving four pillars:

1. Holistic system thinking
2. The power of information
3. Product or throughput focus
4. Organizational purpose

In this chapter we aim to develop an understanding of the crucial dynamics surrounding reliability for Dominion Virginia Power by using concepts from resilience engineering and socio-technical systems design. Subsequently, we describe a process model that integrates core aspects of knowledge management through training in the utility setting. In the final paragraph, we explain how this model is being used within Dominion to develop training.

In this utility case study, the methodological framework presented is a way of building expertise and creating high-reliability work approaches.

THE GRID
The electric power system is the infrastructure that supplies, transmits, and delivers electricity to where it is used. It is a system of systems that includes physical networks like power plants, electric transmission and distribution networks, information and control systems, and networks of regulated relationships. This system of systems is "the grid." The grid is a challenging work environment revolving around complex issues, including integrated management of load and generation and real and reactive power flows. Technical issues and the increasing pace of change pose challenges for legacy grid planning and operational practices. One of

the drivers of change in the US grid is the rapid and increasing deployment of renewable electricity. The Energy Policy Acts of 1992 and 2005, and the resulting diverse industry response in turn, significantly increased the complexity of utility planning and operations. Pending increasing employee retirements pose an ongoing concern that many organizations are currently facing.

The operations work in this case study is that electricity production and demand must be dynamically balanced at all times. This is a real challenge for operation of the power systems because of the variability and uncertainty of load (ratcheted up with the advent of intermittent renewables), as well as equipment failures that can affect the generation and delivery of electricity. There are significant consequences for failure to maintain this dynamic balance—not the least of which is putting customers in the dark.

The North American Electric Reliability Corporation (NERC) defines electric system reliability as "the ability to meet the electricity needs of end-use customers, even when unexpected equipment failures or other factors reduce the amount of available electricity. Maintaining reliability involves ensuring that adequate resources are available to provide customers with a continuous supply of electricity, as well as having the ability to withstand sudden, unexpected disturbances to the electric system" (NERC, n.d.).

Maintaining reliability is a complex enterprise that requires trained and skilled operators, sophisticated computers and communications, and careful planning and design. A key component to reliable power-system operation is continuous monitoring and controlling of the system in real time. Failures in those areas may cause widespread, uncontrolled, cascading outages.

In retrospective analysis following events such as the 2003 blackout, the historical sharp-end view of error described by Woods and his colleagues (2010) remains prevalent in utilities. That is, it has historically been easier to place the blame on the last operator whose hand was on the controls than to find the real causes of errors and adjust work approaches and the training that supports them, accordingly. Motivation, organizational learning, and work approaches have been problematic issues as a result.

The emphasis in this case study moves away from the sharp end toward the innovative future to recognize and integrate the blunt-end factors of performance. Creation of a training program that focuses on *why things go right* rather than *why things go wrong* is an efficient and humane work approach for a complex socio-technical system.

This is not an easy endeavor. High reliability is an important but elusive goal involving a fundamentally dynamic set of properties, activities, and responses. There is no stepwise approach to transform an organization's work into a high-reliability organization. Reliability and safety are difficult to observe and achieve partially because it is easier to recognize when it is *not* happening (catastrophic error) rather than identifying what *is* happening (timely human adjustments and adaptive decision-making).

So reliability and safety become *dynamic nonevents* (Reason 1997):

- *Dynamic* in that reliability and safety result from managing continuous change and,
- *Nonevents* in the recognition of safety and reliability via the absence of other things like errors and accidents.

High reliability and resilience engineering are compatible but not identical approaches. The conceptual overlap is found in an organization's capability to develop or "engineer" a culture that is more reliable and better able to bounce back from errors. High reliability is not a state that an organization can ever fully achieve but only continue to aspire to. Reliability is characterized by a dynamic set of properties, activities, and responses. The principles of high-reliability organizing include processes and practices that facilitate an organization's focus on emergent problems and deploying the right combination of resources to address them. This includes noticing and responding to small issues and vulnerabilities before they escalate into a bad event. Smaller issues are easier to deal with but more difficult to spot. Resilience engineering does not have an agreed-on definition in the literature. Rather, it is more of a conceptual framework. The authors understand the cogent argument of resilience engineering as designing systems, processes, and work that optimize safety (rather than the traditional view focused on identifying the factors that undermine existing safety).

This Dominion case study hones in on the intersection of the perspectives as they relate to training for resilience, building rich and complex mental models, adaptive decision-making, and a wide-area view of the work. The next section describes how this is accomplished through leveraging the cognitive aspects of increasing intuition while building expertise through training.

NATURALISTIC DECISION-MAKING IS HOW THE WORK IS DONE

Naturalistic decision-making (NDM) based on the work of Gary Klein (1989) describes how people actually make decisions in real-world settings. People in general and experts in particular do not make decisions according to prescriptive approaches. Instead, experts lean on their intuition. This is particularly true in difficult circumstances such as those involving limited time, uncertainty, high stakes, vague goals, and unstable conditions. These are the conditions that occur in complex socio-technical systems, involving mostly nonroutine work, within real-time operations-utility work environments. Expertise is trainable using specific principles of deliberate practice to achieve accurate intuition. The best-quality decision approaches and work environments encourage the blending of intuition and analysis in work environments—intuition for the nonroutine and analysis for the routine.

Instead of prescribing a single sequence of steps for decisions, Dominion considers how electric-utility professionals actually make decisions and solve problems. Then cognitively based skills that support natural ways of deciding are identified. The training to build the skills is fundamental to the successful work approaches needed for the best-quality decision-making.

For grid operations, decision theory provides little help. There is no empirical evidence that the use of classical decision theory improves performance (Lipshitz and Strauss 1997). The naturalistic research studies show that ideal decisions are unrealistic in complex and time-pressured situations characteristic of high-reliability organizations. Decision makers must recognize and adapt to the evolving nature of the situation, evoking the essence of resilience. According to Gary Klein:

> The culprit is an ideal of analytical decision-making that asserts that we must always generate options systematically, identify criteria for evaluating these options, assign weights to the evaluation criteria, rate each option on each criterion and tabulate the scores to find the best option. We call this a model of concurrent option comparison, the idea being that the decision maker deliberates about several options concurrently...These strategies sound good, but in practice they are often disappointing. They do not work under time pressure because they take too long. Even when there is enough time, they require much work and lack flexibility for handling rapidly changing field conditions (Klein 1989, 56).

A solution for building the flexibility (and resilience) that Klein describes can be found in recognizing the work as decision-making rather than merely task completion and then creating a development and training path that builds expertise. Using this approach as a foundation for a training progression, Dominion is integrating the principles of resilience engineering and high reliability at the individual level, including metrics for the workers and the work. At both the individual and organizational level of analysis, the progression of knowledge is a critical success factor.

KNOWLEDGE DEVELOPMENT

We argue that knowledge development must include a strong foundation of explicit and tacit knowledge applied to real-time decisions at the individual level of work analysis. Optimal knowledge development as a progression of expertise must be embedded within an organizational work environment, with a focus on recognizing that errors will occur. Correctly learning from adverse outcomes with a view that goes beyond the last action prior to an event creates a system that is better able to support adaptive work practices. Our premise is that these aligned approaches are mutually beneficial and support a high level of reliability for the workers and the work outcomes.

According to Calvin Pava (1983), knowledge development is the transformation process of knowledge work, in which organizational learning is accomplished through nonroutine tasks. In 1990, Purser extended this definition and further divided the knowledge-development process into knowledge availability, utilization, and conceptualization. Consistent with Dreyfus (1981), progression with a focus on development of quality tacit knowledge, and Ericsson and his colleagues' (2006) deliberate practice to achieve expertise, Nanoka and Takeuchi (1995) define knowledge development as *the interaction between tacit and explicit knowledge.*

DELIBERATION

Deliberation, according to Pava (1983), is an ongoing exchange between people beginning when an issue is identified and ending when resolution is achieved. Deliberations are the gist of knowledge work—providing the context and subtext of decisions, including anything that enables a change in knowledge. Deliberation does not play a role in defining tasks and operations to be performed; rather, it is the mechanism for identifying issues. For instance, in operations work, alarms can help or sometimes hinder quality decision-making. Deliberation informed by decision-support research can effectively determine the optimal alarm settings.

It is important to recognize that deliberations in knowledge work happen—whether they are planned or not because nonroutine tasks cause uncertainty, which in turn requires resolution. Proper work design including planning and management of deliberations through training can reduce variances that stand in the way of knowledge development and organizational learning. There is not one agreed-on way to approach this important responsibility.

A challenge in planning for knowledge development is that learning and knowledge creation are conceptualized in different ways. Some authors, such as Tannenbaum and Rastogi, define knowledge as fairly static, going through processes where knowledge is gained in an incremental way in which the first outcomes must be achieved before one progresses to the next level. This linear approach is neither adequate for nor descriptive of how utility-system-operations job knowledge is gained.

The Dominion case-study project has an alternative focus on knowledge models more consistent with Nonaka and Takeuchi's (1995) Socialization, Externalization, Combination, Internalization [SECI] dynamic, an iterative approach aligned with Pava's concept of deliberation. That is, in addition to formal training, novice operators engage in socialization with expert operators, and knowledge is shared. This has historically been known as "tribal learning." Novices are able to combine concepts and internalize them. The questions of novices often press experts to explain why decisions are made in a particular way. Mental models for the range of knowledge levels continues to be built and strengthened through the deliberation process and formal training. The SECI model integrates explicit and tacit knowledge, an element that provides an important linkage to the progression of expertise and also supporting NDM.

In the SECI model, these "equations" apply:

Explicit = Knowing "what" through theory and knowledge that is easy to describe and lacks content.

Tacit = Knowing "how" through practice and knowledge that is intuitive and hard to articulate.

PROCESS MODEL

To enhance the perspective making that individuals bring to knowledge development, Nonaka and Takeuchi (1995) combined modes of knowledge creation with enabling conditions to create a useful process model for Dominion.

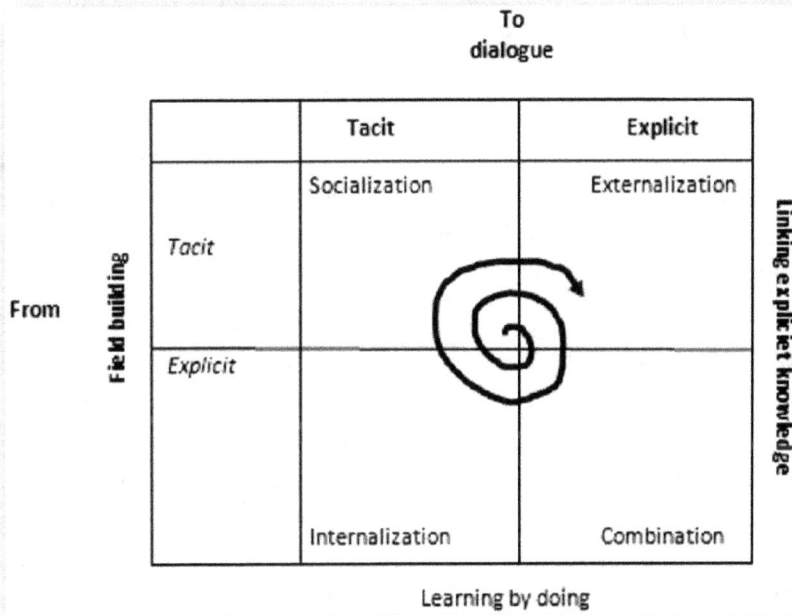

Figure 14.1 The knowledge-development process (Nonaka and Takeuchi 1995)

SOCIALIZATION PROCESS—TACIT KNOWLEDGE EXCHANGE

In the utility sector, it is effective when workers search for knowledge while defining the issue as it is unfolding while they work. Historically and successfully, utility operators have relied on task narrative forums, described by Boland and Tenkasi (1995) to help narrate experiences and share with others. Although the knowledge fundamentals of system operators are drawn from training, the bulk of learning often comes from informal story swapping among operators about their experiences in particular scenarios. Experts (either informally or through structured learning)

help individuals assemble contextual materials and build links and representations to assist novices and less experienced operators think about
thinking. The goal for this Dominion case project is to enhance the knowl-
edge-seeking behaviors by providing access to knowledge sources concurrently with direction about the issue or scenario to be resolved.

EXTERNALIZATION PROCESS—TACIT TO EXPLICIT KNOWLEDGE EXCHANGE

At Dominion, workers are transferring knowledge, giving voice to ideas,
sharing mental models, and creating concepts. Common barriers to recognize and overcome during training include lack of common frame of
reference and lack of shared meaning. The goal is to enhance knowledge
through identification of goals and divergent values of participants.

COMBINATION PROCESS—EXPLICIT KNOWLEDGE EXCHANGE

Knowledge is transferred once it has become explicit. Experts typically
have a difficult time making their tacit knowledge explicit. Part of the
Dominion project includes conducting structured interviews for expert
knowledge capture. To support the knowledge of experts, Dominion
seeks to assimilate and organize documents, like procedures, and coordinate ideas to be used throughout the knowledge development at all
stages. The goal are to determine decision protocol, screen criteria for
evaluating technical alternatives, and negotiate optimal trade-offs.

INTERNALIZATION PROCESS

At Dominion, trainees at novice stages will internalize by adding tacit
knowledge to their individual knowledge bases, and experts help contribute to the shared organizational knowledge base. Internalization leads to
the next spiral upward toward expertise for all individuals involved, back
to the socialization phase, in which workers at different stages will integrate this newly established tacit knowledge. The goals are to build the
knowledge base and codify learning experiences, which are integrated to
future training, and in turn enhance the business unit and Dominion as a

learning organization. Mental models are honed, skills are improved, and knowledge interdependencies are updated.

CONCLUSION

Dominion Virginia Power is embracing an evidence-based approach to training and work in an industry historically driven by retrospective analysis of events that are anomalies. Some organizations create tasks and attempt to make them synonymous with procedures in an effort to increase safety and reliability through preventing errors. But Dominion recognizes that demonstrating capability to perform tasks is not enough to ensure system reliability. Decision making is the stuff of system operations in complex systems like the grid. Although the NDM movement is well recognized, the electric-utility industry has not approached full integration in training programs.

The legacy of this approach is a focus on the characteristics of high-reliability organizations, in which the work approaches for grid operations are built around being reliable and resilient rather than preventing errors. Two particular points are emerging as useful for organizations to consider: *Knowledge cross-leveling* and *adaptive capacity*.

CREATED KNOWLEDGE IS EXPANDED ACROSS THE ORGANIZATION

Organizational learning is essential for high-reliability work approaches. This is predicated on organizational knowledge creation as a never-ending iterative process that upgrades itself continuously. New concepts that have been vetted move on to a new cycle of knowledge creation at a different ontological level. This interactive, upward-spiraling process takes place individually and organizationally while always building a more resilient and reliable culture.

ADAPTIVE CAPACITY

Adaptive capacity is a large framework for working. At the forefront, Dominion Virginia Power is a leadership example of workers in utility environments developing adaptive capacity to deal with new complex and dynamic circumstances. Dominion Virginia Power is pioneering the method and framework for learning to thrive in less static and less predictable environments than previously existed. Today's workplace brings dramatic increases in interdependence and connectivity among individuals, groups, and the systems that control the grid, including the following:

- Complexity
- Ambiguity
- Novelty
- Diversity of opinions, people, issues, technology, and more
- Vanishing shelf life of knowledge

The challenge for humane work approaches is to enable individuals and organizations to learn to better meet adaptive *challenges* specifically and adaptive *changes* more broadly.

System-operations jobs are classic socio-technical systems, yet very few utility organizations approach job and work design—and the training that supports it—through this lens. We purport that there are different reasons for different organizations. The reasons that have emerged through grounded-theory-approach interviews include these common themes:

- Span of authority—Project control that would positively impact work approaches is seldom under the control of an individual charged with the goal of the appropriate socio-technical systems decision-making.
- Lack of alignment—Incremental projects for humane work approaches are often prioritized by business units that do not share a common goal related to improving the significant aspects of the socio-technical system.
- What you look for is what you find—There is more effort to looking at work approaches at the system level, and it requires more coordination and collaboration.

We encourage more conversation about well researched, underused evidence-based approaches to work design in utility-sector socio-technical systems. Dominion Virginia Power is leveraging a training-focused framework to enhance operations expertise. The framework will use work approaches that support resilience engineering work practices within complex socio-technical systems.

REFERENCES

Boland, R. J., and R. V. Tenkasi. July–August 1995. "Perspective Making and Perspective Taking in Communities of Knowing." *Organizational Science* 6 (4).

Csete, M., and J. Doyle. March 2002. "Reverse Engineering of Biological Complexity." *Science 1*, 295 (5560): 1664–69.

Ericsson, K. A., N. Charness, P. Feltovich, and R. Hoffman. 2006. *The Cambridge Handbook of Expertise and Expert Performance.*.London: Cambridge University Press

Holling, C. S. 1987. "Simplifying the Complex: The Paradigms of Ecological Function and Structure." *European Journal of Operational Research* 30 (2): 139–46.

Hollnagel, E., D. Woods, and N. Leveson. 2006. *Resilience Engineering: Concepts and Precepts*. New York: Ashgate.

Klein, G. 2011. *Streetlights and Shadows: Searching for the Keys to Adaptive Decision Making*. New York: Bradford Books.

Klein, G. 1989. "Recognition-Primed Decisions in Advances in Man-Machine Systems Research." W. B. Rouse (ed.). Freenwich, Conn.: JAI Press. 47–92.

Lipshitz, R., and O. Strauss. 1997. "Coping with Uncertainty: A Naturalistic Decision-Making Analysis." *Organizational Behavior and Human Decision Processes* 69 (2): 149–63.

McDermott, R. 1999. "Why Information Technology Inspired But Cannot Deliver Knowledge Management." *California Management Review* 41 (4): 103–16.

McDermott, R., W. M. Snyder, and E. Wenger. (2002). *Cultivating Communities of Practice: A Guide to Managing Knowledge*. Boston: Harvard Business School Press.

Nanoka, I., and H. Takeuchi. 1995. *The Knowledge-Creating Company*. Oxford: Oxford University Press.

Pava, C. 1983. *Managing New Office Technology: An Organizational Strategy*. New York: The Free Press.

Taylor, J. C., and D. F. Felten. 1993. *Performance by Design: Sociotechnical Systems in North America*. Englewood Cliffs, New Jersey: Prentice Hall.

Tversky, A., and D. Kahneman. 1997. "Judgment under Uncertainty: Heuristics and Biases." *Science*, New Series, 185 (4157): 1124–31.

Weick, K., and K. Sutcliffe. 2007. *Managing the Unexpected: Resilient Performance in an Age of Uncertainty*. New York: Jossey-Bass.

Weick, K., K. Sutcliffe, and D. Obstfeld. 1999. "Organizing for High Reliability: Processes of Collective Mindfulness," in R. S. Sutton and B. M. Staw (eds.), *Research in Organizational Behavior*, vol. 1. USA: Elsevier Science/JAI Press, xii, 331 pp.

Woods, D., S. Dekker, R. Cook, L. Johannesen, and N. Sarter. 2010. *Behind Human Error*, second ed. Burlington, Vermont: Ashgate Publishing.

www.nerc.com

Fifteen

Enid Mumford: the ETHICS methodology and its legacy

Peter Bednar and Christine Welch

INTRODUCTION

There is evidence of a paradigm shift in the field of information systems (IS) development away from a focus on alignment of IS and business goals toward a recognition that value is created by people, demonstrating IS capability. Overby (2011) suggests that "Business outcomes from technology investments are all that really matter." She goes on to quote Dave Aron, vice president and fellow in Gartner's CIO Research group, who states, "The next step on the journey is to move from alignment to engagement." Developing capability to generate and use information will have a number of dimensions (e.g., in the field now known as business intelligence, searching, gathering and modeling techniques are recognized to be important and are rendered possible by applying appropriate supporting technologies. To focus on information and communication technologies, in isolation from their use by capable professionals is reduced to an academic exercise. Business-process design and capability development are at the heart of modern IS development activity.

Capability is embedded in people, and it follows that an effective IS will be one designed as a socio-technical whole in which available technologies are considered in the light of the desires of those who will use them. Thus, this is a good time to reexamine the work on socio-technical systems associated with members of the Tavistock Institute in the years following World War II. In particular, Enid Mumford's work on the ETHICS methodology, honed over forty years of practice in a variety of industrial and organizational contexts, forms a useful source of inspiration for twenty-first-century designers. This methodology is discussed in the next section of the chapter. For a more detailed discussion of ETHICS, interested readers are referred to *Designing Human Systems—The ETHICS Method*.[16] Mumford's work always demonstrated her desire to "look beyond" accepted practice to the pursuit of further adaptation. It is this that enables contemporary researchers to develop the potential of the socio-technical approach. Hirschheim and Klein (1994), for instance, present a modification of ETHICS for the purpose of incorporating ideals of neohumanism. In Mumford's research discourse, the purpose of an information system can be perceived as twofold: to support people in informing themselves and/or to support people in helping others to inform themselves. Her approach has sometimes been criticized as too elaborate and time-consuming to be practical. We believe, on the contrary, that it is reflective of the intensity of end-user engagement required to effect successful design—the difficult, creative, (and therefore time-consuming) learning processes lying at the heart of successful analysis and transformation of sociocultural organizational practices.

SOCIO-TECHNICAL DESIGN AND THE ETHICS METHODOLOGY

Founder members of the Tavistock Institute, such as Eric Trist and Fred Emery, looked to harness social-science methods for the benefit of society. They adopted what is now known as "action research," believing there could be "no theory without practice, no practice without theory" (Mumford 2006, 320). Socio-technical design was envisaged as a means by which human intelligence and skill could be harnessed in conjunction

---

16 *Designing Human Systems: The ETHICS Methodology*, available online at http://www.enid.u-net.com/index.htm.

with newly emerging technologies in the postwar period to bring about radical improvements in work and life. Two key values underpinned their work: a desire to improve job design to create safer and more enjoyable work systems and a wish to see greater democracy in both the workplace and in wider society. Members of the institute put forward a coherent set of socio-technical principles (Cherns 1976). They believed that a work system should be seen as a set of activities coming together to form an integrated whole, as opposed to a collection of separate tasks (i.e., an open system interacting with an environment that influences its behavior). Furthermore, alongside all of these principles, an idea of participative design prevailed (i.e., if work was to be democratic and enriching, so also should be the process by which work systems were designed). Mumford and Weir (1979) reflect that "A work system that is designed to achieve objectives defined solely in technical terms is likely to have unpredictable human consequences. The reason for this is that technical decisions taken at an early stage of the design process will impose constraints on the organization of the human part of the system" (1979, 9).

Mere examination of a social dimension in addition to technical matters does not suffice. Participative design methods were therefore put forward by a number of authors, such as Stowell and West (1985) and Friis (1991), who perceived it to have benefits both for the self-actualization needs of people and the efficiency needs of organizations. However, "Participation" is a term capable of more than one interpretation, depending on whose perspective is considered. Participants enjoy varying degrees of engagement with the process—from consultative or representative participation through to a full "consensus' approach" (Mumford and Henshall 1979). Ongoing acquisition of relevant "knowledge" is needed for informed decisions to emerge. Thus, participation involves learning and development of effective relationships. Power within participating groups will also be an issue. Morgan (1997), drawing on Plato, reminds us that people can become trapped within their own constructed "realities." This entrapment can prevent individuals and groups from espousing new knowledge that conflicts with established patterns (Argyris 1990), inhibiting learning and hence processes for effective work design. Individuals need to be motivated and supported to think and express themselves and to overcome any inhibitions they feel about expressing their ideas. Confrontation sometimes results if controversial opinions are expressed or if people feel that their ideas could be thought eccentric or unworkable and are reluctant to express them (Bednar and Welch 2006). Groups are more than collections of individuals and have dynamic, emergent qualities of their own. Members may react in a hostile way to individuals perceived as nonconforming and even ostracize them. Individual behavior within groups may demonstrate manipulative strategies designed to bring about outcomes that best suit individual preferences (see Robinson 2004 and Hoyt 1997). Mumford highlights an important role for facilitators in participative design but emphasizes that control should rest with the participants themselves. This position is supported by Nissen (1984, 2002), Stowell and West (1985), and Friis (1991). The facilitator's role is "to help the design group choose and implement an appropriate problem-solving methodology, to keep the members interested and motivated toward the design task, to help them resolve any conflicts, and to make sure that important design factors are not forgotten or overlooked. The facilitator must in no circumstances take decisions for the design group or persuade them that certain things should be done or not done" (Mumford 2003, 41).

The material within the ETHICS methodology can be seen to have at least three main audiences within business organizations. First, it addresses the engaged actors and stakeholders who are pursuing change in their activities (participating employees). The second group are those tasked with managing those engaged actors; and third, there are facilitators (sometimes termed "change magicians") who support the employees and the managers in achieving a desired change.

Because the needs of these audiences differ, ETHICS involves a combination of engagements. The creation of documentation supports dialogue about issues, which otherwise are easily missed. In fact, the process of creating this documentation is more important than the documents themselves. During discussions and preparation of the various types of documentation, people learn about their current situation and desired future situation. This dialogue forms the foundation for change. Much of the work and discussions involved in ETHICS are inherently qualitative. But questionnaires and surveys also can be used as part of the method. The surveys are there to support creation of an overview of the situation from a more quantitative approach. The power of numbers should not be underestimated in these dialogues. The summaries of these surveys help people to discuss their positions within a group of others. The resulting conclusions and summaries often act as an eye-opener both for individual employees and their managers. Thus, far from being a burden on those engaged in change, the documentation created within ETHICS acts as a catalyst for discovery of issues, ideas, and facts people were not previously aware of. Once uncovered, these aspects can be discussed and perhaps addressed. For a facilitator, it can be helpful to have surveys as a complement to the qualitative materials, in discussions with both individual employees and management. For the employees, it provides supports for them to discover their individual positions in the light of others, and similarities and differences can be explored by the facilitator together with the individual employee, as well as the group.

Thus, the tools of ETHICS support learning by the project participants, in line with observation of others. There is then a question of how to extend what has been learned beyond the project participants to the whole organization—in itself a very demanding task. The design challenge: ETHICS has three objectives related to the management of change:

1. It seeks to legitimate a value position in which the future users of computer systems at all organizational levels play a major part in the design of these systems.
2. It enables groups concerned with the design of computer systems to set specific job-satisfaction objectives in addition to the usual technical and operational objectives.

3. It ensures that any new technical system is surrounded by a compatible, well-functioning organizational system.

ETHICS has been described with different numbers of steps, dependent on which literature is being used as a source (e.g., between five and fifteen steps). Figure 1 shows the fifteen steps most commonly found in descriptions of ETHICS made by Enid Mumford herself. The fifteen "steps" below are supported with more than twenty methods and templates.

Fifteen Steps in the ETHICS Methodology (Mumford, 1983–2006):

[1].   Change analysis: Why change?
[2].   System boundaries
[3].   Analysis of existing and future system
[3a].   Logical analysis of system: Input-output analysis
[3b].   Complexity and vertical analysis
[4].   Key objectives analysis
[5].   Key task analysis
[6a].   Key information needs analysis
[6b].   Coordination of objectives, tasks, and information needs
[7a].   Diagnosis of efficiency needs
[7b].   Key variance analysis: Matrix
[8a].   Knowledge and psychological contract
[8b].   Support/control and task contract
[9].   Future analysis
[10a]. Specification of efficiency and social goals
[10b]. Resolution of efficiency and social goals
[11].   Organizational possibilities
[12].   Technical possibilities
[13].   Achieving objectives
[14].   Implementation diagnosis
[15].   Evaluation and self-reflective element

It seems unlikely that Enid Mumford would have suggested that she proposed a radically different epistemology. The question would arise, "Different from what?" Perhaps different from the rationale in methods that suggest beneficial change can be brought about on behalf of participants by "project teams." Perhaps Mumford's work should be viewed as a critique of, and reflection over, "narrowmindedness" and "linear thinking." It also serves to highlight the traps that we create for ourselves when we think "inside our box" (Argyris 1990). But discussion of epistemology probably requires us to engage with a number of different aspects of reflective participation, engagement, employee empowerment, and learning. Here, one of the key issues is related to reflection over self and reflection over relationship of self to others, and vice versa. This of course necessitates recognition of a thinking self in relation to thinking selves of others, the interrelatedness from an individual human reflective self—and the many potential traps within. Perhaps the "radicalness" of Mumford's epistemology lies in her refusal to separate any human epistemology from efforts to make explicit ones axiology, praxeology, and ontology "in context."

Having set out the ETHICS methodology as a toolbox for organizational change, Mumford addresses both the potential for application areas and theory for practice in her work titled *Redesigning Human Systems* (2003). She explores key aspects of socio-technical design in practice through the following topics: the problems of managing change, participation in practice, designing for problem prevention, and designing for an uncertain future. She also gives an overview of experiences of using her approach in a variety of different organizational settings, using nine different cases, which she divides in three categories. Each of these organizational change endeavors represents a different purpose for which socio-technical facilitation can provide support, with rich examples from real-world practice.

Designing for manual workers:

a. Analyzing problem situations: The dock workers of Liverpool
b. Work design: The coal industry
c. Considering structure: Different organizational solutions in the automobile industry

Designing for office workers:

a. New problems in banking
b. Involving employees in design: Rolls Royce
c. Designing an expert system

Designing for companies:

a. Senior management, decision making, and design
b. Companywide participation in air products
c. Quality and environmental issues at Shell International

The choice of a facilitator with the right qualities is crucial to progress of a project. It can be seen today that professional analysts' abilities to understand the challenges facing the business itself are as crucial as their technical expertise.

CRITICISMS OF THE ETHICS APPROACH

In the more than fifty-year history of socio-technical design practice, critics have of course suggested some problems that needed to be addressed (see Baxter and Sommerville 2011). Perhaps the most common is that terminology is inconsistent. However, this is due to the demands of reaching agreement about the social and technical factors that need to be considered and analyzed in the change process. The approach does explicitly support participatory user engagement and employee empowerment. It does not provide a simple recipe for successful change! If the methodology appears abstract, it is due to the challenge of defining a problem space, including determining system boundaries. The approach draws on the natural and professional language already used by the stakeholders, which helps them overcome potential problems of abstraction.

Conflicting value systems within any context of change can be seen as problematic, including difficulties with communication and coordination. This is a potential challenge arising from multidisciplinarity of the team involved in a practical, socio-technical inquiry. It may also occur as employees and managers apply different values, social and managerial. The socio-technical approach offers methods and tools for organized, systemic dialogue and clarification of differences in values; and so supports constructive collaboration and problem resolution.

Some critics have pointed to an apparent lack of effective metrics to assess the application results of socio-technical practices. The approach does include methods for participatory reflection and evaluation, to clarify and describe system expectations in such a way that they can be managed. This focus on creation of an axiology for change in context may be regarded as a strength. Similarly, those who are in search of a panacea to remove all complexity and uncertainty from change projects will be disappointed that ETHICS offers no clear solutions. This is due to the challenges of moving from boundary critique and problems space analysis to suggestion and design of appropriate change. The approach includes specific tools and techniques that help stakeholders to develop resolutions to problems rather than promising to do this for them.

In the past, socio-technical concerns have been attributed to only a marginal role in organizational changes and innovation in ways of working. There has not been much pragmatic use of stakeholder analysis, either. Methods such as ETHICS can therefore lack credibility or seem unduly daunting. However, the approach incorporates several stakeholder analyses and also explores different types of participation and empowerment, which allows reflection over engagement and involves stakeholders in their own definition of desirable change practices and system boundaries.

CONCLUSION

Enid Mumford continued to develop and redevelop her approach throughout her lifetime. In 1994, for example (Mumford and Beekman 1994) she incorporated lessons learned from business-process reengineering with her ETHICS method. The result was a methodology that the authors called "PROGRESS," which was intended to bring forth the best of both worlds.

In 1996, she took this further (Mumford 1996) and explored a more explicit engagement with ideas from Stafford Beer's Viable Systems Model. While she had long been using ideas from VSM, in this book they are clearly incorporated in the ETHICS approach. She also included further ideas from Deming (1986) and expanded the discussion on total quality. The overall approach, however, stays the same as before, and the expansions are pragmatically incorporated in the ETHICS approach. In 1999, Mumford turned her attention to issues with technology change—how problems become more and more complex while established practices for decision-making and problem solving become less and less effective. As main examples, she used drugs and cybercrime to demonstrate how critical yet apparently insoluble problems could be addressed. She showed a way forward and presented a viable method for approaching all complex problems with competence and efficiency.

Mumford's discussion in one of her last articles (2006) raises a number of important issues. She points out that an open-systems perspective is needed if the benefits of socio-technical methods are to be realized. The interconnections with the wider system within which a particular work system is situated must be considered. Any organization subsists from moment to moment as an emergent property of the interactions among the people who are its members, creating systems that are not just open but dynamic (Bednar 2009). In the context of networked organizations, dynamic complexity is not merely expanded but radically altered. The role of ICTs in a networked society is not simply to create connections between individuals and organizations but to support transformations in organizational life as it is lived (Mumford et al. 1984).

Innovative information systems will change how organizations function. Therefore, we must redesign organizations in the context of the possibilities offered by IS. However, information systems are not simply applications of ICT but synergies supporting human activity. Socio-technical, systemic approaches will ensure that new kinds of technical and organizational systems are built in harmony. There is a need to consider transformation as a process and not merely to focus on management of resultant change. Multiple perspectives on transformation from all engaged actors must be considered (Bednar and Welch 2005, Baxter and Sommerville 2011).

Participation at all levels in work-system design is an important socio-technical principle that is not always realized (or realizable) in practice. However, limitations to participation may be damaging to the usefulness of any designed system because the contextually dependent knowledge of unique individuals will be lost in the design process. Individuals must be empowered to join in co-creaion of their system, surfacing their contextual understandings, and participating fully in ownership and control of their project. This may be a primary reason why many fashionable techniques of the past thirty years have continued to disappoint(e.g., TQM, BPR).

Mumford's approach had its roots in progressive social policies at the end of the 1940s, but its value persists today through its emphasis on the tacit knowledge of the individuals who are members of a particular organization at the point where change in work systems appears desirable. The discourse of knowledge management shows that organizations are aware of the business value of the know-how that is embedded in their staff and the business processes executed by them. The ETHICS methodology, with its emphasis on surfacing the working knowledge of individuals and groups to inform change, clearly has much to offer organizations wishing to create, preserve, and exploit this know-how. Coakes (in Avison et al. 2006) encapsulates this in describing her experience of discussing with Mumford their experience of involvement with business process reengineering: "It became obvious to me, as I reflected not only on Enid's words but also on my own practical experience, that as processes were reengineered, much of the understanding of how they operated, especially under times of uncertainty, was being lost to organizations...the tacit understanding of exceptional circumstances was linked closely to the process workers' experiences, both with that particular process and also other processes both related and unrelated." As this issue of "sticky knowledge" (Coakes 2004) grows in importance for business organizations, it is probable that methodologies such as ETHICS will acquire a renewed importance.

REFERENCES

Avison, D., N. Bjorn-Anderson, E. Coakes, et al. 2006. Enid Mumford: A Tribute. *Information Systems Journal* 16 (4): 343–382.

Argyris, C. 1990. *Overcoming Organisational Defenses—Facilitating Organisational Learning.* Boston: Allyn and Bacon.

Baxter, G., and I. Sommerville. 2011. "Socio-technical Systems: From Design Methods to Systems Engineering." *Interacting with Computers* (23): 4–17.

Bednar, P. M. 2009. "Contextual Analysis: A Multiperspective Inquiry into Emergence of Complex Sociocultural Systems," in G. Minati, M. Abram, and E. Pessa (eds.), *Processes of Emergence of Systems and Systemic Properties: Toward a General Theory of Emergence.* Singapore: World Scientific. 299–312.

Bednar, P. M., and C. Welch. 2005. "IS, Process, and Organizational Change and Their Relationship to Contextual Dependencies." *Proceedings of Thirteenth European Conference on Information Systems.* University of Regensburg, Germany, May 25–28, 2005.

Bednar, P., and C. Welch, 2006. "Structuring Uncertainty: Sponsoring Innovation and Creativity," in F. Adam, P Brezillon, S Carlsson & P Humphreys (eds.), *Creativity and Innovation in Decision-making and Decision Support,* vol.2. London: Decision Support Press.

Bednar, P. M., M. Sadok, and V. Shiderova. January 2014. "Socio-technical Toolbox for Business Analysis in Practice: Smart Organizations and Smart Artifacts." Lecture notes in *Information Systems and Organisation,* Leonardo Caporarello, Beniamino Di Martino, and Marcello Martinez (ds.).Heidelberg, Germany: Springer International Publishing. 219–27.

Beer, S. 1985. *Diagnosing the System for Organizations*. London and New York: John Wiley.

Cherns, A. 1976. Principles of Socio-technical Design. *Human Relations* 2: 783–92.

Coakes, E. 2004. "Knowledge Management: A Primer." *Communications of the Association for Information Systems* 14: 406–89.

Deming, W. W. 1986. *Out of the Crisis*. Cambridge: MIT Center for Advanced Engineering Study.

Friis, S. 1991. "User-Controlled Information Systems Development— Problems and Possibilities Toward Local Design Shops," in *Information and Computer Science*. Sweden: Lund University Publications.

Hirschheim, R., and H. K. Klein. March 1994. "Realizing Emancipatory Principles in Information Systems Development: The Case for ETHICS." *MIS Quarterly*.

Klein, H. K. 2004. "Seeking the New and the Critical in Critical Realism: Déjà Vu?" *Information and Organization* 14: 123–44.

Mumford, E. 1983. *Designing Human Systems for New Technology: The ETHICS Method*. Manchester Business School.

Mumford E. 1999. *Dangerous Decisions: Problem Solving in Tomorrow's World*. Dordrecht: Kluwer Academic Publishers.

Mumford, E. 2003. *Redesigning Human Systems*. Cambridge: IRM Press, London University Press.

Mumford, E. 2006. "The Story of Socio-technical Design: Reflections on Its Successes, Failures, and Potential." *Information Systems Journal* 16: 317–342.

Mumford, E, and D. Henshall. 1979. *A Participative Approach to Computer System Design*. New York: Wiley.

Mumford, E., and M. Weir. 1979. *Computer Systems in Work Design—The ETHICS Method*. New York: John Wiley.

Nissen, H.-E. 1984. "Acquiring Knowledge of Information Systems—Research in a Methodological Quagmire," in Mumford et al. 1984. "Research Methods in Information Systems." *Proceedings of the IFIP WG 8.2* Colloquium, Manchester Business School, 1984: 39–52. North Holland, Amsterdam.

Overby, S. May 12, 2011. "IT Value Is Dead: Long Live Business Value." *CIO Magazine* http://www.cio.com/article/2408200/business-alignment/it-value-is-dead--long-live-business-value-.html?nsdr=true.

Stowell, F., and D. West. 1985. *Client-Led Design: A Systemic Approach to Information Systems Definition*. London: McGraw Hill.

Sixteen

Applying Enterprise Information Technology from a Socio-technical Perspective

MARK J.G. GOVERS AND PIM SUDMEIER

INTRODUCTION

Strangely, information technology (IT) has never played a major role in (re)designing organizations and workplaces from a socio-technical systems (STS) perspective. Mumford (2006) was the rule rather than the exception (see chapter 15). Regardless, her value insights at the time never became a mainstream routine in STS thinking and practice. Three reasons "force" STS thinking to change this ignorant routine urgently. First, IT systems profoundly determine organizational design choices. Especially, enterprise IT systems, like ERP, are not a derivate of organizational design choices anymore. They have built-in organizational designs that are enforced in organizations and on humans in workplaces. Second, IT creates the technical context in which many workplaces and organizations are operating. In many cases, IT is the context in which work takes place. Therefore, it is essential to take valuable, new-business-model opportunities but also potential social negatives coming from IT into consideration during organizational and workplace design processes. If not, the delicate balance between social and technical pivoting for STS is interfered beyond repair. And third, information, especially the quality of information, is becoming vital in dynamic and turbulent settings in which more and more organizations and workplaces operate. In all, quality of information developed into a major design parameter along with quality of organization and quality of work. For this, IT requires attention from STS practitioners as it creates the architecture in which organizations and humans operate. Inspired by Ashby's Law on Requisite Variety—that is, STS's core principle—we are opening with this contribution the door to such a view for STS and IT practitioners—specifically, from an enterprise perspective.

ALL IN ONE AND ONE FOR ALL AS DOMINANT TENDENCY OF IT EXPERTS

Standardization of work processes has proven its value also within the STS practice. With the introduction of enterprise IT systems, like ERP, standardization thinking is, however, overstretched, with devastating effects on agility and therefore on productivity and the health of humans and organizations over time. It results in complex work processes that can be observed during the implementation process of enterprise systems. Heaping everything together is a time-consuming IT technical as well as a political process. It explains why ERP projects often run over time and budget and why maintaining enterprise systems is a pain. Why? The popular ERP concept, for instance, is grounded on integrating all business functions in such a way that they meet in a work process. The ERP concept is grounded on integrating all business functions in such a way that they meet in a work process. Most operational work processes, like a client process, entail sales as well as logistical and financial aspects (process steps). With ERP, an organization can run these process steps in one step of a client process. But in most organizations, more similar processes take place. They differ in having various inputs and/or outputs or in having various process steps. In other words, there is variety. In the enterprise IT practice, unlike the STS, the attempt is to heap all the variety together in one uniform process design and control model. It is done in denial of Ashby's Law—a core STS principle. Embracing variety is considered to go against the concept of standardization of work processes. Actually, the applied concept standardization is "uniformization. "It combines two different forms of integration. The first can be called "horizontal standardization." It heaps process steps together in a coupled process flow. The second can be called "vertical standardization." It is about optimizing process steps into one generic process step capable of dealing with many process varieties. Figure 16.1 shows how both work.

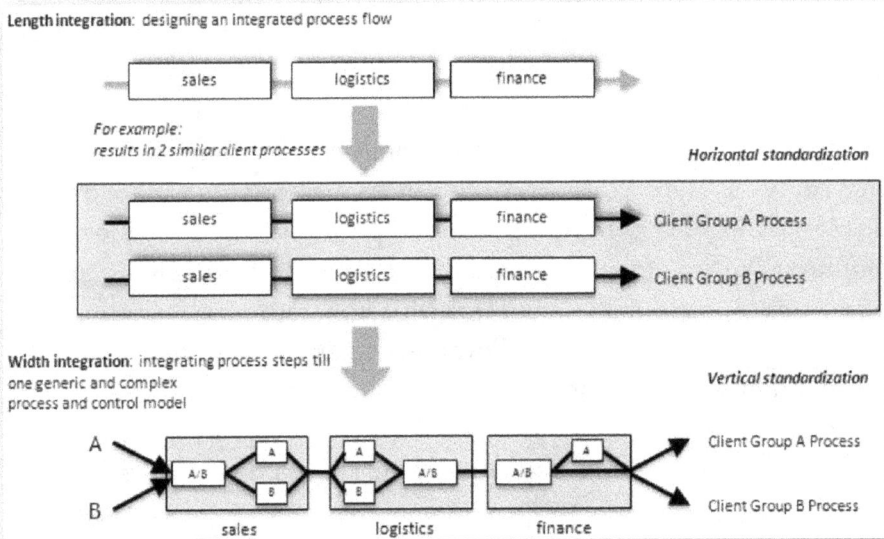

Figure 16.1 Horizontal and Vertical Standardization

The result of these two standardizations is twofold. Independent process flows (in the figure: different sale processes) are made dependent. The process design seems to be simpler as all variety is put into one standard. However, it seems to slip one's mind that various more independent process flows are integrated. With this self-inflicted dependency, the standardized process flow seems more complex than is actually the case in reality. One uniformed process flow was created consisting of several independent process-flow varieties. The assumption is that future changes affect these varieties in a similar manner over time. For organizations operating in predictable and stable contexts, this is correct. Changes can be implemented in a gradual and planned manner. Efficiency advantages of the uniformed approach remain. If changes increase in number and frequency, the uniformed approach works counterproductively. It takes more time and cost to change the way processes are computerized because it creates a domino effect. A required change in one variety leads directly to changes in the connected other varieties. Why? Due to vertical standardization, the actually independent process flows are made interdependent. This vertical standardization needs to be redesigned, which impacts all connected process flows. The persistency of vertical standardization does not limit itself to purely IT thinking and acting. It is also deeply rooted in control-oriented management disciplines like accounting. ERP projects often start with the implementation of the financial module. These control disciplines get the opportunity to pour their control with concrete into the enterprise system. The primary, logistical processes have to find their way in the solidified framework. The variety of such primary processes gets into a scrape and have to nestle themselves into the set standard. The consequence is a width-way expanding standard: an overstretching standardization. In short, the bureaucratic dangers of vertical standardization hit double hard—from one site from the technology and from the other site from the dominance from overly control-focused management routines.

ASHBY'S LAW AS INSPIRATION

Having an eye for variety and dynamics is essential to avoid bureaucratic effects of ERP and IT in general. Ashby's Law of the requisite variety offers, from an STS perspective, a different direction to use IT, even ERP, in a nonbureaucratic manner. Inspired by Ashby (1956), two viewpoints are key—first, to determine which type of computerization is needed and second, to determine how to computerize (primary) processes in enterprise IT systems. Variety plays a role in computerization in two ways:

- How dynamic are information needs: static (low) vs. dynamic (high)?
- How dynamic is the information provisioning: static (low) vs. dynamic (high)?

This implies four types of enterprise computerization, as shown in figure 16.2.

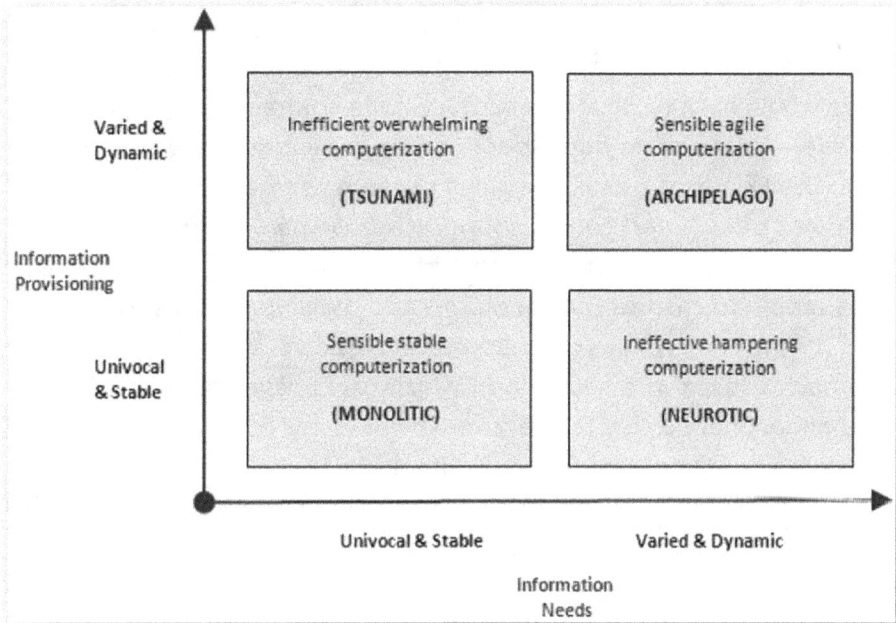

Figure 16.2. Types of Enterprise Computerization

Monolithic enterprise computerization is efficient and effective if the information needs are stable and univocal. Consequently, the information provisioning can be stable and univocal as well. For example, an ERP solution is feasible for the context of the following producer of ship engines. Their product assortment consists of eight main engine types (cubic inches) with a few known variations per engine type (diesel, gas, ship, land, etc.). The production routings differ sporadically, and sales are quite stable. A monolithic computerization makes sense here.

Neurotic enterprise computerization occurs when a monolithic approach is used in a situation in which information needs vary and are dynamic. In a way, the computerization is overwhelmed by users' ever-changing information needs. It is tough—often impossible—to fulfill these information needs on time. To illustrate such information stress, we offer an example from our own practice. As a company, we were looking forward to shifting to iPhones. One colleague, though, wanted to stick with his Nokia. It might seem that it would be no problem, and all we would have to do is extend our phone contracts with our telecom provider. After half an hour spent calling to headquarters and clicking through all kinds of menus, the caller became stressed. The salesperson could not offer varied contract forms because he could not get in into his computer. Luckily, another provider could, as his system allowed salespeople to change contract forms and draw up varied agreements.

Tsunami enterprise computerization occurs when a monolithic approach is used in a situation in which users have stable and simple information needs. Users are overwhelmed by computerization that offers too many options (variety) without information needs requiring them. As a consequence, certain users cannot see the wood for the trees anymore. Hospitals are exemplary. The number of IT systems and digital protocols is so large that many users have difficulties with patient-information requests. Quite often, doctors and nurses have no idea how to find the simplest information needed. This creates a different type of information stress: In need of information (provisioning) but having difficulties finding it in the system. Without knowing, many organizations work with tsunami and neurotic computerizations and are in a situation of structural information stress. Information stress implies a misbalance between the used and offered information provisioning and the actual information needs in an organization and in workplaces. In IT jargon, it is called "misalignment" (Henderson and Venkatraman 1993).

Like work stress (Karasek 1979), information stress affects quality of work and organization (De Sitter 1994, see also: Vriens and Achterbergh 2011) negatively. Knowing that in the current information era IT affects organizations and humans, the necessity grows for having information provisioning capable of dealing with various and dynamic information needs. Govers (2003) calls this "archipelago computerization".

ARCHIPELAGO THINKING AS AN STS ALTERNATIVE

The socio-technical ordering principle of De Sitter (1994, see also Vriens and Achterbergh 2011) grounds the outlook for archipelago enterprise computerization that suits STS-designed organizations and workplaces. This design principle for designing organizations and workplaces offers guidance for designing computerization as well. Translated to computerization, it boils down to the following design order:

1. Reduce information needs via complexity reduction by creating independent primary-process flows.
2. Increase information provisioning by creating the requisite information variety for each primary-process flow.

Information needs can structurally be reduced by complexity reduction. For this, De Sitter (1994, see also Vriens and Achterbergh 2011) offers an effective design framework for the diversification of primary processes. It reduces the complexity of relations with the environment and reduces the internal interdependencies. Looking for independent parallel market or production flows (streams) is the first step. Within these streams, looking for segments of strongly coherent activity, is step two. Both steps, applied by designing enterprise computerization, implies that each stream gets, ideal typically, its own computerization to deal with the variety and dynamics of that stream. Basic data, like customer information, are computerized and connected "under the water line" to provide overall management information; a data warehouse architecture can be used for this. "Above the water line," each process stream has its own options and progress of primary and supporting processes. Like an archipelago, islands are connected under the water line and are disconnected above the water line. In practice, an archipelago enterprise computerization (see fig. 16.3) can consist of various (here, three) parallel, independent enterprise systems instead of having an all-embracing one.

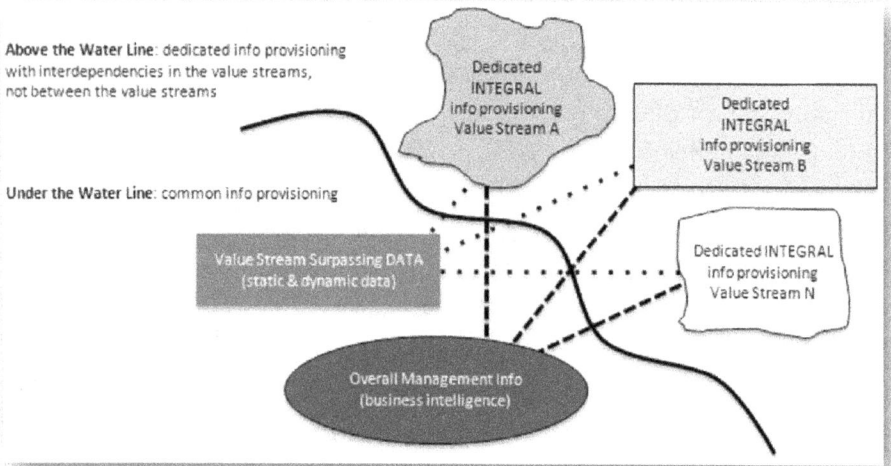

Figure 16.3 Archipelago enterprise computerization

A light version of archipelago can be a menu-card structure. Like in a cafeteria, a menu of an enterprise system is built around clear-cut, varied processes. Figure 16.4 shows the difference between having everything in one purchase process design and having the different varieties in a purchase-menu-card design. Related to the previously discussed horizontal and vertical standardization, it recommends avoiding vertical standardization. We need to avoid it because creating interdependencies of process steps increases the probability of information stress. Besides that, it causes time and money to consume implementation and maintenance, as explained before.

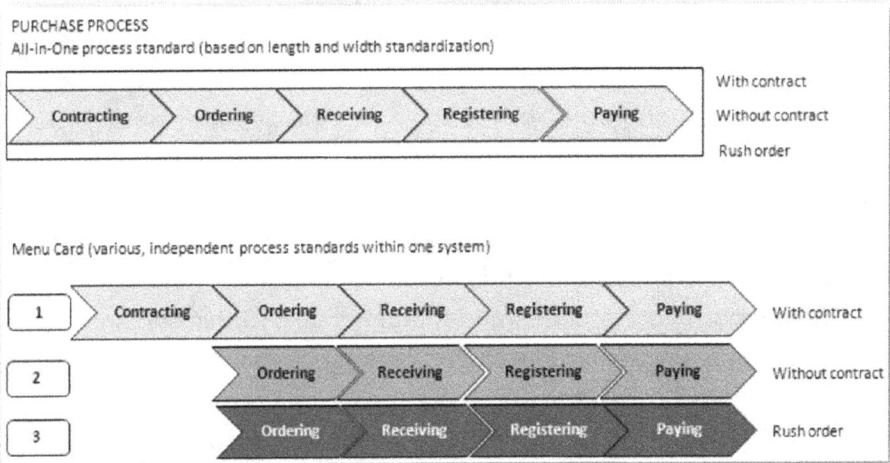

Figure 16.4. Menu-card concept

UNLEARNING OLD AND LEARNING NEW ROUTINES

Archipelago enterprise computerization is more than just architecture; it requires that IT and organization-design experts let go of routines. IT design experts who distance themselves from the routine "avoid redundancy." IT experts are shy about taking similar processes in parallel if parts (steps) look alike. They prefer to apply vertical standardization. Giving each parallel process stream its own data is even more taboo. With modern IT, this is not an issue anymore; even with ERP systems. It's almost dogmatic that holding on to "avoid redundancy" and vertical standardization are not necessary anymore. By letting go of both routines, IT design experts help prevent IT-driven bureaucracy. For organizational-design experts, it implies that they have to let go of the routine that IT has to support the organizational architecture they designed. They have to understand that production of product and (especially) services happens more and more within the context of IT. Computerization is not a derivative of an organizational design anymore. As IT and computerization create a technical framework in which work processes and workplaces are taking place, the information (computerization) design has to work parallel with the organizational design. Changing both routines also implies that both experts need to start working with each other as a team instead of "against" each other.

Sole monolithic IT routines are the wrong answer to facilitate healthy and productive organizations and workplaces. At least two new, archipelago, IT routines need to be learned that build on STS thinking. Instead of focusing with a functional view on business processes (finance, purchase, HR, etc.), we have to start focusing with an integral view on primary processes from input to output. And instead of searching for the greatest common deviator, we have to start searching for the smallest deviating variety when designing work processes. As shown in figure 4, we should not look to bring the three various purchase processes together in one if they have some steps in common. Instead, we should embrace variety and design three processes independent from each other, and as such computerize the three. If not, the varieties are made interdependent, which has undesired effects in terms of time and cost when confronted with dynamics, as explained before. It is not self-evident to apply these new routines. It requires leadership to dissociate IT and business professionals from their common, functional, differentiated and "uniformization" thinking and acting.

UPCOMING NEW IT APPROACHES AND TECHNOLOGIES

In the meantime, the IT world is not sitting still. In terms of project management, so-called "scrum'" and "agile" are new ways of developing software that are focusing on teamwork (Agile Manifesto 2001)—similar to STS. Emphasizing teamwork to develop software, "scrum and agile" have no outspoken view on organizational and workplaces design. In a scrum and agile way of working, the mentioned routines of having a functional-differentiated and vertical standardization (standardization) are not brought into discussion. Scrum and agile help speed up the IT design processes, but this does not imply new—like archipelago—design routines for organizations and workplaces. STS has to be aware of this because scrum and agile are getting so popular in the IT world that what really needs to be changed remains untouched. This is the outcome of the IT design process: an archipelago architecture, if information needs are various and dynamic (see fig. 16.2). STS can help the IT world not only to speed up IT processes but also to help them deliver aligned information provisioning.

In addition to project management, also new IT technologies are of interest like "always-on" connectivity, cloud computing, and apps. By means of "always on," users can be online and have access to systems and information any place and any time. With cloud computing, data are stored in databases and accessible with the Internet any time, any place, and from any device. Apps offer user the opportunity to assemble (construct) their own information provisioning out of small applications. We assume that apps focusing on enterprise-related information needs—so-called "enterprise apps" (Kerschberg 2015)—are of particular interest for STS. Enterprise apps provide the tools to design specific and dedicated information needs for value streams. Even more, we predict that an information architecture built with enterprise apps will be easier to maintain and renew.

For STS, the upcoming development of "enterprise apps" is especially interesting. More organizations, or parts of them, work in turbulent fields. In such fields, the life cycle of value streams is low. It means that value streams decay more frequently and rapidly, and consequently, new ones have to be created and designed. A trend is to create such value streams in co-creaion with other organizations in temporary network settings. Such value streams require dedicated, agile, and information provisioning crossing organizational boundaries. We believe that enterprise apps positioned in an archipelago architecture offers the framework for this. Upcoming IT approaches and technologies we have mentioned offer new opportunities for designing organizations and workplaces. The archipelago architecture offers an integral framework to position these in conjunction with enterprise IT systems for value streams.

The impact of new IT opportunities and enterprise computerization is far reaching. Besides, the traditional impact of technology on work and coordination relations, information becomes an imperative aspect for designing work in teams, value streams, organizations, and even organizational networks to stay tuned with the changing ecosystems that organizations interact with. Information can no longer be approached as a derivative of the design of work and organizations. Information and information technology have evolved into a key design issue for work and organizations.

Monolithic enterprise computerization designs are becoming absolute and are migrating to varied and dynamic information archipelago architectures. This shift offers new perspectives for STS experts to apply STS design principles to help organizations and IT experts design such information architectures. Besides executive and regulation tasks, STS experts have to start embracing information tasks in their designs as well. It boils down to design questions like: What information is needed in teams to perform efficiently and effectively?" and "How do you design such information tasks effectively in agile information architectures?"

CONCLUSION

It may sound paradoxical: STS design principles offer a toolkit for designing nonbureaucratic computerization without being aware of it. Based on one of its core grounds, Ashby's Law, the notion and effect of variety and dynamics are made clear for designing information provisioning aligned with changing information needs. The key is to understand that information needs are not univocal and stable. They are becoming more varied and dynamic and therefore ask for varied and dynamic information provisioning as well. In this contribution and for that purpose, archipelago enterprise computerization was introduced and developed. Archipelago thinking asks to depart from old routines and embrace new routines. The old, bureaucratic-determined routines like taking a functional-differentiated view on business processes and overstandardization processes are fatal for rapidly designing flexible computerizations. For this, STS determined that new routines are required, like focusing on the primary process (again) and on looking for the smallest deviating variety. This shift in routines is in urgent need of STS experts with an eye for information technology or IT experts with an eye for socio-technical thinking and acting. Upcoming IT trends offer new options to engage IT and STS into mutual strengthening efforts to design healthy and productive organizations and workplaces.

REFERENCES

Agile Manifesto. 2001. *Manifesto for Agile Software Development.* http://www.agilemanifesto.org. January 25, 2015.

Ashby, W. R. 1956. *An Introduction to Cybernetics.* London: Chapman and Hall.

de Sitter, L. U. 1994. *Syngertisch Produceren (Synergetic Producing).* Assen: Van Gorcum.

Kerschberg, B. 2015. "Four Critical Reasons to Build Enterprise Apps." *Forbes* TECH, January 15, 2015.

Govers, M. J. G. 2003. "Met ERP-Systemen Naar Moderne Bureaucratieën?" ("Setting Out for Modern Bureaucracies with ERP Systems"). PhD dissertation. Radboud University Nijmegen.

Govers, M. J. G., and P. Sudmeier. 2011. "De Sitter in the Informatietijdperk." *M en O: Tijdschrift Voor Organisatiekunde en Sociaal Beleid* 65 (2) 31–45.

Govers, M. J. G. December 5, 2012. "Gevraagd: Nieuwe Agile IT Principles" ("Wanted: New Agile IT Principles"). *Automatiseringsgids.*

Henderson, J. C., and N. Venkatraman (1993). "Strategic Alignment: Leveraging Information Technology for Transforming Organizations." *IBM Systems Journal* 32 (1): 4–16.

Karasek, R. A. 1979. "Job Demands, Job Decision Latitude, and Mental Strain: Implications for Job Design." *Administrative Science Quarterly* 24: 285–308.

Mumford, E. 2006. "The Story of Socio-technical Design: Reflections on Its Successes, Failures, and Potential." *Information Systems Journal* 16: 317–42.

Vriens, D., and J. Achterbergh. 2011. "Cybernetically Sound Organizational Structures I: De Sitter's Design Theory." *Kybernetes* 40 (3): 405–24.

Seventeen

Lowlands Socio-technical Design Theory and Lean Production

JAC CHRISTIS AND ERIK SOEPENBERG

INTRODUCTION

Lean Production (LP) can be regarded as a design approach in search of a theoretical foundation. In this chapter, we show that Lowlands Socio-technical Design Theory (STSL) could function as such a foundation. To reach this goal, we first describe STSL as a system theoretical reformulation of Original Socio-technical Theory (OSTS). Then we introduce the Toyota Production System as the origin of LP and the challenge it poses for the academic field of organization design. Next we give an exposition of Lowlands Socio-technical Design (STSL) as a structural design approach based on developments in system theory. We conclude by reformulating LP in STSL terms and show that LP is a subcase within the more general theory of STSL. We discuss the merits of both approaches and clarify some misunderstandings of Lean, both outside and inside the Lean community. Embedding LP in the more general language of STSL should enable us to discover similarities and differences, to start a process of mutual learning, and to integrate diverse design approaches in a theory of organizational design.

THE ORIGIN OF LOWLANDS SOCIO-TECHNICAL DESIGN THEORY AND LEAN PRODUCTION

THE ORIGIN OF STSL (LOWLANDS SOCIO-TECHNICAL DESIGN)

STSL was developed in the Netherlands by Ulbo De Sitter(see chapter 5). In the opinion of de Sitter, OSTS was correct in its practice. Instead of adapting workers to existing Tayloristic structures, it aimed at the transformation of that structure itself. Because the structure of the division of labor is also a structure of power relations, it struck at the heart of the organization—its power structure. However, De Sitterwas dissatisfied with both the concepts and design tools of OSTS. So he gave himself the task of a system theoretical reformulation of OSTS. At the conceptual level, he considered the distinction between technical and social subsystems to be a reification of what are, in fact, interconnected aspects of the same system. Redesign should be aimed not at the joint optimization of so-called social and technical subsystems but at integral design. The organizational structure should be designed in such a way that all aspects are improved simultaneously, including the quality of the organization (in terms of costs, quality, and time), the quality of work (in terms of stress, risks, and learning opportunities), and the quality of labor relations (in terms of cooperation and shared decision making).

THE ORIGIN OF LEAN: THE TOYOTA PRODUCTION SYSTEM

The Toyota Production System (TPS), now known as Lean Production (LP) or Lean Thinking (LT), was developed by the Toyota Motor Company as an answer to two problems it met after WWII. First, a small home market for different types of cars necessitated a flexible way of producing cars: "Toyota did not have the resources or the market to support many plants, and the product mix was too eclectic to justify dedicated plants" (Standard and Davis 1999, 60). Second, because of shortages on the capital market, it needed short cycle times (as the sum of processing time and waiting time). The time between purchasing raw materials and being paid by the customer had to be as short as possible. The result of years of experimenting with solutions to those problems was the TPS, a system that differed in essential ways from the mass-production systems of Ford and General Motors. So why didn't Toyoda take the Ford production system from the Rouge plant back to Toyota? There was too much material, floor space, time, and investment tied up for too long. Instead, the Toyota executives developed a completely different way of thinking about manufacturing (Standard and Davis 1999, 61).

According to Hopp and Spearman (2008), what was so revolutionary about the TPS was the fact that they did not take the existing production system with its functional structure, large batches, long setup times, and high levels of inventories as a given. Instead, they simplified the production system by introducing a flow system of just-in-time (JIT) production that necessitated small batches, short setup times, and continuous process improvement. This enabled them to install greatly simplified planning systems (pull systems such as KANBAN) and cost-accounting systems (known as Lean accounting).

LEAN AND ORGANIZATION DESIGN

According to Standard and Davis, Lean is a design approach in search of a scientific foundation. The science of organization design should assess its success and generalize it by embedding it in more abstract concepts and theories to be able to respecify it for different manufacturing and nonmanufacturing contexts. Lean is a success story (Schonberger 2008), and in this paper, we concentrate on embedding Lean in a more general theory. Within the field of operations management, Hopp and Spearman's *Theory of Factory Physics* (2008, third edition) has been called the science of Lean (as in Standard, Davis, 1999). It explains in a scientific way the success of Lean and clears up some (self-)misunderstandings of Lean. However, it concentrates on manufacturing and, within manufacturing, on discrete parts production on disconnected flow lines (Hopp and Spearman 2008, 11). Others try to embed Lean in Goldratt's theory of constraints (Levinson and Rerick 2002, Levinson 2007). In this chapter, we offer STSL as a noncompeting but complementary scientific foundation of

Lean. It offers a general system language that encompasses applications of Lean in other contexts such as high-variety/low-volume manufacturing (Suri 1998, 2010), service organizations (Seddon 2005), construction (Ballard 2008), and public organizations (Seddon 2008). It enables us to discover both general similarities and context-specific differences to start a process of mutual learning, to integrate all these insights in a theory of organizational design, and to add content to redesign proposals of, for example, the health care system as proposed by Porter and Teisberg (2006) and Christensen et al. (2009).

DESIGN PARAMETERS

Here we describe the design parameters that we then use to reformulate Lean in STSL concepts. To enable understanding of the STSL design parameters by non-Lowlands readers, we start with the way Mintzberg introduced the concept of design parameters.

MINTZBERG ON DESIGN PARAMETERS

Mintzberg (1983) introduced four groups of design parameters in his book *Structure in Fives:* design of positions, design of superstructure, design of lateral linkages, and design of decision-making systems. It is not difficult to recognize the first two groups as the design of the production structure and the last two groups as the design of the control or governance structure. According to Mintzberg, unit grouping (a parameter of the super structure) is the strongest parameter of all. As we will see, it is an enabling constraint both "downward" with respect to the design of positions (job design) and "upward" with respect to the design of the control structure (decision-making system and lateral linkages).

UNIT GROUPING: FUNCTIONAL AND MARKET-BASED STRUCTURES

We owe Mintzberg the insight that all bases for grouping can be reduced to two: functional and market grouping. In fact, we comprise all the bases for grouping discussed above to two essential ones: (1) market grouping, comprising the bases of output, client, and place; and (2) functional grouping, comprising the basis of knowledge, skill, work process, and function...In effect, we have the fundamental distinction between grouping activities by ends, by the characteristics of the ultimate markets served by the organization—the products and services it markets, the customers it supplies, the places where it supplies them—or by the means, the functions (including work processes, skills, and knowledge) it uses to produce its products and services (Mintzberg 1983, 53–54).

The same distinction is used in STSL, although with a different terminology. A primary process has as its end the transformation of a requested order (a customer, client, or patient with a wish) in a delivered order. The activities or operations carried out in the primary process are the means to reach that end. So you can group by means. You then look inside the organization in search of similar activities/operations that are grouped together into the same functionally specialized unit. In STSL this is called "operations-based grouping." In an operations-based structure, all operations are potentially or actually coupled to all customer orders.

That is what makes them heterarchical structures with all network elements being interrelated. And that is why these structures are so complex, prone to disturbances, and difficult to control.

You can also group by ends. You then look outside your organization at the market in search of similar order types. The different and interdependent operations that are needed for the production of a restricted set of similar orders are then placed together in the same organizational unit. In this way, you create independent or pooled streams around similar orders. That is why this is called "stream-based grouping" in STSL and "value streams" in Lean. According to Mintzberg, you will find market grouping at the higher and functional grouping at the lower levels of organizations, as in the divisionalized form. Both STSL and Lean propose to apply market grouping "all the way down" till you reach the level of cross-functional teams or cells as the lowest-level building blocks of your organization. This is one of the reasons you will not find this kind of organization in Mintzberg's configurations (see also Sabel 2006). In general, by stream-based grouping, you try to reduce variability in input, process, or output. Because an order is a customer/client with a wish (for a product or service), stream-based or market grouping can be the following:

- Product-based: Similar wishes for different customers (as often in manufacturing)
- Customer-based: Similar customers with different wishes (as often in services).[17;]
- Project-based: Similar projects in which unique wishes of customers are handled (as in architect bureaus)

The functional and market structures have different "downward" and "upward" effects. A functional structure enables job specialization at the job level and constrains the possibilities of job enlargement, enrichment,

17 The local cross-functional district teams of Buurtzorg Nederland and the local branches of Svenska Handelsbanken are examples of customer-based groupings.

and cross-functional teamwork. The opposite is the case with market grouping. The functional structure also leads to both a centralization of decision making and a proliferation of lateral linkages. The opposite is the case with market grouping: In effect, the functional structure lacks a built-in mechanism for coordinating the work flow. Unlike the market structures that contain the work-flow interdependencies within single units, functional structures impede both mutual adjustment among different specialists and direct supervision at the unit level by management. The structure is incomplete; additional means of coordination must be found. The natural tendency is to let coordination problems rise to higher-level units in the hierarchy, until they arrive at a level where the different functions in question meet. The trouble with this, however, is that the level may be too far removed from the problem (Mintzberg 1983, 59).

THE DESIGN PARAMETERS OF STSL

Here we present the parameters that we present in the next paragraph to reformulate Lean in terms of STSL's parameters. The parameters refer to the production structure (the grouping and coupling of performance operations) and the control structure (the grouping and coupling of control operations). The performance operations are subdivided into the categories of preparatory, making, and support operations. The preparatory functions include quoting, engineering, order processing, and procurement. The support functions include quality control, maintenance, logistics, accounting and control, and personnel. For reasons of space, we concentrate on the parameters of the production structure, including the parameter of separation/integration of performance and control:

- Functional concentration versus deconcentration. This parameter refers to the way of grouping of making functions: functional versus market grouping.
- Functional specialization versus despecialization. This parameter refers to the centralization versus decentralization of preparatory and support functions.

- Functional differentiation versus integration. This parameter refers to the level of division of labor or job specialization within the preparatory, making, and support functions.
- Separation versus integration of performance and control. This parameter refers to the separation versus integration of conception and execution.

Note that the three parameters of the production structure refer to the same phenomenon (functional or market grouping) applied both to different parts and to different levels of the primary process. The parameters are used in both a descriptive and a normative way: in complex and dynamic environments, the combination of functional deconcentration, despecialization, and integration enhances the quality of the organization, work, and labor relations.

FUNCTIONAL STRUCTURE: ECONOMIES AND DISECONOMIES OF SCALE

A typical functionally concentrated, specialized, and differentiated organization with separation of performance and control would look like figure 17.1 (and note that in Mintzberg's divisionalized form, this is the internal structure of the divisions and/or business units it is composed of):

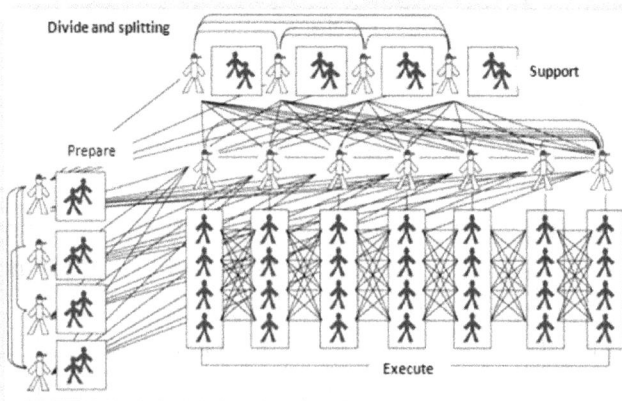

Figure 17.1 A Complex Organization with Simple Jobs (De Sitter1983, 138

The underlying idea of such an organizational structure is that cost reductions can be best achieved by exploiting economies of scale. At the same time, the diseconomies of scale that are created in this way are accepted and even made invisible. The idea of cost reduction by economies of scale informs not only the design of organizational structure but also the design of incentive and reward structures. As such, the functional structure is entrenched and difficult to change: you have to change both taken-for-granted ways of thinking (cultural change) and of doing (structural change). In a nutshell, the idea tells you that to reduce costs, you should group in a functional way, and you should optimize the functionally specialized parts or segments of the organization by aiming at job specialization (to economize on wage costs), maximal capacity utilization (to avoid idle capacity), and large batch production (to amortize setup times). Paradoxically, this leads to a suboptimization of the whole: it disrupts the order flow; creates excessive inventories with negative effects on costs, quality, cycle time, and flexibility; and increases coordination costs immensely, which necessitates high staff levels and the installment of complex planning and cost-accounting systems. Overhead costs will rise, and the paradox result of cost reduction in this way is a worsening of performance in terms of quality, time/speed, and costs. The system dynamics are shown in figure 17.2.

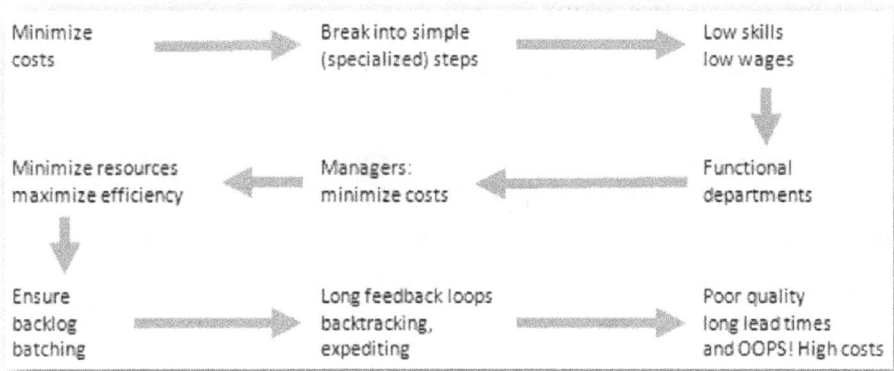

Figure 17.2 Diseconomies of scale (adapted from Suri, 2010, 45)

A SYSTEM THEORETICAL REFORMULATION OF LEAN

HOW NOT TO CHARACTERIZE LEAN

For some, Lean is about waste reduction (the seven forms of *muda*) and/ or continuous process improvement. This is a misleading characterization of Lean. First, waste reduction is neither a goal nor a manufacturing strategy: Is losing weight the definition of a good diet? No; it is better health, increased capabilities, and longer life. So it must be for Lean. More fittingly, Lean employs a large set of concepts and tools to reduce delays and quicken response in all processes. That is fundamental Lean, with time compression as its main focus (Schonberger, 2008, 45). Standard and Davis concur: "If eliminating waste is the central theme of an improvement effort, the benefits will be superficial...System improvement focuses on improving how material and information flow through the plant. Its objective is to minimize cycle time (Standard and Davis 1999, 134). So does Suri (2010). It's about time.

Second, if all important forms of waste are caused by functional batch-and-queue production, it isn't helpful to try to reduce waste within that structure. Improvement within those structures is called "kamikaze kaizen" by Womack and "paintball kaizen" by Standard and Davis (1999, 134). The most important gain is in substituting "organizing with the flow" for "organizing across the flow."

THE LEAN STRATEGY: FLOW PRODUCTION WITH CAPACITY BUFFERS

According to Hopp and Spearman (2008), in an ideal world without variability, demand and transformation can be perfectly aligned. However, the real world with variability necessitates buffers. Variability comes in two forms: demand and process or transformation variability. And buffers can take only three forms: time (when demand waits for products/ parts), inventory (when product is finished before demand), and capacity (which reduces the need for the other two buffers). For traditional bureaucratic organizations, idle capacity is the main waste. The guiding idea for organizing production is maximum resource utilization, which is best realized in a functional structure (Modig and Ahlstrom 2012). But such a manufacturing strategy necessarily produces waste in the form of time and/or inventory buffers (and, according to de Sitter, adds internal variability to demand variability). In contrast, the Lean strategy is aimed at flow efficiency (Modig and Ahlstrom 2012). The most important wastes are time end inventory buffers. To reduce those buffers, Lean introduces a flow structure, installs a pull planning system, and then starts a process of continuous improvement to further reduce process variability. But such a manufacturing strategy *necessitates capacity buffers*. Toyota exploited its understanding of the science of operations by using a 30 percent capacity buffer to support its strategy to drive consistent, low cycle times. Most Lean practitioners would label such a capacity buffer as non-cvalue-added and try to eliminate it...Toyota chose to pay for inventory reduction, low cycle times, and continuous-improvement efforts with its capacity buffer. The cost of the capacity buffer was outweighed by the ability it provided Toyota for buffering against variability to achieve lower inventories, reduced scrap, and better response time. This was the right choice for Toyota and was reflected in its financial statements (Pound, Bell, and Spearman 2014, 175–76).

PARAMETER 1. FLOW PRODUCTION: FUNCTIONAL DECONCENTRATION OR MARKET-BASED GROUPING

The evildoer for both Lean and STSL is functional batch-and-queue production; both turn over the production structure from a functional to a market-based one (functional deconcentration). In Lean, market-based groupings are called "value streams." The best way to think about a value stream is as a business segment focused on a product family, or sometimes, customer family. There is probably nothing more effective, in process improvement, than breaking up the functional silos and realigning the processes by the work flow in a product family. The work cell is a microcosm of this realignment. The focused factory and plants in a plant are enlarged variants. Linking a focused factory to a supply chain or customer chain extends the scheme further (Schonberger 2008, 106).

Lean is based on both a different way of thinking (the idea of economies of flow or flow efficiency) and of doing (designing organizational structures and reward and incentive systems that are informed by this idea). To create a flow, you take a restricted set of similar orders (for example, all titanium bicycles, as in Womack and Jones 2003), determine the operations/machines you need to produce this subset of orders, unfasten them from the floor, and place them together in a cross-functional value stream and/or manufacturing cell. The advantages are many. First, you reduce the complexity of the production structure by placing interdependent activities in the same unit. This reduces coordination needs and enables you to install immensely simplified planning and cost-accounting systems. Both planning and cost accounting are directed at the higher levels of value streams and manufacturing cells, not at individual levels of machines and operations, as in traditional planning and cost-accounting systems. In terms of costs, you reduce overhead costs, decrease the number of lateral linkages, and introduce performance criteria that are targeted at the optimization of the process as a whole.

Second, by introducing flow production, you lower inventories with positive effects on costs (less capital tied up in inventories, smaller storage space, less material handling, less risk of obsolescence), quality (early discovery of defects, less scrap and rework, and improvement of root-cause analysis), cycle time (shorter cycle times and less variability of cycle times), and flexibility (shorter cycle times postpones committing resources to production and thus enables adaptation to changes in customer orders). Instead of pitting costs against quality and time, Lean stresses the cost aspects of quality and time. By concentrating on improvements in quality and speed, costs will be reduced as a consequence, and new business will be generated.

PARAMETER 2. FLOW PRODUCTION: FUNCTIONAL DESPECIALIZATION OF PREPARATION AND SUPPORT FUNCTIONS

Functional despecialization is the same as functional deconcentration but is now applied to the preparatory and support functions. It means that formerly centralized preparatory and support functions are decentralized to the different value streams (as in the Bromont case, in which each cross-functional product unit has its own support unit). It's the same in Lean/QRM. Notice that each cluster (focused factory) has its own staff of engineering (manufacturing, quality, design), maintenance and material support (Nicholas and Soni 2006, 195). In QRM, this is called an "office cell." In QRM, shop-floor and office cells are always designed around a Focused Target Market Segment (FTMS). An office cell is based on the same design principles as applied to a shop-floor cell and is defined as "a closed-loop, collocated, dedicated, multifunctional, cross-trained team responsible for the office processing of all jobs belonging to a specific FTMS. The team has complete ownership of the cell's operation, and the primary goal of the team is reduction of the cell's [cycle time]" (Suri 2010, 14). Former overhead is now contained within the value streams and/or cells, which greatly simplifies both planning and cost accounting.

Functional despecialization corresponds to Mintzberg's horizontal and vertical decentralization or decentralization of staff and line functions, as in the divisionalized form. According to Mintzberg, decentralization can be selective and parallel. This corresponds to STSL's distinction between aspectual and integral control. Parallel decentralization or integral control is logically associated with market-based grouping. Each unit or division is decoupled from the others and is given the power necessary to make all those decisions that affect its own products, services, or geographical areas. In other words, parallel vertical decentralization is the only way to grant market-based units the power they need to function in a quasiautonomous manner (Mintzberg 1983, 102). Note that in Mintzberg's divisionalized form, market-based grouping and parallel decentralization stop at the divisional level, while in both STSL and Lean they are applied "all the way down" to the level of cross-functional teams or cells. That is one of the reasons why socio-technical and Lean organizations do not fit any of Mintzberg's five configurations[18]

PARAMETER 3. FLOW PRODUCTION: FUNCTIONAL INTEGRATION AND CROSS-TRAINING

After introducing flow in the manufacturing process and decentralizing preparatory and support functions to the value streams, functional deconcentration can now be applied to the internal structure of the cells (and or value streams). In each cell, different and interrelated operations are carried out on a restricted set of similar orders. The result is cross-functional teams that contrast with the functional teams of the functional structure. Application of cross-training makes the team members multiskilled and the team a flexible one. To record the level of cross-training, both STSL and Lean use the flex matrix. The vertical axis of the matrix contains all direct and indirect team tasks, and the horizontal axis contains all team members. Within the matrix, you can see who is able to carry out which task. According to Mintzberg, there is a trade-off between efficiency and quality of work: "Job enlargement pays to the extent that the gains from better-motivated workers in a particular job offset the losses from less-than-optimal technical specialization" (Mintzberg 1983, 31). Against this, both Lean and STSL can explain why organization and job design have direct and simultaneous positive effects on both efficiency and quality of work. They both point to the necessary macro- and meso-level preconditions for job enlargement and enrichment in conditionally autonomous teams at the job level. In this way, they create simple organizations with complex jobs and thus improve both the quality of the organization and the quality of work.

---

18 And because he thinks the distinction between functional and market grouping is irrelevant for professional bureaucracies, he misses the innovations that actually take place in health care and education; see Christis 2011.

PARAMETER 4. FLOW PRODUCTION: INTEGRATION OF PERFORMANCE AND CONTROL

According to Lazonick (2005), functional and hierarchical integration is one of the characteristics of the innovative enterprise (the other two being strategic control and financial commitment). All organizations have a certain level of functional or horizontal and hierarchical or vertical specialization. Most organizations also apply a deep level of division of labor. By functional differentiation and segmentation on the horizontal axis, they necessitate further hierarchical differentiation and segmentation on the vertical axis. The result is a bureaucratic, complex organization with simple jobs. A small vanguard of innovative organizations introduce functional and hierarchical integration in their organization. Lean and STSL do so by designing an organization that is composed of smaller organizations (the principle of modularity). They make these modules conditionally autonomous by delegating control tasks to those modules. "Operators in work cells typically have autonomy to make decisions and perform their own basic equipment maintenance, changeover, quality control, and job-scheduling (and) also engage in continuous-improvement efforts, data collection, and performance management, and even materials procurement from vendors" (Nicholas and Soni 2006, 79).

	Cost-based	Time-based
Organization:	Functional	Cellular (cross-functional manufacturing and office cells)
Management:	Top-down control	Team ownership
Teammembers:	Narrow, specialized	Cross-trained
Mind-set:	Efficiency and utilization goals	Relentless focus on cycle time reduction

Figure 17.3 Key transformations (adapted from Suri 2010, 46)

CONTINUOUS IMPROVEMENT AND ROUTINES

Most of the advantages of Lean are a consequence of its JIT flow system, with shorter cycle times and lower inventory levels. At the same time, this makes them extremely vulnerable to disruptions of the flow. Inventories act as safety buffers. Lowering them means lowering the safety buffers. So introducing flow structures at the same time makes process disruptions visible (by lowering inventory levels), creates the urgency to remove them (to prevent disruption of the flow), and creates the possibilities to do so (by multiskilled workers who have an overview of the interrelated operations of the process). Note that the design sequence is this: First install flow production (value streams and cells) and pull planning systems. Only then start the process of continuous improvement. Without continuous improvement at the process level, the system would fall apart. And without the introduction of flow and pull at the system level, process improvement makes little sense: Process improvement alone cannot produce systemwide advantages, and system improvement requires that specific processes within the system be modified (Standard and Davis 1999, 127).

Routines are an important part of the process of continuous improvement. In the Lean literature, a distinction is made between work standards and standard work. The former refers to the standards or routines formulated by Mintzberg's techno-structure and imposed on the workers. It is an example of the separation of conception and execution. *Standard work* refers to standards or routines that are developed, critically reviewed, and updated by the frontline workers themselves. It is an example of the integration of conception and execution: "Whereas the former [standard work] relies mostly on the efforts of shop-floor teams to develop standards, the latter [work standards] imposes standards that are developed by staff specialists and engineers." (Nicholas and Soni 2006, 163–64).

CONCLUSION

COMMONALITIES

We showed that Lean corresponds to the prescriptive STSL parameters: Lean combines functional deconcentration, functional despecialization,

functional integration, and integration of performance and control functions. Both STSL and Lean regard cross-functional teams or cells as the
basic building blocks of the organization. The advantages of the shift
from functional to cross-functional units are many:

- Cells eliminate inventory (and so frees cash flow).
- Cells shorten cycle time (and so creates cash flow and generates
  new business).
- Cells draw interrelated processes together in time and place (and
  so enables continuous improvement of quality, speed, and costs).
- Cells eliminate overhead costs (by simplifying planning and cost-
  accounting systems).
- As the first customer of product engineering, cells enable design
  for manufacturing.

However, designing value streams and/or cells can be a difficult affair.
There are many ways of grouping similar orders, and finding the right one
can be a hard nut to crack. Designing streams and/or segments within
streams can take different forms according to the situation you start with.
To simplify matters, De Sitterdistinguishes three different design contexts
or start situations: crisscross or spaghetti streams, latent streams, and one
single stream (fig. 17.4). These are called heterogeneous, semihomogeneous, and homogeneous streams in Kuipers and van Amelsvoort (1990).

Crisscross streams	Latent streams	One stream
Many different products/variants	Mainly product-variants	One product with different design
Many differences in operational combinations and sequences	Differences in operational combinations but less in sequences	Identical operations and fixed sequences
Hundreds of routings	Dozens of routings	One routing
Example: part supplier	Example: Producer of furniture	Example: Assembly of mass product

Figure 17.4 Design situations (de Sitter 1994, 245)

These correspond to Hopp and Spearman's distinction (based on Hayes and Wheelwright 1979) between the jumbled flow (job shop), the disconnected line flow (batch production), and the connected line flow (assembly line).

DESIGN PRINCIPLES AND CONTEXTS IN MANUFACTURING

We can first use these different design contexts to resolve a debate that is raging in the Lean community: Is QRM the same as or totally different from Lean? Lean in its classical, Toyota, form was developed for high-volume/low-variety production. It was then applied to the different design situations of semihomogeneous and heterogeneous streams. In the way it had to invent new tools because tools such as value stream mapping, KANBAN, and leveled production make no sense in the high-variety/low-volume situation (crisscross streams). Suri developed QRM to meet the high-variety/low-volume situation. In this way, he developed tools that are applicable in the other design situations. So both apply the same higher-level principles to different lower-level design contexts. Both are extensively covered in De Sitter1987 and 1994. De Sitteroffers a set of analytical tools for introducing flow production in these different situations that are broader than and partly overlap with the tools offered in the Lean/QRM literature. On the other hand, STSL was never as creative as Lean in developing simplified planning and cost-accounting systems and visual-control systems.

The discussion of STSL and Lean seems to focus on the design of the assembly line. The general idea of De Sitteris to redesign the assembly line into parallel flows with less stations in which less people carry out more interdependent tasks in longer "takt" or work-cycle times. This can take the form of phase groups, minilines, dock groups, and preassembly in module groups and can cumulate in assembly groups in which the complete product is made in a few phases by one or a few groups (as in the Volvo Uddevalla plant in Sweden). Apart from the effect on the quality of work, this would drastically reduce system losses: takt time is inversely related to system losses of the line structure such as stochastic losses, balancing losses, and so on. In Womack, Jones, and Roos (1990), the assembly groups of Uddevalla are presented as a naïve return to a lost time of craft production. On the other hand, the average Japanese takt time was ninety seconds, which is long when compared to European firms (thirty-two seconds for the Fiesta in Belgium and forty seconds for the Peugeot in France, according to de Sitter). This explains at least part of the Japanese success. Moreover, when confronted with a tight labor market, Toyota started to experiment with "Scandinavian" forms of work in restructuring at the assembly line (Pill and Fujimoto 2007).

LEAN AND MEAN?

The time has come for the socio-technical community to shed its prejudices on Lean. The first one is that Lean concentrates on process improvement and neglects organizational design. As we showed, this is an absurd accusation. A second one is that Lean neglects quality of work. Bromont is a star case of Lean/Six Sigma within General Electric. Those who visited the plant and spoke with the workers and team leaders know, again, that this is an absurd accusation. Its structure, with cross-functional manufacturing and support cells, can be called socio-technical, and we all admired the way frontline workers are involved in the continuous process of improvement and innovation of the plant. Long ago, Lean added the underutilization of human capacities as a form of waste, and the spirit of Lean is well captured by Schonberger (2008): *"Lean is hard on processes and soft on people."* By substituting capacity buffers for time and inventory buffers, Lean enables frontline workers to participate in the process of continuous improvement. The opposite is the case in functional, bureaucratic structures: By aiming at maximum capacity utilization, these organizations are hard on people and soft on processes. These are the real mean organizations.

REFERENCES

Achterbergh, J., and D. Vriens. 2009. *Social Systems Conducting Experiments*. Berlin: Springer.

0

1

Ashby, W. 1956. *Introduction to Cybernetics.* London: Chapman and Hall.

Ballard, G. 2008. "The Lean Project Delivery System: An Update." *Lean Construction Journal* 2008, 1–19.

Barnard, C. 1938. *The Functions of the Executive.* Cambridge: Harvard University Press.

Beer, S. 1979. *The Heart of Enterprise.* New York: Wiley.

Black, J., and S. Hunter 2003. *Lean Manufacturing Systems and Cell Design.* Dearborn: Society of Manufacturing Engineers.

Christensen, C.J. Grossma, J. Hwang 2009. *The Innovator's Prescription. A Disruptive Solution for Health Care.* New York: McGraw Hill.

Christis, J. 1998. *Arbeid, Organisatie en Stress.* Amsterdam: Spinhuis.

Christis, J., and B. Fruytier 2006. "Competentiemanagement : Een Kritiek en Een Alternatief." *Tijdschrift Voor HRM* 4: 6–16.

Christis, J. 2009. *Wat Is Slim Organiseren?* Groningen: Hanzehogeschool.

Christis, J. 2010. "Organization and Job Design: What is Smart Organizing?" In: H. van Lieshout, L. Polstra, J. Christis, and B. Emans, *Managament of Labour: Societal and Managerial Perspectives.* Groningen: KCA.

Christis, J. 2013. *Handleiding Competentiemanagement Instrument.* Groningen: KCA.

Christis, J. 2014. *Netwerkanalyse.* Groningen: KCA.

de Sitter, L. U., A. Vermeulen, P. van Amelsvoort, L. van Geffen, P. van Troost, F. Verschuur 1987. *Het Flexibele Bedrijf.* Deventer: Kluwer.

de Sitter, L. U. 1994. *Synergetisch Produceren*. Assen: Van Gorkum.

Hopp, W., and M. Spearman. 2008. *Factory Physics*. New York: McGraw-Hill.

Hayes, R, and S. Wheelwright. 1979. "Link Manufacturing Process and Product Life Cycles." *Harvard Business Review* (January–February), 133–140.

Kuipers, H., and P. van Amelsvoort. 1990. *Slagvaardig Organiseren*. Deventer: Kluwer.

Lazonick, W. 2007. "Varieties of Capitalism and Innovative Enterprise." *Comparative Social Research* 24: 21–69.

Lawrence, David. 2002. *From Chaos to Care. The Promise of Team-Based Medicine*. Cambridge: Da Capo Press.

Levinson, W. 2007. *Beyond the Theory of Constraints*. New York: Productivity Press.

Levinson, W., and R. Rerick 2002. *Lean Manufacturing: A Synergistic Approach to Minimizing Waste*. Milwaukee: ASQ Quality Press.

Mintzberg, H. 1983. *Structure in Fives*. New Jersey: Prentice Hall.

Pound, E., J. Bell, and M. Spearman. 2014. *Factory Physics for Managers*. New York: McGraw Hill.

Porter, M., and E. Teisberg. 2006. *Redefining Health Care*. Boston: Harvard Business School Press.

Nicholas, J. and A. Soni. 2006. *The Portal to Lean Production*. New York: Auerbach Publications.

Porter, M. 2008. "Value-Based Health Care Delivery." *Annals of Surgery* 248 (4): 503–10.

Roberts, K. 1990. "Some Characteristics of One Type of High-Reliability Organization." *Organization Science* 1 (2): 160–76.

Sabel, C. 2006. "A Real-Time Revolution in Routines." In C. Heckscher and P. Adler (eds.), *The Firm as a Collaborative Community*. Oxford: Oxford University Press.

Schonberger, R. 2008. *Best Practices in Lean Six Sigma Process Improvement*. New York: Wiley.

Seddon, J. 2005. *Freedom from Command and Control: Rethinking Management for Lean Service*. New York: Productivity Press.

Seddon, J. 2008. *Systems Thinking in the Public Sector*. Axminster: Triarchy Press.

Simon, H. 1996. "The Architecture of Complexity," in Simon, *The Sciences of the Artificial*. Cambridge: MIT Press.

Simon, H. 1997. *Administrative Behavior*. New York: Free Press.

Standard, C., and D. Davies. 1999. *Running Today's Factory*. Cincinnati: Hanser Gardner Publications.

Suri, R. 1998. *Quick-Response Manufacturing: A Companywide Approach to Reducing Lead Times*. New York: Productivity Press.

Suri, R. 2010. *It's About Time*. New York: Productivity Press.

Takahiro, F., and F. Pil. 2007. "Lean and Reflexive Production." *International Journal of Production Research* vol. 45 (16): 3741–62.

Thompson, J. 1967. *Organizations in Action*. New Brunswick: Transaction Publishers.

Weick, K., and K. Sutcliffe, K. 2007. *Managing the Unexpected: Resilient Performance in an Age of Uncertainty,* second edition. San Francisco: John Wiley and Sons, Inc.

Womack, J. and Jones, D. (2003). *Lean Thinking*. New York: Free Press.

Womack, J., D. Jones, and D. Roos. 1990. *The Machine That Changed the World: The Story of Lean Production*. New York: Rawson.

Eighteen

Changing the Nature of Work: Toward Total Workplace Innovation

INTRODUCTION

Turbulence, turbulence, and even more turbulence—that is the environment in which organizations are operating nowadays. Change, change, and even more change—that is the response that today's organizations have adopted. Organizational change therefore seems to have become one of the main social problems or risks in contemporary society. Yet study after study indicates that the rate of change is not quite as fast as it would appear. However, it appears that a radical change is gathering momentum. In this chapter, we explore the underlying reason. First, we focus on the hows and whys of the traditional organization. Then we present an environmental overview. It will not come as a surprise that customers nowadays have different expectations from those of half a century ago. In the labor market too, we have reached a milestone in history; we appear to be on the verge of a new era. It is time for a paradigmatic shift. Next, we examine the new paradigm. *Total Workplace Innovation*, which is the issue at stake, is an integrated version of various design theories and traditions. We conclude our chapter by looking ahead to the end of this century.

THE TRADITIONAL MANNER OF WORKING

From the eighteenth century onward, when employees were first gathered together under one roof in workshops, the organization of work became a major issue. Before then, farmers and artisans largely determined, of their own accord, when and how they worked. The rise of these workshops drastically changed this. A constant factor in the evolution is the increasing specialization of work, toward processing. As production workshops grew in size, the work could increasingly be subdivided into specialized tasks. Workers no longer made products but only performed a specific procedure. The Scottish moral philosopher Adam Smith observed this advanced division of labor during his visits to factories in the eighteenth century. He advocated the rapid dissemination of specialization; he anticipated that it would result in major productivity gains. The reasons for this are the increased expertise employees acquire when carrying out simple activities—no time is lost switching between different tasks and tools, and there is the potential to use machines to perform simple tasks and to limit the necessary training period. As a result, it becomes possible to recruit cheaper laborers.

At the end of the nineteenth century, the American engineer Frederick Taylor was a major proponent of this standardization. He felt that by letting employees themselves work out how best to approach their work, the capitalist/entrepreneur of the time was missing out on the opportunity to earn large profits. In those days, piecework pay was commonplace. The general assumption is that employees work harder when they are paid per piece. The reality is very different. If they did this, they would produce a greater "supply," whereas the "demand" remains the same. A burgeoning supply while demand remains level makes the price plummet. The employees under Taylor's command knew this very well and were therefore dragging their feet. They worked sufficiently slowly to ensure that the supply produced remained just lower than the demand, to keep the price artificially as high as possible. Taylor was aware of the practice because he had been a laborer himself for a while. As long as the laborers kept the production process under their control, the company and society would remain deprived of potential productivity gains. This required a separation between managers and workers in the organization, with the managers specializing in the scientific development of the preparation and support of the work and the workers needing to ensure that these rules were actually followed. A new social category was born: *management*. It is a professional group that has continued to grow to this day. In addition to specialization or better simplification in executing the work, another specialization focused on thinking about performing the work. The preparation and support of the work were assigned to numerous specialized departments.

This method for organizing work was widely disseminated in the last century—not only in factories, but also in offices and educational and care organizations. Anyone who thinks this method of organization has now become obsolete has been hoodwinked by management talk of a "horizontal, learning organization in the knowledge economy." It remains the dominant organization method. Surgeons performing operations in specialist treatment wards for cataracts, knees, or hips are examples of a contemporary application of the organization principles developed early last century. Highly skilled knowledge workers in call centers, reciting imposed scripts that must be completed within three minutes, populate one of the fastest-growing sectors of our economy.

Most large organizations operate on the basis of an impressive number of departments and subdivisions, according to the "process" that needs to be completed for the product or service. The customer order to be processed (a product or service) is split into the elementary components that are subjected to the processing. The result is that the product or customer needs to travel long distances between departments, facing delays on every occasion and a risk of disruption. What is happening here, on every occasion? The organization first and foremost looks "inward," to the activities it performs. Next, similar activities will be accommodated within the same organizational unit. The result is a *functional structure*.

In such a structure, the employee forms part of a functional team in which similar actions can be carried out on all orders. Little cohesion exists between the activities at the team level and unit level, so there is little cooperation. Employees who belong to the same department or team in a functional structure often have the illusion that they are *collaborating*.

They are not collaborating in the sense that they are completing a common product or service together, through each other's work. A team of tax inspectors checking up on different taxpayers does not collaborate. According to Marx, these employees are alienated from each other because they perform work that is (functionally) detached. Why do they retain the illusion that they are collaborating? They are working in close proximity to each other, but that is all these colleagues actually have in common.

At the level of the organization as a whole system, there is close collaboration among the different components of the structure. After all, they may all be linked to the orders. This results in a complex organization with fragmented subtasks, and every subtask is, in principle, linked to every other subtask. The functional-organization method is often associated with short-cycle work, still driven by Ford and the call centers. In fact, it is a special version that applies fragmentation to an extreme level. But this comes at a price. We already learned this during our days in the Scouts, with the game "Chinese whispers," when we whispered a message from the start to the end of the chain, losing some of the content in the process. With every whisper-and-listen interaction—with every step of the process-oriented production process—we run the risk of something going wrong. We have lost sight of those system losses. While the focus is placed on the specialist operation, in search of economies of scale, the question arises: *Who is actually looking after the customer?*

PROBLEMS CAUSED BY A CHANGING ENVIRONMENT

The traditional manner of working was hugely successful in the last century. The functional organization is designed for an environment that is *stable, secure, simple,* and *transparent.* However, since the 1970s, organizations have needed to meet other, more pressing requirements. The environment became VUCA: *volatile, uncertain, complex,* and *ambiguous.* In the market, the emphasis increased on high-quality products and services, in addition to competition on *price.* Japanese automobile manufacturers suddenly started to compete with Western car manufacturers, based on the *quality* of the cars they made. In the following decade, they piled on the pressure with fast delivery in a twenty-four-hour economy, partly due to globalization. The variety in the range of goods on offer also increased drastically due to the individualization of society. The 1980s were characterized by a drive to increase *flexibility.*

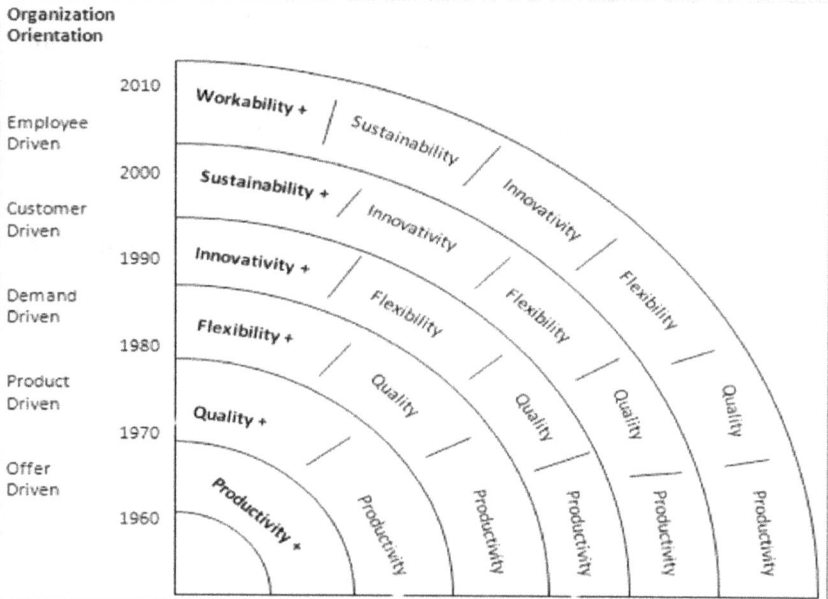

Figure 18.1 Demands Imposed by the Market in the Past Few Decades, adaption based on P. Bolwijn and T. Kumpe, 1991.

The end of the 1980s saw a geopolitical landslide. There was glasnost in Poland, the Berlin Wall came down, and the Chinese communist party changed direction. The Western economy woke up in a new global economy and realized that comparatively high wages could be maintained only if *innovation* became the hallmark of our economy. As we entered the twenty-first century, the requirement for *sustainability* was added to this. The realization that our ecological footprint needs to shrink eventually also reached the boardrooms of virtually every organization. Since 2010, we can add another demand to the list. Following two consecutive baby booms in the previous century, we have operated in a plentiful labor market over the past fifty years. We are now in a completely different situation. Given the combination of a decline in the number of young people and the aging population, a growing number of people are exiting the labor market. We have now grown used to the idea that we will need to work longer to compensate for this. The job itself will need to make this feasible. Organizations must therefore need to offer *healthy* work.

Figure 18.1 shows that these criteria do not replace each other but exert cumulative pressure on organizations. Under the pressure of this combination of requirements, organizations applying a traditional, process-oriented, or functional job division are facing an increasingly difficult time. Managing them in the rapidly changing environment becomes increasingly complex; internal communication is challenging, and the response time is excessive. The troubleshooting potential of their employees is too small, their internal relationships become more strained, and they are faced with a higher risk of stress. In virtually every sector, this becomes manifest through a number of generic bottlenecks. A frequently used metaphor to visualize this type of organization is a row of contiguous silos. Between the silos, there is a never-ending occurrence of coordination problems. The tragic aspect is that the harder each silo (and every employee) tries to do its utmost to achieve its own (suboptimal) targets, the harder they find it to reach harmony, and the more coordination problems and conflicts arise as a result. Customers demand ever-shorter delivery times, which makes it more important to be informed of each other's field of activity and to make clear agreements with the others.

The increase in knowledge in particular adds further pressure. As a result, there is a growing need for a multidisciplinary approach, but the functional design of organizations is completely unsuited to that purpose. A functional design results in a fragmented approach to the customer because every department or silo is responsible for only part of the customer's requirements, whereas nobody has the overall responsibility. It seems paradoxical, but it is absolutely typical of functionally structured organizations that they do not focus on the customer but rather on their own departments and their own processes. Managers therefore take the most obvious action, which is to impose more rules and procedures. This conflicts with the need for autonomy in a VUCA world.

This situation can easily end up in a vicious circle of bureaucracy. This is illustrated by the law of Van Hootegem: "There is no such thing as a perfect rule. Any imperfections of an intrinsically imperfect rule are, as a rule, replaced by a new, intrinsically imperfect rule. The latter imperfections are, as a rule, replaced by a new, intrinsically imperfect rule." To express it in Weber's words, "Mankind has locked itself inside an iron cage" (Weber, 1904–1905). In numerous organizations, it seems even more apt to refer to a "gilded cage" (Vranken 2013, 355).

CHALLENGES IN THE LABOR MARKET

The Western population is simultaneously aging and experiencing a reduction in the proportion of young people. The group of young people potentially entering the labor market is becoming gradually smaller compared with the group of people reaching retirement age. In 1990 in Flanders, there were still 124 young people (fifteen- to twenty-four-year olds) for every 100 older employees (aged over fifty-five). Nowadays, there are already fewer young people than people over fifty-five. In 2025, there will be only 74 young people for every 100 older employees. Meanwhile, the group of people aged over sixty-five is clearly getting bigger. It is therefore logical that many sectors are making efforts to maximize the inflow of young people, encouraging them to choose bottleneck occupations such as those in the care sector, the IT sector, or engineering. However, that is far from being the only way to resolve the staff shortage. Working on the quality of working life itself ensures that employees remain in work for longer and that the sector's appeal increases at the same time. To get an idea of the jobs considered "high-quality," we can use the stress model designed by Karasek (1979). This model indicates that the job demands of the work itself do not cause stress; rather, it the combination of work-related demands and the scope for decision making is associated with job control. If that scope is limited, high work-related demands cannot be met, which causes stress symptoms. Inversely, having sufficient scope for decision making makes it possible to handle work-based demands adequately. As a result, these demands are instead experienced as challenging and motivating, and the job provides opportunities to learn (fig. 18.2). Karasek's model offers a positive message. After all, it not only shows that there is a way to prevent risks, but also that the absence of these risks in turn results in greater learning opportunities, satisfaction, motivation, drive, innovative employee behavior, and eventually better performance by employees. It is therefore not only about avoiding risks but also about providing all sorts of opportunities.

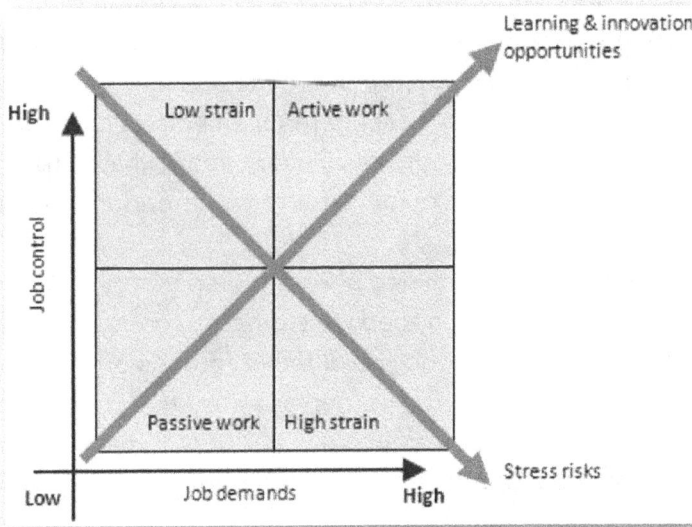

Figure 18.2 Job Demands Control Model
(Karasek and Theorell, 1996)

The data gathered through the ECWS survey (European Foundation, 2011) nevertheless spells out a disappointing message. Working in an economy dominated by functional organizations carries a high risk of ill health. Less than one third of Europeans (26 percent, to be precise), are employed in a workplace that is potentially bad for their health. In other words, 154,660,000 salaried Europeans risk falling ill due to the fact that they are insufficiently in control of their job demands and their jobs). Converting exhausting jobs to active jobs requires adjustments in the way the work is organized.

TOTAL WORKPLACE INNOVATION (TWIN)

For a good customer focus, organizations must look "outward" to the customers and their preferences before grouping similar customers or customer requests (referred to as "orders"). We advocate an order-oriented organization as an alternative to its functional counterpart.

Total workplace innovation follows a specific design sequence (see also chapter 6). For this purpose, we must first perform a mission and vision exercise. It is highly recommended that the design is drafted with the help of co-creaion. *"Fetch the whole system into the room"* is the best guarantee for success. Based on the mission and vision, a strategy is developed, along with practical job requirements to meet the performance. It is crucially important to calculate not only what output we wish to achieve but also what it could cost and which performance requirements are less important.

What needs to be determined after the preparatory work has been completed is what the value-added work process consists of. It is helpful in that respect to work out who the different (groups of) customers are. These questions seem superfluous, perhaps absurd, but many organizations wrestle with them. One example is the printer manufacturers who now predominantly sell ink. Or the producers of coffee machines, who are currently only after the sales of coffee. Once all these questions have been answered, we will have identified the value-adding activities that our organization creates for its customers. By agreement, that is what we refer to as the *executing* activities. The following step is to *sort* the customers and their orders. This must be done by going in search of customers (orders) with common characteristics. We go in search of sub-sets of customer families (orders) showing great homogeneity in terms of quality requirements. That in turn imposes identical claims on the manner in which the production process must be carried out. We are therefore looking for criteria to divide patients, students, lingerie, biomass power stations, episodes of a soap, and so on, into relatively homogeneous subsets. Around those subsets, a miniature organization is formed that completes the process from A to Z for this group of customer orders. We refer to the process described above as *parallelization*. We create parallel order streams that each have major interdependence within the stream but re minimally dependent on each other.

In principle, preparatory and supporting activities are kept close to the value-adding process. This makes the organization more versatile and dynamic in its response to customer requests. Further, that makes it possible to create active and manageable jobs because we make *job demands* and *job control* interact. The cherry on the cake is still to come. The control structure is addressed once these design choices in the core work processes have been made. We design it bottom up. Here we apply the same creed: "Do it decentrally, *unless...*" It leaves room to maneuver with regard to the customer, the employee, and society in search of active work. This allows for a more democratic organization to be created, with fewer managers. In this organization, managers are in principle no longer concerned with extinguishing fires but with strategic decisions that matter and that make a difference. By designing the management structure last and by doing it bottom up, the design sequence for Total Workplace Innovation is complete.

The result of this design work consists of a number of parallel order units and teams, ideally specialized according to the type of customer or order. There is great internal cohesion, empowerment, independence, and entrepreneurship. The design is immensely flexible. Depending on market developments, streams can be closed down or cloned. The organization is therefore sufficiently agile to respond to market developments without the need for restructuring. The interference between the streams is kept to a minimum, but it requires attention. The tanker (the functional organization) is converted into a group of smaller "boats" that differ from each other. However, a group of boats alone doesn't make a fleet. There is a constant need for vigilance and instruments for horizontal coordination.

The design work we have carried out so far must be situated in Lowlands socio-technical design theory. This is a theory about how to organize things differently and better. It first saw the light in the 1950s at the Tavistock Institute in Great Britain.

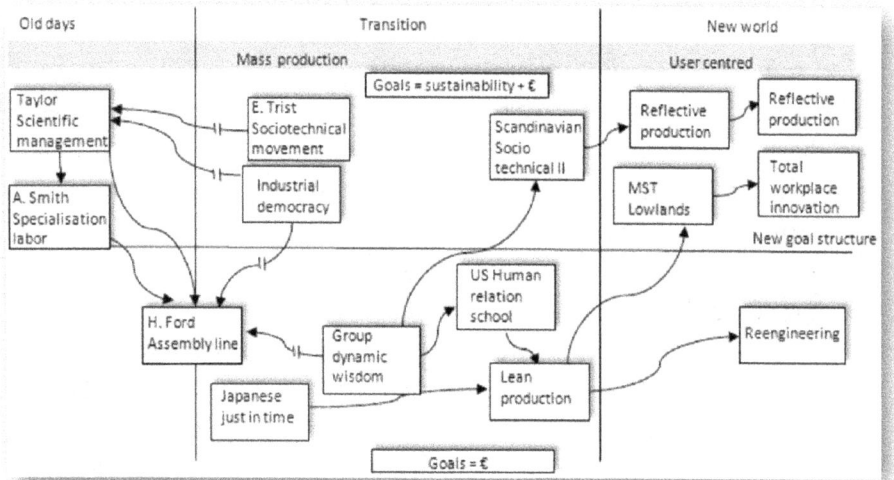

Figure 18.3 Theoretical genealogy of Total Workplace Innovation
(Adaption based on figure designed by R. Karasek)

Figure 18.3 illustrates the theoretical genealogy that is developed in greater detail here. Based on research and consultancy work on the subject of technological innovations in British mines, Trist, Bamforth, and Emery concluded that the technical and social systems needed to be designed in a congruent manner. In this chapter, the theoretical foundation can be found in our Low Countries. De Sitterplayed a leading role in that regard. He developed a theory on production processes, which was partially based on the social-systems theory.

Hence the plea to let the modern socio-technical systems approach evolve into a full-fledged theory (van Hootegem 2000). During the current evolution, a dialogue was organized with other prominent organizational concepts. The Lean philosophy and its associated toolbox were launched by means of a business management book that almost reads like a thriller: The *machine that changed the world* (see also chapter 19). Because this publication treated the Volvo experiments with small autonomous groups as a laughing matter and because modifications to the conveyor-belt system are considered revolutionary, the socio-technical systems community originally took a firm stand against this new, currently still-continuing management hype. "Lean," which can mean slim as well as frugal, is a collective name for various types of systems innovations that were developed within the Toyota group and have found their way into virtually all sectors around the world. Lean distinguishes seven different forms of waste (muda). The list fails to include the cost inflicted by poor quality of working life. This cost is felt when we train people without making the most of their talent in the functional structure because the same is expected from everyone in the same job. Anyone capable of achieving more derives no benefit from demonstrating it because the system— set up for boring uniformity—cannot handle that much talent. This is a major difference from the socio-technical design, in which we develop job specifications tailored to the preferences and competencies of the employees (job crafting). Any underutilization of talent in the functional organization is a cost. Lean considers goods that are put into storage as a cost. The Lean philosophy completely ignores competencies that are not used and are therefore put into storage as far as society is concerned. The same goes for costs caused by jobs being of inferior quality. Lean does not give a second glance to absenteeism, attrition, shorter working lives, most of all, a great deal of human suffering. However, all these issues cost our society, which indirectly includes the organizations, enormous sums of money. For that reason, we go in search of *Total Workplace*

Innovation (TWIN) by integrating Lean into the modern socio-technical systems approach by listing *eight and a half types of waste.*

The Lean tools can be easily integrated in the manner in which we design our order streams. Creating a flow, a smooth flow of movement, the constant endeavor is to be customer-friendly; these aspirations are shared by both organizational concepts. It moved Christis to provocatively conclude that the modern socio-technical systems approach is in fact the theoretical cradle of Lean (Christis, 2011) (see chapter 19). A word of warning seems appropriate during this integration exercise. Lean places a heavy focus on standardization. Its followers have elevated the participative development of standard operating procedures (SOPs) to virtually an art form. It seems only logical to look for the most appropriate standard for any operations that occur frequently. It seems less logical to record them bureaucratically in protracted procedures than to continue the collective search for increasingly better procedures from a dynamic learning perspective. An attempt is made to establish standards that everyone would need to adhere to. This may work in mass-production environments, but in organizational contexts with professionals, a standardizing practice of this nature will soon be met by resistance.

If TWIN is to fulfill all expectations, the integration process is not yet complete. So far, this chapter has dealt with the level of the *structure of the division of labor.* Starting out from design requirements and specifications, design parameters are applied to separate the labor, resulting in a network of jobs and associated roles. This is how a network of mutual behavioral expectations is created. The *Relational Coordination* theory, developed by Gittel (2003), has helped us complete the realization of the network. The theory is used to examine precisely what sets efficient airlines and hospitals apart from their less efficient competitors. Her answer: "The relationships among the employees!" Next she lists the interventions that efficient organizations use to safeguard the coordination of their internal relationships. Her list is quite diverse in nature. Some interventions come directly from the modern socio-technical systems recipe book. By contrast, others are mainly related to the structure of the division of labor. In a functional organization, the division of labor is by definition static. Mobility among different workplaces within a task-oriented division or silo is slightly surrealistic because it is a move to the same. Conversely, shifting between the silos is difficult because completely disparate competencies are mobilized in different silos.

An entirely new mobility perspective is created in a socio-technically designed organization. There will be a diversity of roles, as a matter of principle. In addition, the organization will include wide-ranging, overlapping roles within the streams, following the flexibility test. By developing a mobility policy on top of this design, organizations will gain widely shared knowledge of their customers and operations. In other words, it will lead to organizational empathy, which will be constantly nurtured. The time span for organizing these coordinated relationships can differ significantly. For example, employees may rotate several times within one working day. Security officers in Scandinavian airports are rotating almost constantly, enabling several employees to keep an eye on travelers from several different observation points. Employees can be mobile and accompany a customer. A group of teachers can follow a group of pupils for a prolonged period, or a nurse can look after a group of discharged patients at home. It can also be a method to create longer cycle times during line work. Employees can be regularly transferred to another stream or branch. Some jobs may be given a more project-based nature, opening up the possibility of temporary tasks.

A chemical company developed a rotation scheme that enabled employees to swap one production job for another. After seven months, they were moved to a job in the maintenance department. Next, they returned to their original production job. To maintain a feel for the maintenance work, employees spend one week in six in maintenance jobs, within the twenty-one months spent in production. In short, mobility patterns can be structured in many different ways. Regardless of the way it is achieved, coordinating relationships through a carefully thought-out mobility policy ensures that employees make a vastly increased number of connections. In addition to the strong ties of employees who retain a functional relationship, weak connections are built up between employees who once used to have a functional relationship. The latter are particularly important for the innovation and mobilization of resources.

We have now gradually unfolded the new world of work (NWOW), at least in one particular meaning. After all, on some occasions NWOW presents itself as a story to facilitate dismissing the era of individual, closed offices to the history bin. Based on activity studies that take us back to the era of the Taylorist *time and motion* studies, collective-activity zones are furnished with trendy furniture. Sometimes this resembles a return of the functional organization. At other times, the picture painted is much more comprehensive. It's a story about other forms of collaboration, about trust, about not being bound by location and time. That is the picture we wish to finish our paper with: integrating the NWOW story into the TWIN paradigm. After all, it should be obvious that the story that is slowly drawing to a close has far-reaching implications for the infrastructural requirements arising in the new organization's environment. Regardless of whether we are looking at factories, offices, schools or hospitals, architecture or interior design, spatial design or IT design, the new organization can prosper only through diversity and pluralism, with internal connections based on its vision, strategy, and common interests. It can simultaneously deliver space and collect space for a bespoke customer-based approach. The organization designed as an archipelago.

CONCLUSION

Many ideas discussed in this chapter have been in existence for some time. It is fair to ask why they have never been picked up before. There are two parts to the answer. In fact, they was only a partial answer to a universal question. The lack of integration was acutely felt. What was needed was a comprehensive concept. Furthermore, the time was not ripe. Scientific insights can be far ahead of their time. The fact that it should work well now is related to a unique, combined momentum. The circumstances in the economy and the labor market are so compelling that organizations will have no other choice. Is it likely that tomorrow we will be working in organizations with the TWIN design label? The short answer is no! Organizations are systems that stabilize behavior—that is what makes them able to achieve what a disparate group of people would be unable to achieve. However, it can also work against them. They find it difficult to handle change. By nature, they are slow to change; in addition, the proposed design significantly shakes up the power balance. We will need brave bosses to provide strong, genuine leadership. There is no doubt that the new organization will win eventually. It took Taylor and Ford a century to become dominant and subsequently irrelevant. What is the forecast? That by 2099, we will all be working in a TWIN organization...

REFERENCES

Bolwijn, P., and T. Kumpe. 1991. *Marktgericht Ondernemen: Management van Continuïteit en Vernieuwing*. Assen: Van Gorcum/Stichting Management Studies.

Christis, J. 2011. "De Moderne Socio-techniek als Theoretische Onderbouwing van Lean" ("The Modern Socio-technical Systems Approach as the Theoretical Foundation of Lean"). *M and O* 65: 96–115.

de Sitter, L. U. 1994. *Synergetisch Produceren: Human Resources Mobilisation in de Productie: Een Inleiding in de Structuurbouw (Synergetic Production: Human Resources Mobilisation in the Production: An Introduction to Building the Structure)*. Assen: Van Gorcum.

_De Smet, M. 2009. *Liefde voor Het Werk in Tijden van Management: Open Brief van Een Arts (Loving the Job in the Days of Management: Open Letter from a Doctor)*, third edition. Tielt: Lannoo. 222.

Ford, H. 1922. *My Life and Work*. London: Heinneman.

Gittell, J. 2003. *The Southwest Airlines Way: Using the Power of Relationships to Achieve High Performance*. New York: McGraw Hill.

Karasek, R. 1979. "Job Demands, Job Decision Latitude, and Mental Strain: Implications for Job Redesign." *Administrative Science Quarterly*, 285–308.

Karasek, R., and T. Theorell. (1990). *Healthy Work, Stress, Productivity, and the Reconstruction of Working Life*. New York: Basic Books.

Kuipers, H., P. van Amelsvoort, and E. H. Kramer. 2010. *Het Nieuwe Organiseren: Alternatieven Voor de Bureaucratie*. Leuven: Acco.

Roos, D., J. Womack, and D. Jones. 1990. *The Machine That Changed the World—The Story of Lean Production*. New York: Rawson/Harper Perennial.

Smith, A. 1776/1986. *An Inquiry into the Nature and Causes of the Wealth of Nations*. Harmondsworth: Penguin Books.

Taylor, F. 1911. *The Principles of Scientific Management*. New York: Harper and Row.

Kuipers, H., P. van Amelsvoort, and E. Kramer. 2010. *Het Nieuwe Organiseren: Alternatieve Voor de Bureaucratie (The New Organisation: An Alternative to Bureaucracy)*. Leuven: Acco.

van Hootegem, G. 2000. *De Draaglijke Traagheid van Het Management: Tendensen in Het Productie- en Personeelsbeleid (The Bearable Slowness of Management: Trends in Production and Personnel Policy)*. Leuven: Acco.

van Hootegem G., P. van Amelsvoort, G. Van Beek, and R. Huys. 2008. *Anders Organiseren and Beter Werken*. Leuven: Acco.

van Hootegem G., R. Huys, and G. Maes. 2014. *Meten en Veranderen: Instrumenten Bij Het Nieuwe Organiseren (Measuring and Changing: Instruments for the New Organisation)*. Leuven: Acco.

Vranken J., G. van Hootegem, and E. Henderickx. 2013. *Het Speelveld, de Spelregels, en de Spelers? (The Playing Field, Game Rules, and Players?) Handboek Sociologie (Sociology Guidebook)*. Leuven: Acco.

Nineteen

The Future of STS-D

BERNARD J. MOHR AND PIERRE VAN AMELSVOORT

OUR DREAM

Our dream of humane and innovative communities of work (i.e., traditional workplaces, virtual workplaces, networks, and ecosystems) is not finished—in fact, it is still in its adolescence! The overwhelming majority of people still experience work to an unacceptable degree as "meaningless, dead-ending, and soul-destroying" far too often. Yes, a lot of workplace change has happened since the days of Frederick Taylor, but there still is a lot work to do. Within emerging economies such as China, Brazil, and India, there is still great opportunity in their production-line workplaces—but also at the offices of knowledge workplaces. However, in what we call the developed world, we have never before seen the levels of employee disengagement that are now being reported, nor have we seen the mishmash of massive economic upheavals, breathtaking advances in technology, widespread political turmoil, unprecedented climate change, radically shifting demographics, and breakthroughs in social relations that have left organizations with a full plate of adaptation challenges. Simultaneously we see "positive deviants"—workplaces where people at *all* levels experience appropriate levels of autonomy, community, significance, and reward, workplaces that seem to flourish economically while also contributing to the many "wicked problems" of today's complex world.

Learning from each other about theoretical insights and sharing of practices around the world is important to improving our communities of practices. Reaching out, sharing, and growing the fundamental STS-D insights with other communities of practices and stakeholders is equally important to our goal of a world replete with humane and innovative organizations.

THIS BOOK

The chapters in this book on socio-technical systems design have exposed sixty years of development in theory and practice. Also, we have shown that developments are still going on. We have seen the three waves in this development. The first wave is about the design of more or less routine work in manufacturing processes, with most "projects" taking place within the four walls of a manufacturing entity; the second is about non-routine work with knowledge workers; and the third is about designing whole organizations, value-realization networks (both internal external), and issue-based ecosystems. These waves of evolution are not discontinuous but rather like Russian Dolls, each working with and encapsulating what has gone before.

In this chapter, we summarize the different approaches and to find common ground. Also we try to formulate the future challenges for this community of practice.

DIFFERENT APPROACHES AND COMMON GROUND

We also notice how original STS-D theory and practice have manifested in and/or influenced other approaches to organization design such as Lean Thinking (see chapter 16), High-Performance Work Systems, (see chapter 2) Total Workplace Innovation (TWIN) (see chapter 18), and Lowlands STS-D (originally called Integral Organization Renewal). They are all different words but, in the end, the same purpose.

These past sixty years have seen both a diffusion and integration of different perspectives and approaches. Discovering common ground can help us all in different cultures and countries. The different STS-D approaches have the same roots in common, characterized by the following three ideas:

1. All have a multiple-stakeholders approach. Each unique STS organizational design is the result of an attempt to balance customer focus, productivity, quality of working life, and employee voice. That is a unique point of STS-D compared to other approaches such as Lean/Six Sigma.

2. STS-D designs are always aligned with organizational purpose and strategy. Different environmental demands require different design possibilities. Designing is therefore not a stand-alone change and actually not a one-size-fits all change process. Important in this is that all participants understand the connection among purpose, strategy, and organizational design. The STS design process ensures a participatory process of co-creaion and collaborative learning.

3. In STS-D, the work, enablers to the work, the organization of the work, and the people are not separate domains. Simultaneous attention is on the technical part of the organization, such as technology; division of labor and control systems; and the social part—culture, people, and behavior. The organization design is seen as an important contributor for developing the desired culture and behavior.

FUTURE CHALLENGES

The past decade or two have seen the field of "design thinking" (in particular, "human-centered design") burst into the consciousness and practice of hundreds, if not thousands, of organizations across the globe—including for-profit, government, and social-enterprise entities. There are few leading organizations that have not heard of, considered, or used, design thinking to address significant challenges.

Yet the overlap of membership between the STS-D community of practice and the Design Thinking community is almost nonexistent. This is true also of the overlap between the Lean Thinking and STS-D communities of practice. However, between them, Lean and Design Thinking have an estimated 90 percent of the market share when it comes to dollars being invested in organizational innovation.

Both the possibilities and the challenges generated by these realities are significant. But seizing the possibilities and overcoming the challenges will require our own STS-D community of practice to accomplish the following:

- Clearly differentiate our unique capability.
- Simultaneously incorporate the best practices and, where appropriate, partner with other non-STS-D practitioners

Not only must we reach out, learn from, and partner with Design Thinking and Lean practitioners; we also need to bridge our practices of designing organization architectures with the practices of information system architects and facilities architects.

Co-designing humane and innovative organizations will always require the active participation of those who will live in the system, but increasingly we need to have working involvement with the many other professionals who are "designing" the organizations, networks, and ecosystems of the future, for example, IT and facility architects

In the process of co-creating this book, we asked our chapter authors to chime in with their ideas about future challenges. Below are two responses.

Frank Pot: "It should be emphasized that STS-D is not only something of the past, referring to the times of the coal mines and industrial mass production. Its basic/general ideas (improving organizational performance, quality of working life, and labor relations simultaneously) and its basic/general design rules are still the same, but organizations, employees, and environments have changed, so the practical content of these ideas and rules has changed as well. This is in line with the principle that STS-D always must be local in its implementation.

Some people say "teamwork" is an outdated concept because most employees have individual targets and because more and more people decide to work as self-employed professionals. In my opinion, this comment stems from a wrong understanding of teamwork. The large majority of working people have to tune their work with others (the self-employed as well). STS-D is about coordination and shared responsibility. "Physical teams" is one possibility; "virtual teams" is another. Other concepts could do as well, such as "relational coordination."

From a strategic point of view, STS-D used to be connected to performance indicators such as productivity, QWL, and quality of product and services. For the past fifteen years, more attention has been paid to the relationship among organizational design, "innovation capacity," and "human talent mobilization." My suggestion would be to show how STS-D is still relevant, or even more relevant, in "the second machine age" (Brynjolfsson and McAfee 2014), *The Second Machine Age: Work, Progress, and Prosperity in a Time of Brilliant Technologies*, New York/London: W. W. Norton.) They write about "the coinvention of organization and technology" (p137, Brynjolfsson and McAfee 2014)) and say, "Creativity and organizational redesign are crucial to investments in digital technologies" (p138, Brynjolfsson and McAfee 2014)) and "This kind of organizational coinvention requires more creativity on the part of entrepreneurs, managers, and workers..." (p138 Brynjolfsson and McAfee 2014).

From an Interview with Brynjolfsson and McAfee in *Harvard Business Review*, June 2015. In the same issue, an article by Thomas Davenport and Julia Kirby says, "Beyond automation. Strategies for remaining gainfully employed in an era of very smart machines."

Wim Sprenger et al. say the following about future challenges for this work:

1. Employee participation is not the same as participation of employee organizations. Most authors dealing with employee participation do not make the difference or do not mention it at all. Only Gustavsen (chapter 9) speaks of the participation in democratic dialogue of labor-market parties. He is rather optimistic and argues that Norwegian unions and employers' organizations have moved toward a mainstream of democratic dialogue, answering the need "to ensure the stable and long-term commitment of major actors in society." We doubt if this is the case for many unions and countries. This makes it clear how important "indirect participation" at a national level can be to provide a mainstream framework in which employee participation and workplace innovation can develop.

2. There is a need for the development of new design tools and competencies for networks and interorganization design.

3. It would be interesting to investigate more deeply the possibilities to combine confrontational and cooperative/deliberative trade-union strategies. In fact, UFW (United Farm Workers does this.

4. A provocative question: If the middle class and its pool of skilled open-ended jobs is shrinking worldwide, will STS-D of the future be mainly a tool shop for a shrinking group of employers and employees on a global scale?

5. How can we develop employee participation and humane and innovative workplaces for low-skilled, peripheral, and nonstandard employees?

An additional challenge includes making our ideas and practices more well known. "Marketing" has never been a strong point of STS-D practitioners, so it needs to be a continuous point of attention. Another challenge is supporting rising economies with cheap labor cost in understanding the value of humane organizations in which attention is also paid to the quality of working life in relation to productivity.

In chapter 1, we mentioned the three waves. We are now in the beginning of the third wave—designing whole organizations' networks and ecosystems. We need considerable work on this third wave to get more insights, instruments, and practices. Building on the ideas of Lowlands STS-D is a good start.

We also need to elevate the codesign of both facilities architecture and information and communications technology (ICT) as part of all STS-D. In this area of work, there are major important issues to explore.

The design choices made for ICT are crucial to the effective functioning of the whole system. When ICT systems inadvertently reinforce old command and control systems based on standardization and mass production, a bottleneck is created in the development of more innovative organizations. Innovative organizations need flexible ICT systems that support flexible work processes that in turn can cope with unpredictable uncertainty. Developing a common language between ICT-systems designers and STS-D practitioners is a prerequisite for addressing this issue. However, we believe that we can have a win-win situation for both.

ICT has and will have a great influence on how we organize our work and lives. The boundaries between organizations, between different places of the world, and between life and work are shifting. Social media connects us to every place in every time, together. Virtual collaboration in teams, communities, networks, and ecosystems is just in the beginning of the development. This raises a lot of STS design questions. What do we do with empty schools, empty offices, and empty manufacturing plants? What works, and what doesn't? Can managers, employees, and unions really cooperate in a long-term dialogue about organizational designs and development based on mutual respect and the search for win-win strategies? What is the role of government policy and support in these larger issues, and how does the government sector participate?

CONCLUSION

We are faced with a multitude of opportunities and challenges in co-creating humane and innovative organizations. The rationale for so doing is inescapable. At the level of the individual, our experience at work determines how we feel, who we are, and how we participate in the world to a remarkable extent. At the societal level, it is our institutions (service, manufacturing, government, and social enterprise) that have the potential to create a better world or to destroy it.

Socio-technical system design and our community of practice have a powerful heritage and wonderful history of innovation. Some of our ideas have been and will continue to be absorbed by others—both effectively and less so. Some of our methods are being replaced with innovations we have "borrowed" from others—both effectively and less so.

Despite the different design practices presented in this book, the three core ideas are important values in the global STS-D community. The question is, does the global community need common global definitions? We don't think so.

In our view, we should be aware of the common values and learn from the variation in theoretical approaches and the diversity of practice. This diversity is a more effective base for learning than standardized definitions and methods. The same can be said about mergers with other approaches as long as we keep our values in mind.

To enforce and continue this learning process, a vibrant global community of practice based on the abovementioned values as a common purpose is an important condition. A learning community has not only this common purpose but is also based on mutual respect, openness, fairness, and friendship.

We live in interesting times. Never before has so much wealth been produced. Never before have the distribution disparities been as great.

Bernard J. Mohr and Pierre van Amelsvoort

Never before has technology been as ubiquitous and disconcerting while being as enchanting. Never before has the world teetered on the verge of unimaginable promise for all while being a step away from global environmental, economic, and military disaster. Never before has a generation demanded us to work in such new and challenging ways.

The world is calling, and the call is clear. We need more workplaces that work better and more workplaces that are better to work in.

www.ingramcontent.com/pod-product-compliance
Lightning Source LLC
Chambersburg PA
CBHW052112270326
41928CB00010BA/1801